THE COMPLETE GUIDE TO
DECKS

A Step-by-Step Manual for Building Decks

Creative Publishing international

CHANHASSEN, MINNESOTA
www.creativepub.com

Contents

**Creative Publishing
international**

Copyright © 2005
Creative Publishing international, Inc.
18705 Lake Drive East
Chanhassen, Minnesota 55317
1-800-328-3895
www.creativepub.com
All rights reserved

Printed in U.S.A. by R. R. Donnelley
10 9 8 7 6 5 4 3 2 1

President/CEO: Ken Fund
Vice President/Publisher: Linda Ball
Vice President/Sales & Marketing: Kevin Haas

Executive Editor: Bryan Trandem
Creative Director: Tim Himsel

For revised edition:
Writer: Paul Currie
Editor: Thomas G. Lemmer
Project Manager: Tracy Stanley
Art Director: Jon Simpson
Photographer: Tate Carlson
Scene Shop Carpenter: Randy Austin
Production Manager: Laura Hokkanen

THE COMPLETE GUIDE TO DECKS
Created by: The Editors of Creative Publishing international, Inc.,
in cooperation with Black & Decker. Black & Decker® is a trademark
of The Black & Decker Corporation and is used under license.

Library of Congress
Cataloging-in-Publication Data

The complete guide to decks : a step-by-step manual for building basic and advanced decks.
 p. cm.
 At head of title: Black & Decker.
 Includes index.
 ISBN 1-58923-200-3 (soft cover)
 1. Decks (Architecture, Domestic)--Design and construction--Amateurs' manuals.
I. Black & Decker Corporation (Towson, Md.) II. Creative Publishing international.
 TH4970.C645 2005
 690'.893--dc22
                                2005008284

Cover photo of redwood deck courtesy of California Redwood Association

Portions of *The Complete Guide to Decks* are taken from *Portfolio of Unique Deck Ideas* and the Black & Decker® books *Building Decks, Advanced Deck Building* and *Great Decks & Furnishings*. Other books in the Black & Decker® Home Improvement Library™ include:

Complete Guide to Bathrooms, Complete Guide to Ceramic & Stone Tile, Complete Guide to Creative Landscapes, Complete Guide to Easy Woodworking Projects, Complete Guide to Finishing Touches for Yards & Gardens, Complete Guide to Flooring, Complete Guide to Home Carpentry, Complete Guide to Home

Masonry, Complete Guide to Home Plumbing, Complete Guide to Home Storage, Complete Guide to Home Wiring, Complete Guide to Kitchens, Complete Guide to Outdoor Wood Projects, Complete Guide to Painting & Decorating, Complete Guide to Roofing & Siding, Complete Guide to Windows & Doors, Complete Photo Guide to Home Repair, Complete Photo Guide to Home Improvement, Complete Photo Guide to Outdoor Home Repair

Introduction

This newest edition of *The Complete Guide to Decks,* the best-selling deck-building manual, again offers everything necessary to help you design, plan, and build the deck of your dreams—and save money in the process. Completely revised and updated, the material collected here features the most up-to-date tools, materials, and construction techniques for building decks that meet current National Building Code standards. You'll also find information on new alternative decking materials and how to bring lighting and power to the deck location.

The first section, Deck Basics, defines and discusses in detail the materials and tools necessary for any deck project. Everything from the location and function of structural components to options in decking patterns, stairs, and railings is covered. Essential information about lumber, concrete, and other necessary hardware and materials is provided. A guide to the hand and power tools required in deck construction is also included, along with those tools that can be found at rental centers.

The Design & Planning section shows you how to plan and design the best deck for your home, including how to schedule the project. This section also demonstrates the best methods for creating precise, easy-to-follow plans which you will need in order to obtain a building permit from your local building code office. Information on everything you need to know about working with your local building officials and codes is also included.

Basic Deck Building Techniques demonstrates how to lay out and install the deck you have designed on paper. Step-by-step instructions are provided, illustrating how to build each component of a basic deck: ledgers, footings, posts, beams, joists, decking, stairs, and railings. The specific tools and materials required for each of these techniques are listed. This section also contains methods for applying a finish to your deck to protect it against moisture, as well as maintenance and repair techniques for keeping your deck structurally sound and looking new.

The Advanced Deck Building Techniques section moves beyond simple construction to show you how to create more complex deck structures and solve problems that may arise on building sites. In this section, step-by-step instructions demonstrate how to work on steep slopes, build multiple levels, construct curves and uncommon angles, and build complex stairways and railing designs. However, before taking on projects in this section, make sure you are capable of performing the basic deck building techniques.

The last two sections of *The Complete Guide to Decks* contain building plans for ten frequently built deck designs and several common deck accessory projects. Each plan provides a materials list and building details that can be modified easily to meet your specific site measurements and local building codes. All that's left is to obtain a building permit before you begin construction. Information about the tools, materials, and techniques necessary to build from any one of these plans is discussed in the previous sections of this book. Additionally, you'll find instructions for providing your deck with power and lighting, including directions for installing low-voltage lighting accessories.

The thorough instructions, helpful tips, and up-to-date information found in this newest edition of *The Complete Guide to Decks* make it the premier deck-building manual. With the help of this comprehensive book, you will be able to build a beautiful, long-lasting deck as quickly, easily, and economically as possible.

Deck Basics

Deck-building Glossary

Baluster — a vertical railing member.

Batterboards — temporary stake structures used for positioning layout strings.

Beam — the main horizontal support for the deck, usually made from a pair of 2 × 8s or 2 × 10s attached to the deck posts.

Blocking — short pieces of lumber cut from joist material and fastened between joists for reinforcement.

Cap — the topmost horizontal railing member.

Cantilever — a common construction method (employed in some of the deck plans in this book) that involves extending the joists beyond the beam. The maximum overhang is specified in the Building Code.

Corner-post design — a construction method that incorporates posts at the outside edges of the deck, so the joists do not overhang the beam.

Decking — the floor boards of a deck (also known as deck boards).

End joists — the joists that are at each end of a series of parallel joists.

Face board — attractive wood, usually redwood or cedar, used to cover the rim joists and end joists.

Footing — a concrete pier that extends below the frost line and that bears the weight of the deck and any inset structures or furnishings.

Horizontal span — the horizontal distance a stairway covers.

Inset — an area of a deck that has been cut out to accommodate landscape features such as trees or to provide access to fixtures.

Joist — dimensional lumber, set on edge, that supports decking. Joists on attached decks hang between the ledger and rim joist.

Joist hanger — metal connecting pieces used to attach joists at right angles to ledger or header joists so that top edges are flush.

Ledger — a board, equal in size to the joists, that anchors the deck to the house and supports one end of the joists.

Open step — a step composed of treads mounted between stair stringers without any risers.

Post — a vertical member that supports a deck, stairway or railing.

Post anchors — metal hardware for attaching deck posts to footings and raising the bottom of the post to keep it away from water. The end grain itself can be protected with sealer as added protection from rot.

Rim joist — a board fastened to the end of the joists, typically at the opposite end from the ledger. Rim joists attach to both ends of a free-standing deck.

Rise — the height of a step.

Riser — a board attached to the front of a step between treads.

Run — the length of a step.

Sandwich beam — a beam design that incorporates a pair of beam timbers attached to either side of the post with carriage bolts.

Span limit — the distance a board can safely cross between supports.

Stair cleat — supports for treads that are attached to stair stringers.

Stair stringer — an inclined member that supports a stairway's treads. A stair stringer may be solid, with treads attached to cleats mounted on the inside face, or cut out, with treads resting on top of the cutouts.

Tread — the horizontal face of each step in a stairway, often composed of two 2 × 6 boards.

Vertical drop — the vertical distance from the deck surface to the ground.

Baluster

Facing board

Joist

Header joist

Concrete footing

Beam

Rail

Cap

Decking

Railing post

Joist hanger

Ledger

Baluster

Tread

Stringer

Outside joist

Deck post

Stairway post

Post anchor

Decking Patterns

Decking is an important element of a deck, and can be installed using a variety of board sizes and design patterns. The decking pattern deter-mines the spacing and layout of the joists. For example, a normal, straight decking pattern requires joists that are spaced 16" on-center.

Diagonal pattern adds visual interest to a deck. Diagonal patterns require joists that are spaced closer together than for straight patterns.

Parquet pattern requires double joists and blocking to provide a support-ing surface for attaching the butted ends of decking boards.

A diagonal decking pattern requires that the joist spacing be 12" on-center. Parquet patterns and some other designs may require extra support, like double joists or extra blocking. For sturdy, flat decking, use 2 × 4 or 2 × 6 lumber. Thinner lumber is more likely to twist or cup.

Framed opening for a tree requires extra blocking between joists. Short joists are attached to blocking with joist hangers.

Border pattern gives an elegant, finished look to a deck. Install trim joists to support the border decking.

Stairways

Most local building codes require that you use pressure-treated lumber for stairway posts and stringers. Install stair treads and risers cut from lumber that matches the surface decking. If possible, create treads that use the same board pattern as the decking. You may cover visible pressure-treated portions of the stairway with lumber matching the decking, too, or stain them to match the decking as closely as possible. Local codes may require handrails on stairways with three or more risers.

Platform steps feature wide treads. Each step is built on a framework of posts and joists.

Stairway Styles

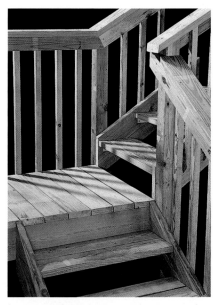

Open steps have metal cleats that hold the treads between the stringers. The treads on this stairway are built with 2 × 6s to match the surface decking.

Boxed steps, built with notched stringers and solid risers, give a finished look to a deck stairway. Predrill ends of treads to prevent splitting.

Long stairways sometimes require landings. A landing is a small platform to which both flights of stairs are attached. See pages 142 to 151.

Railings

Railings usually are required by building code on any deck that is more than 24" high. Select a railing design that fits the style of your home.

For example, on a low, ranch-style house, choose a deck railing with wide, horizontal rails. On a Tudor-style home with a steep roof, choose a railing with closely spaced, vertical balusters. See pages 180 to 195 for information on how to build other railing styles, including a curved railing.

Some areas may require an easily gripped hand rail for stairways (pages 190 to 191). Check with your local building inspector.

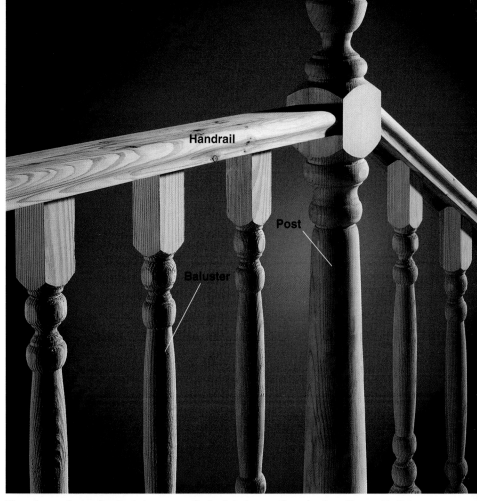

Preshaped products let you easily build decorative deck railings. Railing products include shaped handrails, balusters, and posts.

Railing Styles

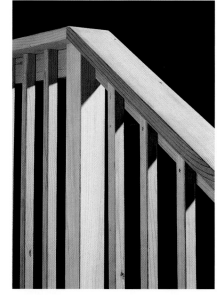

Vertical balusters with posts and rails are a good choice for houses with strong vertical lines. A vertical baluster railing like the one shown above is a good choice where children will be present.

Horizontal railings are often used on low, ranch-style homes. Horizontal railings are made of vertical posts, two or more wide horizontal rails, and a railing cap.

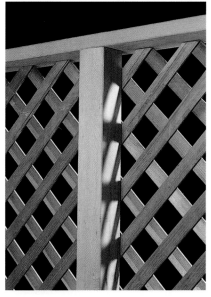

Lattice panels add a decorative touch to a deck. They also provide extra privacy.

Pressure-treated lumber stamps list the type of preservative and the chemical retention level, as well as the exposure rating and the name and location of the treating company.

Cedar grade stamps list the mill number, moisture content, species, lumber grade, and membership association. Western red cedar (WRC) or incense cedar (INC) for decks should be heartwood (HEART) with a maximum moisture content of 15% (MC15).

Lumber

When constructing a deck, select a wood that is not prone to rot or insect attack. Three types are recommended: heart cedar, heart redwood and pressure-treated lumber.

The heartwood of cedar and redwood is highly resistant to decay; the sapwood is not, and must be treated with a preservative when used for outdoor structures.

Because cedar and redwood are somewhat expensive, many deck builders use these woods only on the visible parts of decks and use less expensive pressure-treated lumber, with its telltale green tint, on less visible parts. The preservatives in pressure-treated wood provide a high resistance to decay. You must, however, wear eye protection, a particle mask and gloves, and cover your skin when working with pressure-treated lumber.

If you live in an arid climate, you can bypass the controversy. Because wood can't rot if its moisture content is less than 20%, decks built in the Southwest and other very dry climates can safely be built from untreated pine lumber. It's always a good idea, though, to use pressure-treated lumber for deck posts.

Another option is to use wood/polymer composites. These composite materials are made of recycled plastics and waste wood, and are used for decking and other nonstructural components.

NOTE: The materials lists for the plans in this book include a waste allowance of 10 to 15%.

PRESSURE-TREATED LUMBER UPDATE

As of January 1, 2004, the lumber industry voluntarily discontinued the use of chromated copper arsenate (CCA) treated lumber for consumer uses, such as play structures, residential fencing, and decks. This was done in conjunction with the Environmental Protection Agency (EPA) in an effort to help reduce exposure to arsenic, a known human carcinogen.

While CCA treated lumber will be available until the remaining stock is sold, two new chemical treatments are already in place to take over: alkaline copper quaternary (ACQ) and copper boron azole (CBA). Both ACQ and CBA provide wood with the same protection from insect attack and decay as CCA, however the treatments are more corrosive to metals. Make sure to follow the lumber manufacturer's recommendations when purchasing deck fasteners and hardware.

If you own a deck or other outdoor structure build with CCA treated lumber, you can reduce exposure to CCA by applying an oil-based, semi-transparent stain once every year or two, depending on the condition of the wood. For more information on CCA lumber, visit www.epa.gov.

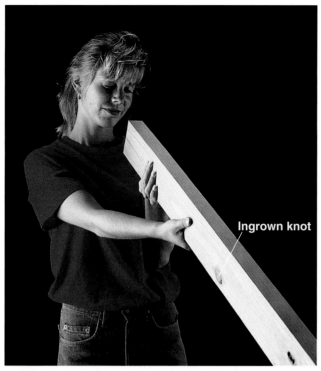

Inspect lumber for flaws. Sight along each board to check for warping and twisting. Return any boards with serious flaws. Check for loose knots. Boards used for structural parts should have only small knots that are tight and ingrown.

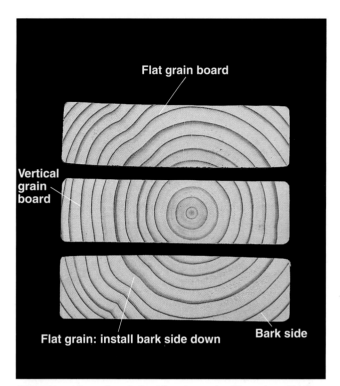

Check end grain of decking boards. Boards with flat grain tend to "cup," and can trap standing water if not installed properly. Research studies indicate that flat grain boards cup toward the bark side (not away from it, as was previously thought in the industry), and should be installed so the bark side faces down.

Store lumber so that it stays dry and warp-free. Use supports to keep the wood stack a few inches off the ground. Use spacer blocks to support each row of lumber, and to allow air circulation between boards. Cover the lumber stack with heavy plastic or a water-proof tarp.

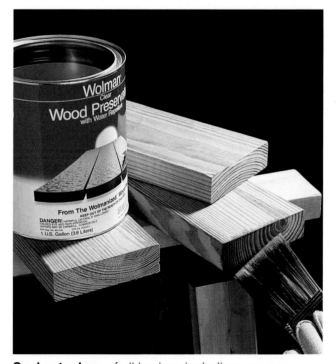

Seal cut edges of all lumber, including pressure-treated wood, by brushing on clear liquid sealer-preservative. Chemicals used in pressure treatment do not always penetrate completely. Sealer-preservative protects all types of wood from rot.

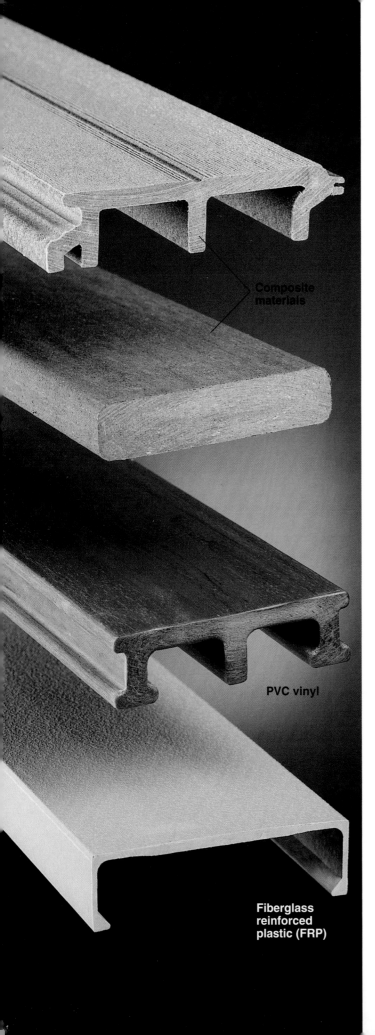

Composite materials

PVC vinyl

Fiberglass reinforced plastic (FRP)

Other Deck Materials

Several other materials may be useful or necessary for your deck building project. Flashing, building felt, and self-sealing membrane prevent moisture damage to a deck and to the area where it attaches to the house. Lattice, lap siding, and preformed fence panels may be used as decorative elements, to provide privacy, or to enclose portions of a deck. Alternative decking materials offer lower-maintenance alternatives to wood.

Although these materials (photo at left) may initially be more expensive than wood decking, they often carry lifetime warranties and can be cheaper than wood over the long run. Most of these products are specifically designed with the do-it-yourselfer in mind. Though the installation methods and fastening systems vary from manufacturer to manufacturer, most are designed to accommodate standard building dimensions, such as 16" joist spacing. Prior to placing an order for any of these materials, check with local building codes, because some areas may have restrictions against certain materials.

Composite materials blend together wood fibers and recycled plastics to create a rigid product that, unlike wood, will not rot, splinter, warp, or crack. Painting or staining is unnecessary. Like wood, these deck boards can be cut to size, using a circular saw with a large tooth blade.

PVC vinyl and plastic decking materials are shipped in kits that contain everything necessary to install the decking other than the deck screws. The kits are preordered to size, usually in multiples of the combined width of a deck board and the fasteners. The drawback of PVC vinyl decking is that it expands and contracts with freeze/thaw cycles.

Fiberglass reinforced plastic (FRP) decking will last a lifetime. Manufacturers claim that the material is three times as strong as wood and not affected by heat, sunlight, or severe weather. The decking is preordered to size but if necessary, it can be cut using a circular saw with a diamond-tip blade or masonry blade.

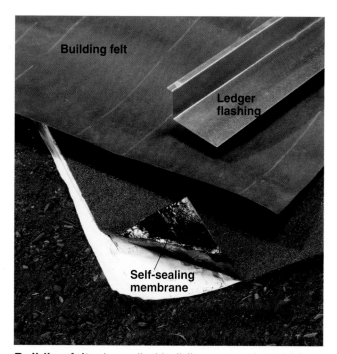

Pressure-treated pine, cedar, or redwood lattice is often used to enclose open areas underneath raised decks or to provide partial-privacy walls at a deck perimeter. Greater privacy is available inexpensively by using preformed fence panels. Lap siding of cedar or redwood lumber can be used to build decorative railing walls and is especially useful for matching existing siding on a house.

Building felt, also called building paper, is used behind house siding materials. Use it to replace felt damaged during a ledger installation. Ledger flashing, or Z-flashing, prevents moisture damage behind the deck ledger (see pages 46 and 48). Self-sealing membrane provides extra protection from moisture in damp climates or in areas where there is snow accumulation. It can be used over flashing or on top of beams and posts (see below), and it self-seals around nails or screws that pierce it.

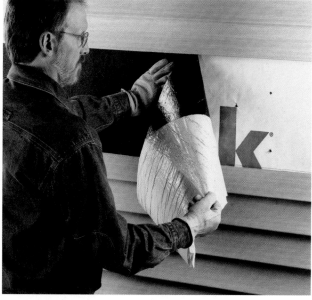

To apply self-sealing membrane, cut a piece to size and position it over the application area. Starting at one end, begin removing the thin plastic backing that protects the adhesive. Firmly press the membrane in place as you remove the backing, working along the installation area. To install long pieces of membrane, enlist the aid of a helper.

Install self-sealing membrane behind the ledger as extra protection from moisture. Apply the membrane over the house wrap or building felt using the same method shown at left.

Hardware & Fasteners

Build your deck with metal lumber connectors, nails, and screws rated for exterior use to help prevent corrosion. Use stainless steel screws or color-plated screws when installing cedar or redwood decking—galvanized screws and nails may react with natural chemicals in these woods to produce staining. Stainless or color-plated fasteners also may be necessary for some pressure-treated lumber, such as ACQ and CBA. Always follow the lumber manufacturer's requirements.

Seal heads of counterbored screws with silicone caulk to prevent water damage.

Metal lumber connectors are used to create strong joints with wood framing members, and are available at lumber yards and home improvement centers.

(Top photo) Deck structural fasteners include: threaded rod with nut, washer, and epoxy syringe (A); J-bolt with nut and washer (B); carriage bolt with nut and washer (C); galvanized lag screws and washers (D); lead masonry anchors (E).

(Bottom photo) Metal connectors and hardware used in deck building include: galvanized flashing (A), nonadjustable post caps (B), post anchor (C), T-strap (D), direct-bearing footing connector (E), adjustable post-beam cap (F), straping plate (G), joist tie (H), skewable joist hanger (I), angled joist hanger (J), joist hanger (K), skewable angle bracket (L), stair cleat (M), H-fit rafter tie (N), seismic tie (O), and angle bracket (P).

Joist ties strengthen and support beams fastened to posts in sandwich beam constuction.

Masonry anchors with lag screws hold the ledger to stone, brick, or concrete blocks.

J-bolts with nuts and washers hold the post anchors to the concrete footings.

Post anchors hold deck posts in place, and raise the base of the posts to help prevent water from entering end grain of wood.

Angle brackets help reinforce header and outside joists. Angle brackets are also used to attach stair stringers to the deck.

Joist hangers are used to attach joists to the ledger and header joist. Double hanger is used when decking pattern requires a double-width joist.

Angled joist hangers are used to frame decks that have unusual angles or decking patterns.

Stair cleats support the treads of deck steps. Cleats are attached to stair stringers with ¼ x 1¼" galvanized lag screws.

Post-beam caps secure beams on top of posts and are available in one-piece or adjustable styles.

19

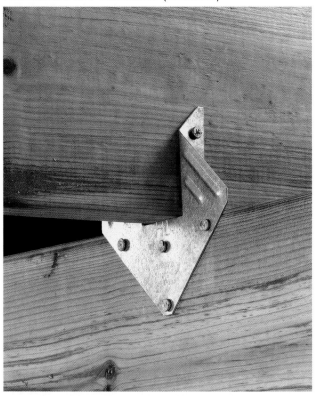

H-fit rafter ties attach 2x joists or rafters to the top of a beam between beam ends.

Seismic ties attach 2x joists or rafters to the top of a beam at its ends.

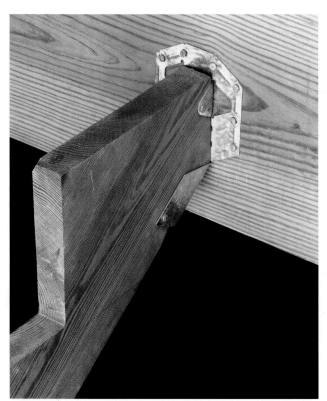

Skewable joist hangers attach 2x lumber, such as stair stringers, to the face of framing at an adjustable angle.

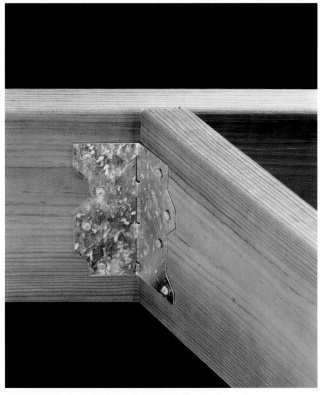

Skewable angle brackets reinforce framing connections at angles other than 90 degrees or at beam ends where 45-degree joist hangers won't fit.

Direct bearing footing connectors attach beams directly to footings on low profile decks.

T-straps reinforce the connection between beam and post, particularly on long beams requiring spliced construction. Local building codes may also allow their use in place of post caps.

Strapping plates, also known as nailing plates, reinforce spliced joints between framing pieces.

Specialty nails and screws, rated for exterior use, are used for deck building. Short metal connector nails (A) are available in 8d and 10d sizes designed to fit holes in the connectors when attaching them to 2× lumber. Galvanized screws (B) are the traditional fastener for framing construction with pressure-treated lumber. Color-plated screws (C) blend in with the decking color, and should be used when working with cedar, redwood, or some of the new variety of pressure-treated lumber because plain galvanized screws may interact with natural chemicals in the wood to produce staining corrosion. Stainless steel screws (D) are the best option to use with any wood species, but are usually significantly more expensive.

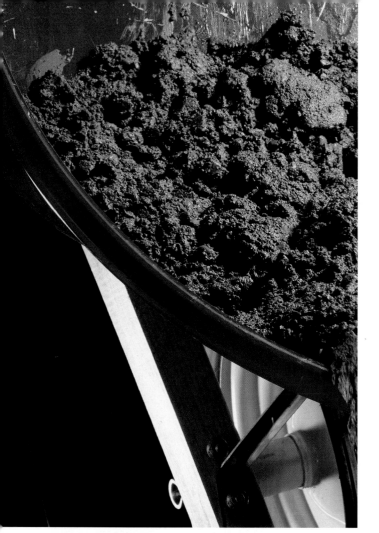

Concrete

Use concrete to make solid footings that will support the weight of the deck (see page 32). Concrete for footings is made from a mixture of portland cement, sand, and coarse gravel (¼ to 1½" in diameter). You can buy bags containing these dry materials premixed at building centers. For larger amounts, buy ready-mixed concrete in trailer loads that you can haul to the job site, or for very large amounts, consider ordering ready-mixed material from a concrete company that will deliver it (see opposite page).

For most deck projects, mixing your own concrete is easy and inexpensive. Combine premixed bags with water following manufacturer's instructions in a wheelbarrow or with a power mixer, available at rental centers. Never use a partial bag of dry premixed concrete because the contents aren't evenly distributed throughout the bag.

The estimation charts below give approximate volumes of concrete. You may have a small amount of concrete left over after pouring footings or stair pads.

Amount of Concrete Needed (cubic feet)

No of 8" Dia. Footings	Depth of Footings (feet)			
	1	2	3	4
2	¾	1½	2¼	3
3	1	2¼	3½	4½
4	1½	3	4½	6
5	2	3¾	5¾	7½

No of 12" Dia. Footings	Depth of Footings (feet)			
	1	2	3	4
2	1½	3	4¾	6¼
3	2⅖	4¾	7	9½
4	3⅕	6	9½	12½
5	4	8	11¾	15¾

Pad Size	Cubic Feet
3 × 3' × 4" thick	3
3 × 4' × 4" thick	4
4 × 4' × 4" thick	5.4

Pre-cast concrete footing piers are available at building centers for use where local Building Codes don't require poured footings. They are particularly useful on low-profile decks because joists can be placed directly in the grooves formed in the pier tops. Piers should be placed on a layer of compactible gravel. When the piers are used to support posts, use post anchors bolted to the piers.

Buying & Mixing Concrete

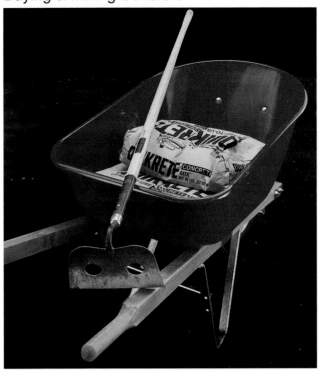

Buy premixed bags of dry concrete for small jobs. A 60-lb. bag creates about ½ of a cubic foot of concrete. A 90-lb. bag creates about ⅔ of a cubic foot.

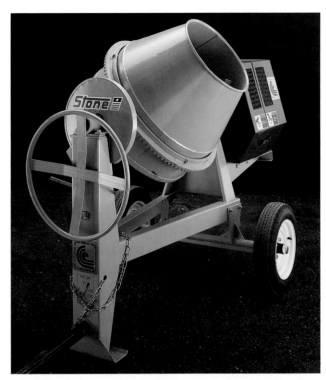

Rent a power cement mixer for larger quantities of premixed bags. It blends 2-4 bags at a time (depending on the size of the mixer) quickly and thoroughly.

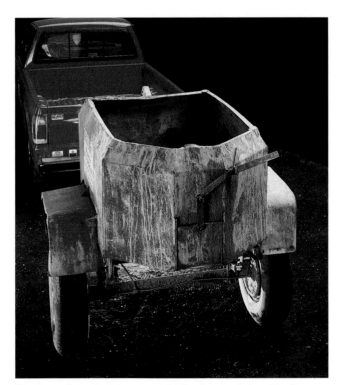

Buy ready-mixed concrete for larger jobs. Trailer loads are available at rental centers, and are sold by the cubic yard. One cubic yard equals 27 cubic feet.

Buy ready-mixed concrete and have it delivered for projects requiring very large amounts. Many suppliers have pumps on their trucks so they can pour concrete directly into footings or pad locations, although they may charge extra for this service.

Mason's string **Quick clamp** **Level**

Small crowbar **Chisel**

Hoe

Tape measure

Shovel **Trowel**

UNION USA

Rubber mallet

Caulk gun

Mason's hammer **Combination square**

Speed square **Flat pry bar**

Line level

Pipe clamp

Scratch awl

Metal snips

Compass

Ratchet wrench and sockets

Plumb bob

22-oz. claw hammer

Chalk line

Putty knife

Framing square **Clamshell posthole digger**

Hand tools for deck building should have heavy-duty construction. Metal tools should be made from high-carbon steel with smoothly finished surfaces. Buy quality hand tools that are well balanced and have tight, comfortably molded handles. There is no substitute for quality.

Tool Basics

With a set of basic hand and power tools, you can complete any of the deck projects shown in this book. You may already own many of the tools needed. If you buy new tools, invest in quality, heavy-duty products that will provide long service.

Some specialty tools, like power miter saws or reciprocating saws, are available at tool rental centers. Or, they can be purchased at home improvement stores.

Always wear eye protection when using tools. Always wear a particle mask and work gloves when sawing or handling pressure-treated lumber, to avoid excessive contact with the chemicals in the wood.

Tools for finishing and maintaining a deck include: rubber gloves (A), shop vacuum (B), 14-gauge extension cord (C), pressure sprayer (D), hydraulic jack and handle (E), eye protection (F), scrub brush (G), paint brush (H), particle mask (I), and orbital sander (J).

Power tools include: power miter saw (A), 14.4-volt cordless trim saw with a 5⅜" blade (B), reciprocating saw with 6" and 8" blades (C), ⅜" drill and bits (D), jig saw (E), and ½" hammer drill and bits (F).

25

Specialty masonry tools are needed when pouring a concrete pad, such as for a stairway landing pad (see pages 65 to 67). Use a wood float (A) to smooth the surface of the concrete, and an edging tool (B) to form a finished edge around the pad's perimeter. Separate setting concrete from the wood form with a tuck-pointing trowel (C).

Drill accurate holes at most angles with a portable drill guide, such as when building a railing with pipe balusters (see pages 194 to 195). A Forstner bit cuts holes with very smooth sides and flat bottoms.

Use a post speed level when setting posts to quickly plumb each post in both directions at the same time.

A laser level works more easily and accurately than a spirit level over long distances. Some units determine level and plumb in several directions—a useful feature when setting and aligning posts and beams.

Water Level

A water level is more accurate and easier to use than mason's string and a line level when laying out a large deck or for one that is built around a house corner. This tool is a long length of clear plastic tubing with clamps at each end (some units have battery-powered sensors that emit a signal when level is reached). Tint the water with red food dye to make it easier to see.

1 Siphon water into the tubing from a bucket. Clamp the lower end of the tubing after water begins flowing from it to prevent trapping water bubbles. Clamp the top end of the tubing when water is 10 to 12" from it.

2 Hold one end of the tubing at the installed ledger (pages 46 to 53). Open the clamp on the tubing and raise or lower it until the water level is aligned with the lower edge of the ledger. Drive a screw through the clamp to hold the weight of the tubing and tape the tubing in place so it is vertical.

3 Lower the other end of the tubing a few inches beneath the bottom edge of the ledger and move to the post you are leveling. Open the clamp and slowly raise the tubing while checking the other end attached to the ledger.

4 Make certain the water level line at the ledger is aligned with its bottom edge, adjusting the tubing at your location in small increments, as necessary. Mark the water level line at the post.

Design & Planning

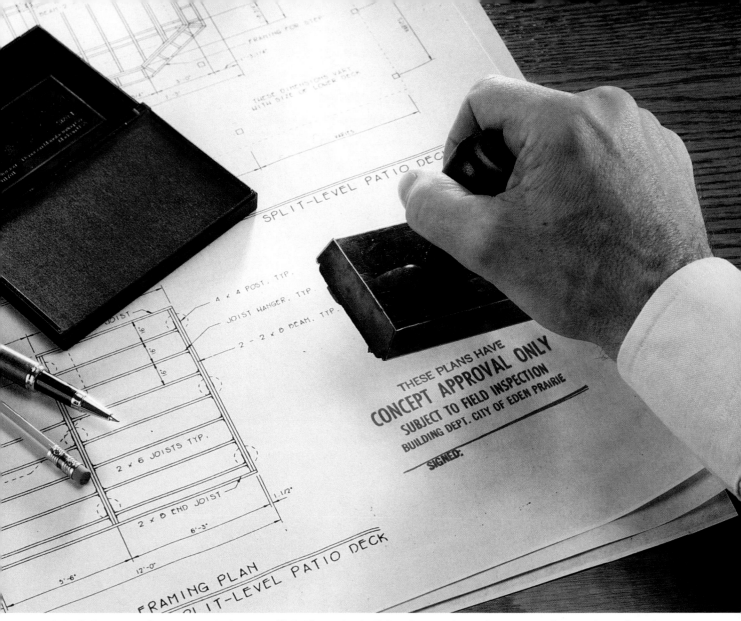

A building permit is granted after an official from the building inspections department has reviewed and approved your deck plans. Consulting a building official early in the planning process can help ensure that the approval process is a smooth one.

Planning Your Project

When building a deck, the importance of planning cannot be overemphasized. Poor planning almost always leads to frustration and disappointment; good planning helps ensure that your new deck will be an attractive, functional space that adds value to your home.

Careful planning helps guarantee that your deck will meet your needs—both aesthetically and functionally. Good planning also makes for a trouble-free construction process. Review the appropriate building techniques to be sure you understand how to build your design.

Begin the planning process by gathering ideas about how you will use your deck and what it will

look like. Then check with your local building office to determine what building code requirements that deck must meet. Use this information and develop your initial idea into detailed plan drawings that will guide construction. Finally, return to the building official; he will review your plans and grant you a permit to begin work.

Keep in mind that adjusting the size of a deck section a few inches may significantly change the amount and cost of lumber you need or the waste. For example, shortening the width of a deck level from 10'6" to 10'3" means 10'-long lumber can be used for 10'-long joists rather than cutting 12'-long lumber down to 10'3".

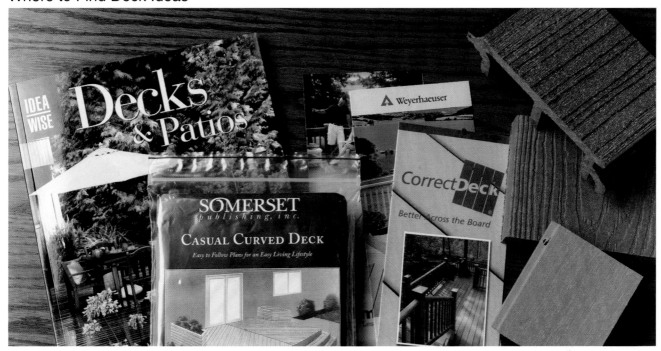

Purchased deck plans, sales literature, and home improvement magazines are good sources of ideas. Deck plans are widely available, but you may need to revise them extensively to make them work for your building site. Sales literature and product samples from lumber suppliers and hardware manufacturers often feature photos and plan drawings of elaborate decks, which you can use to develop your own design.

A great source of creative inspiration for your deck planning are books that contain color photographs of deck and landscape design, such as these.

Personal scouting is perhaps the best source of ideas. Whenever you go out for a drive or walk, keep an eye open for unique, attractive decks. Carry a camera to photograph construction details—after getting the consent of the property owner.

GAL. JOIST HANGER NAILS

TWO PIECE POST CAP

⅝" x 3" LAG SCREWS

DECK JOIST TIES

⅝" x 2" LAG SCREWS

POST ANCHORS

SIDE VIEW   FRONT VIEW

Draw detailed illustrations of the joinery methods you plan to use on all structural members of your deck. Your building official will want to see details on post-footing connections, post-beam joints, beam-joist joints, and ledger connections.

Working with Building Officials

In most regions, you must have your plans reviewed and approved by a building official if your deck is attached to a permanent structure or if it is more than 30" high. The building official makes sure that your planned deck meets building code requirements for safe construction.

These pages show some of the most common code requirements for decks. But before you design your project, check with the building inspection division of your city office, since code regulations can vary from area to area. A valuable source of planning information, the building official may provide you with a free information sheet outlining the relevant requirements.

Once you have completed your deck plans, return to the building inspections office and have the official review them. Make certain you know how many copies of the plans they require before you go. If your plans meet code, you will be issued a building permit, usually for a small fee. This process often takes a few days. Regulations may require that a field inspector review the deck at specified stages in the building process. If so, make sure to allow for the review schedule in your project schedule.

Plan-approval Checklist

When the building official reviews your deck plans, he or she will look for the following details. Make sure your plan drawings include this information when you visit the building inspection office to apply for a building permit.

- Overall size of the deck.
- Position of the deck relative to buildings and property lines. The deck must be set back at least 5 ft. from neighboring property.
- Location of all beams and posts.
- Size and on-center (OC) spacing of joists.
- Thickness of decking boards.
- Height of deck above the ground.
- Detailed drawings of joinery methods for all structural members of the deck.
- Type of soil that will support the concrete post footings: sand, gravel, or clay.
- Species of wood you will be using.
- Types of metal connectors and other hardware you plan to use when constructing your deck.

Footing diameter and depth is determined by your building official, based on the estimated load of the deck and on the composition of your soil. In regions with cold winters, footings must extend below the frost line. Minimum diameter for concrete footings is 8".

Tips for Working with Building Officials

Metal flashings must be used to prevent moisture from penetrating between the ledger and the wall.

Beams may overhang posts by no more than 1 ft. Some local building regulations require that, wherever possible, beams should rest on top of posts, secured with metal post-beam caps.

Engineered beams, such as a laminated wood product or steel girder, should be used on decks with very long joist spans, where standard dimension lumber is not adequate for the load. Engineered beams for decks must be rated for exterior use.

Railings are usually required by local Codes for decks more than 24" above the ground and must usually be at least 36" in height. Bottom rails must be positioned with no more than 4" of open space below them. Balusters, whether vertical or horizontal, can have no more than 4" between them.

Stairs must be at least 36" wide. Vertical step risers must be between 4" and 8" and uniform in height within a staircase. Treads must have a horizontal run of at least 9" and be uniform in size within a staircase. Stair railings should be 34" to 38" above the noses of the step treads, and there should be no more than 6" of space between the bottom rail and the steps. The space between the rails or balusters should be no more than 4".

Determining Lumber Size

A deck has seven major structural parts: the ledger, decking, joists, one or more beams, posts, stairway stringers, and stairway treads. To create a working design plan and choose the correct lumber size, you must know the span limits of each part of the deck. The ledger is attached directly to the house and does not have a span limit.

A span limit is the safe distance a board can cross without support from underneath. The maximum safe span depends on the size and wood species of the board. For example, 2 × 6 southern pine joists spaced 16" on-center can safely span 9'9", while 2 × 10 joists can span 16'1".

Begin planning by first choosing size and pattern for the decking. Use the tables on the opposite page. Then determine the size and layout of the joists and beams, using the information and span tables on pages 36 to 37. In general, a deck designed with larger-size lumber, like 2 × 12 joists and beams, requires fewer pieces because the boards have a large span limit. Next, compute the correct size for posts, using the table on the opposite page. Finally, choose the stair and railing lumber that fits your plan, again using the tables on the opposite page.

Use the design plans to make a complete list of the quantities of each lumber size your deck requires. Add 10% to compensate for lumber flaws and construction errors. Full-service lumberyards have a fine lumber selection, but prices may be higher than those at home improvement centers. The quality of lumber at home centers can vary, so inspect the wood and hand-pick the pieces you want or add a larger percentage to compensate for lumber flaws. Both lumberyards and home centers will deliver lumber for a small fee and you can usually return unused, uncut lumber if you keep your receipts.

Nominal vs. Actual Lumber Dimensions: When planning a deck, remember that the actual size of lumber is smaller than the nominal size by which lumber is sold. Use the actual dimensions when drawing a deck design plan.

Nominal	Actual
1 × 4	¾" × 3¾"
1 × 6	¾" × 5¾"
2 × 4	1½" × 3½"
2 × 6	1½" × 5½"
2 × 8	1½" × 7¼"
2 × 10	1½" × 9¼"
2 × 12	1½" × 11¼"
4 × 4	3½" × 3½"
6 × 6	5½" × 5½"

Recommended Decking Span Between Joists: Decking boards can be made from a variety of lumber sizes. For a basic deck use 2 × 4 or 2 × 6 lumber with joists spaced 16" apart.

Decking Boards	Recommended Span
1 × 4 or 1 × 6, laid straight	16"
1 × 4 or 1 × 6, laid diagonal	12"
2 × 4 or 2 × 6, laid straight	16"
2 × 4 or 2 × 6, laid diagonal	12"
2 × 4, laid on edge	24"

Recommended Post Size: Choose post size by finding the load area for the deck. To find the load area, multiply the distance between beams by the distance between posts. For example, on a deck that has one beam spaced 10 feet from the ledger, with posts spaced 7 feet apart, the load area is 70. If this deck is less than 6 feet high, the recommended post size is 4 × 4.

	Load Area Multiply distance between beams (feet) by the distance between posts (feet).				
Deck Height	48	72	96	120	144
Up to 6 ft.	4 × 4	4 × 4	6 × 6	6 × 6	6 × 6
More than 6 ft.	6 × 6	6 × 6	6 × 6	6 × 6	6 × 6

Minimum Stair Stringer Sizes: Size of stair stringers depends on the span of the stairway. For example, if the bottom of the stairway lies 7 feet from the deck, build the stringers from 2 × 12s. Stringers should be spaced no more than 36" apart. Use of a center stringer is recommended for stairways with more than three steps.

Span of Stairway	Stringer Size
Up to 6 ft.	2 × 10
More than 6 ft.	2 × 12

Recommended Railing Sizes: Size of posts, rails, and caps depends on the spacing of the railing posts. For example, if railing posts are spaced 6 feet apart, use 4 × 4 posts and 2 × 6 rails and caps.

Space Between Railing Posts	Post Size	Cap Size	Rail Size
2 ft. to 3 ft.	2 × 4	2 × 4	2 × 4
3 ft. to 4 ft.	4 × 4	2 × 4	2 × 4
4 ft. to 6 ft.	4 × 4	2 × 6	2 × 6

Many building centers will help you design and create deck plan drawings if you purchase your lumber and other deck materials from them. Their design capabilities include determining a detailed lumber and materials list based on the exact deck plan created.

Developing Your Deck Plan

Before you begin drawing plans, determine everything you want your deck to include. The size, shape, and location of your deck can be affected by several questions: Will the deck be used for entertaining? Will you do outdoor cooking on it? Do you need privacy? Consider how the features of the house and yard influence the deck design. Weather, time of day, and seasonal changes affect deck usage. For example, if your deck will be used mainly for summertime evening meals, look at the sun, shade, and wind patterns on the planned site during this time of day.

Building plans help you estimate lumber and hardware needs, and provide the measurements needed to lay out the deck and cut the lumber. You will need two types of drawings for your deck plans and to obtain a building permit. A plan view shows the parts of the deck as they are viewed from directly overhead. An elevation shows the deck parts as viewed from the side or front.

Calculator Conversion Chart

8ths	16ths	Decimal
	1	.0625
1	2	.125
	3	.1875
2	4	.25
	5	.3125
3	6	.375
	7	.4375
4	8	.5
	9	.5625
5	10	.625
	11	.6875
6	12	.75
	13	.8125
7	14	.875
	15	.9375
8	16	1.0

Tips for Developing a Deck Plan

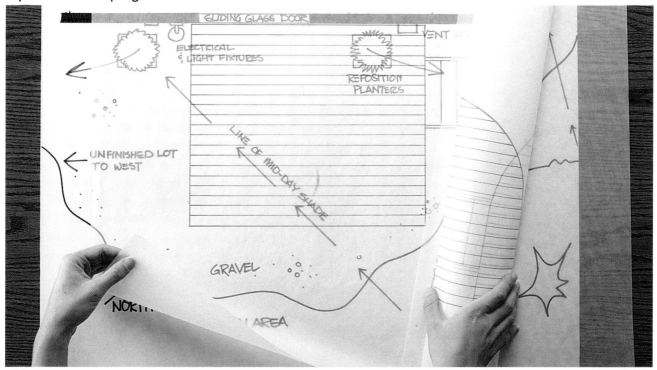

Use tracing paper to sketch different deck layouts. Then, test your ideas by overlaying the deck sketches onto a drawing of your building site. Make sure to consider sun patterns and the locations of existing landscape features when developing a deck plan.

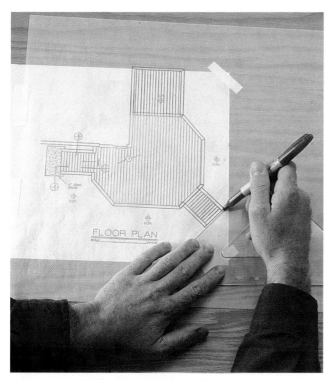

Adapt an existing deck plan, either borrowed from a book (like those on pages 198 to 289) or magazine, or purchased in blueprint form. Tracing paper, pens, and measuring tools are all you need to revise an existing deck plan.

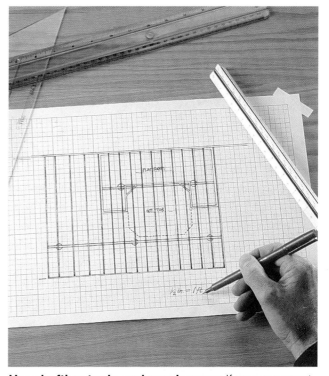

Use drafting tools and graph paper if you are creating a deck plan from scratch. Use a generous scale, such as 1" equals 1 ft., that allows you to illustrate the deck in fine detail. Remember to create both overhead plan drawings and side elevation drawings of your project.

Plan view drawings must show locations and dimensions for ledgers, footings, posts, beams, and joists.

To avoid confusion, do not try to show all parts of the deck in a single plan view, especially for a complicated or multilevel deck. First, draw one plan view that shows the deck outline and the pattern of the decking boards. Then make another plan view (or more) that shows the underlying ledger, joists, beams, and posts.

Elevation drawings must include deck dimensions, size and type of hardware to be used, beam sizes (if visible in drawing), and footing locations and their dimensions. Also indicate the grade of the ground in the deck area. Make multiple elevation drawings if necessary for complicated or multilevel decks.

Basic Deck
Building Techniques

Building Decks:
A Step-by-Step Overview

Review the design plan (pages 38 to 41) and the directions on pages 46 to 107 before beginning deck construction. Build the deck in several stages, and gather tools and materials for each stage before beginning. Arrange to have a helper for the more difficult stages.

Check with local utilities for the location of underground electrical, telephone, or water lines. Apply for a building permit, where required, and make sure a building inspector has approved the deck design before beginning work.

The time it takes to build a deck depends on the size and complexity of the design. A rectangular deck, about 10 ft. × 14 ft., can be completed in two or three weekends.

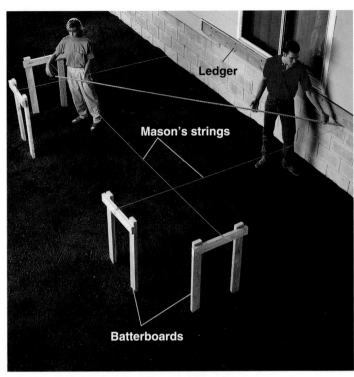

1 Install a ledger to anchor the deck to the house and to serve as reference for laying out footings (pages 46 to 53). Use batterboards and mason's strings to locate footings, and check for square by measuring diagonals (pages 54 to 59).

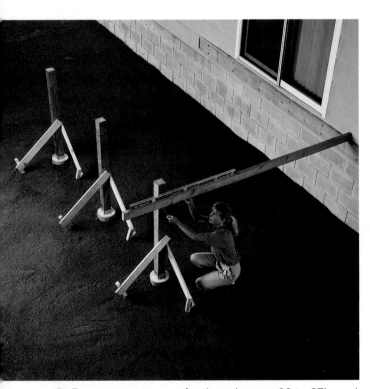

2 Pour concrete post footings (pages 60 to 67), and install metal post anchors (pages 69 to 70). Set and brace the posts, attach them to the post anchors, and mark posts to show where beam will be attached (pages 71 to 73).

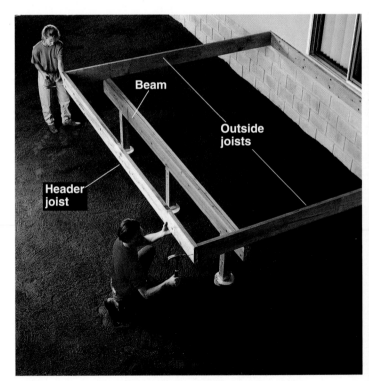

3 Fasten the beam to the posts (pages 74 to 79). Install the outside joists and header joist, using galvanized nails (pages 80 to 81).

44

4 Install metal joist hangers on the ledger and header joist, then hang the remaining joists (pages 82 to 85). Most decking patterns require joists that are spaced 16" on center.

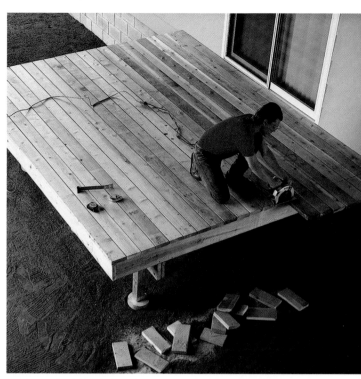

5 Lay decking boards, and trim them with a circular saw (pages 86 to 93). If desired for appearance, cover pressure-treated header and outside joists with redwood or cedar facing boards (page 89).

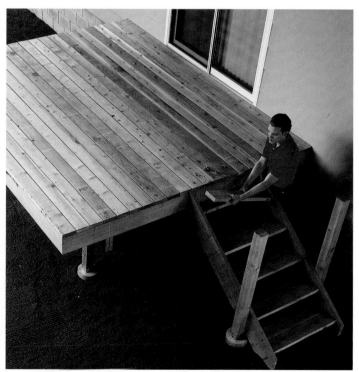

6 Build deck stairs (pages 94 to 99). Stairs provide access to the deck and establish traffic patterns.

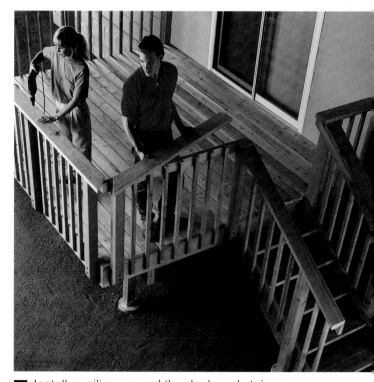

7 Install a railing around the deck and stairway (pages 100 to 107). A railing adds a decorative touch and may be required on any deck that is more than 24" above the ground. If desired, finish the underside of the deck (pages 108 to 111).

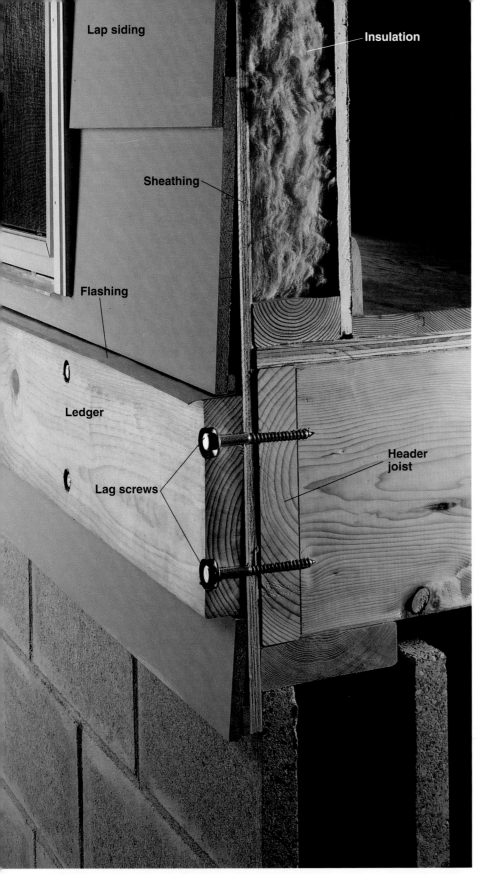

Lap siding

Insulation

Sheathing

Flashing

Ledger

Lag screws

Header joist

Ledger (shown in cross section) is made from pressure-treated lumber. Lap siding is cut away to expose sheathing and to provide a flat surface for attaching the ledger. Galvanized flashing tucked under siding prevents moisture damage to wood. Countersunk ⅜ × 4" lag screws hold ledger to header joist inside house. If there is access to the space behind the header joist, such as in an unfinished basement, attach the ledger with carriage bolts, washers, and nuts.

Installing a Ledger

The first step in building an attached deck is to fasten the ledger to the house. The ledger anchors the deck and establishes a reference point for building the deck square and level. The ledger also supports one end of all the deck joists, so it must be attached securely to the framing members of the house.

Install the ledger so that the surface of the decking boards will be 1" below the indoor floor level. This height difference prevents rainwater or melted snow from seeping into the house.

Everything You Need

Tools: pencil, level, circular saw with carbide blade, chisel, hammer, metal snips, caulk gun, drill and bits (¼" twist, 1" spade, ⅜" and ⅝" masonry), ratchet wrench, awl, rubber mallet.

Materials: pressure-treated lumber, galvanized flashing, 8d galvanized common nails, silicone caulk, ⅜ × 4" lag screws and 1" washers, lead masonry anchors for ⅜" lag screws (for brick walls).

Supplies: 2 × 4s for braces.

How to Attach a Ledger to Lap Siding

1 Draw an outline showing where the deck will fit against the house, using a level as a guide. Include the thickness of the outside joists and any decorative facing boards that will be installed.

2 Cut out siding along outline, using a circular saw. Set blade depth to same thickness as siding, so that blade does not cut into sheathing.

3 Use a chisel to finish the cutout where circular saw blade does not reach. Hold the chisel with the bevel-side in.

4 Measure and cut ledger from pressure-treated lumber. Remember that ledger will be shorter than overall length of cutout.

(continued next page)

5 Cut galvanized flashing to length of cutout, using metal snips. Slide flashing up under siding.

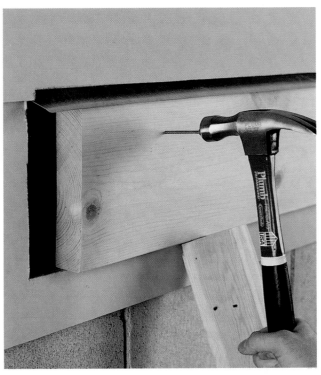

6 Center the ledger in the cutout, underneath the flashing. Brace in position, and tack ledger into place with 8d galvanized nails. Apply a thick bead of silicone caulk to crack between siding and flashing.

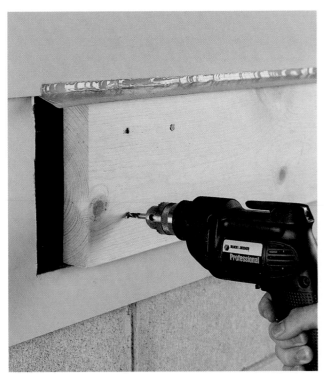

7 Drill pairs of ¼" pilot holes spaced every 2 feet, through the ledger and sheathing and into the header joist.

8 Counterbore each pilot hole to ½" depth, using a 1" spade bit.

9 Attach ledger to wall with ⅜ × 4" lag screws and washers, using a ratchet wrench.

10 Seal lag screw heads with silicone caulk. Seal the crack between the wall and the sides and bottom of the ledger.

How to Attach a Ledger to Masonry

1 Measure and cut ledger. Ledger will be shorter than overall length of outline. Drill pairs of ¼" pilot holes every 2 feet in ledger. Counterbore each pilot hole to ½" depth, using a 1" spade bit.

2 Draw a outline of the deck on the wall, using a level as a guide. Center ledger in outline on wall, and brace in position. Mark the pilot hole locations on wall, using an awl or nail. Remove ledger.

(continued next page)

3 Drill anchor holes 3" deep into masonry, using a ⅝" masonry bit.

4 Drive lead masonry anchors for ⅜" lag screws into drilled holes, using a rubber mallet.

5 Attach ledger to wall with ⅜ × 4" lag screws and washers, using a ratchet wrench. Tighten screws firmly, but do not overtighten.

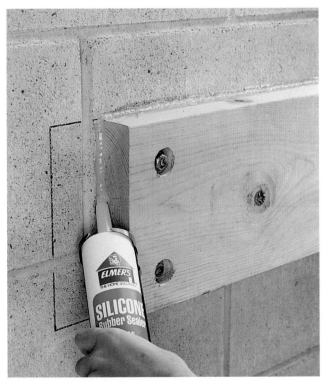

6 Seal the cracks between the wall and ledger with silicone caulk. Also seal the lag screw heads.

How to Attach a Ledger to Stucco

1 Draw outline of deck on wall, using a level as a guide. Measure and cut ledger, and drill pilot holes (page 49, step 1). Brace ledger against wall, and mark hole locations, using a nail or awl.

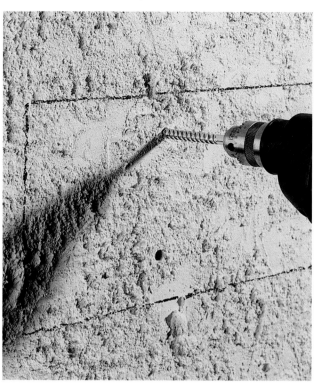

2 Remove ledger. Drill pilot holes through stucco layer of wall, using a ⅜" masonry bit.

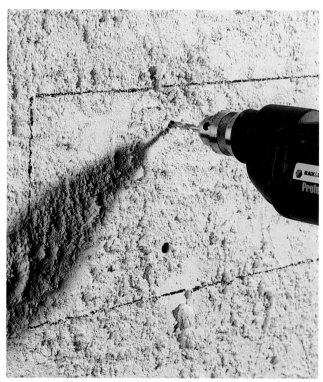

3 Extend each pilot hole through the sheathing and into the header joist, using a ¼" bit. Reposition ledger and brace in place.

4 Attach ledger to wall with ⅜ × 4" lag screws and washers, using a ratchet wrench. Seal the lag screw heads and the cracks between the wall and ledger with silicone caulk.

How to Attach a Ledger to Metal or Vinyl Siding

Deck height, finished

Outside of fascia

Lower cutout mark

1 Mark the length of the ledger location, adding 1½" at each end to allow for the rim joists that will be installed later. Also allow for fascia board thickness if it will be added. Then mark the top and bottom edges of the ledger at both ends of its location. Snap lines for the ledger position between the marks. Check the lines for level and adjust as necessary. You may be able to use the siding edges to help determine the ledger location, but only after checking to see if the edges are level. Don't assume siding is installed level.

2 Set the circular saw blade depth to cut through the siding. Use a metal cutting blade for metal siding; a 40-tooth carbide blade works well on vinyl siding. Cut on the outside of the lines along the top and sides of the ledger location, stopping the blade when it reaches a corner.

3 Snap a new level line ½" above the bottom line and make your final cut along this line. This leaves a small lip of siding that will fit under the ledger.

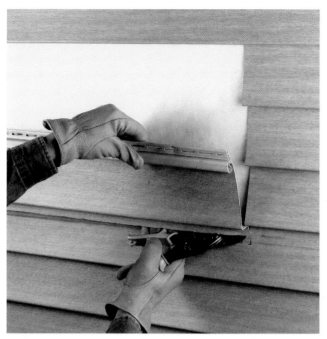

4 Complete the cuts in the corners, using tin snips on metal siding or a utility knife on vinyl siding. A hammer and sharp chisel also may be used.

5 Insert building felt underneath the siding and over the existing felt that has been damaged by the cuts. It is easiest to cut and install two long strips. Cut and insert the first strip so it is underneath the siding at the ends and bottom edge of the cutout and attach it with staples. Cut and insert the second strip so it is underneath the siding at the ends and top edge of the cutout, so that it overlaps the first strip by at least 3".

6 Cut and insert galvanized flashing (also called Z-flashing) underneath the full length of the top edge of the cutout. Do not use fasteners; pressure will hold the flashing in place until the ledger is installed.

7 Cut and install the ledger board (see pages 48 to 49).

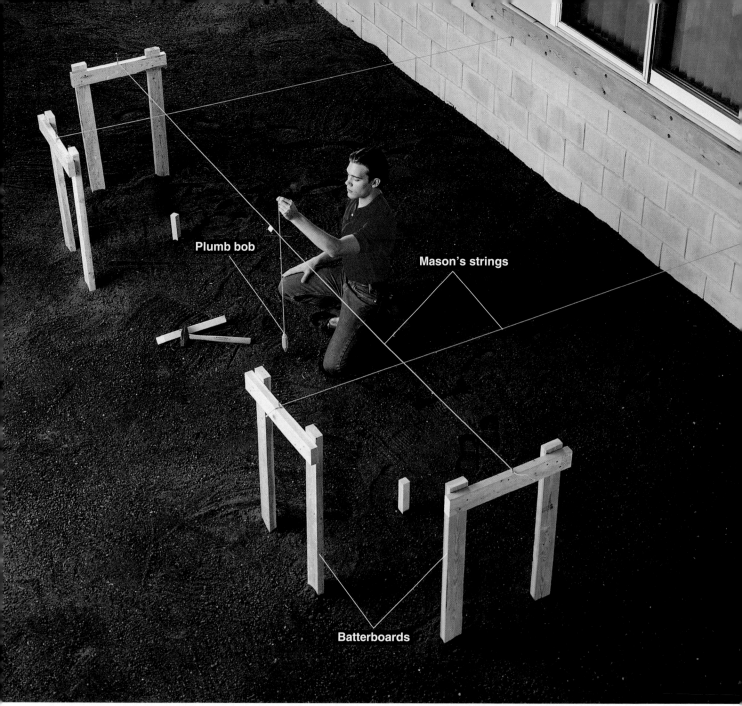

Plumb bob

Mason's strings

Batterboards

Mason's strings stretched between ledger and batterboards are used to position footings for deck posts. Use a plumb bob and stakes to mark the ground at the exact centerpoints of footings.

Locating Post Footings

Establish the exact locations of all concrete footings by stretching mason's strings across the site. Use the ledger board as a starting point. These perpendicular layout strings will be used to locate holes for concrete footings, and to position metal post anchors on the finished footings. Anchor the layout strings with temporary 2 × 4 supports, often called batterboards.

Everything You Need

Tools: tape measure, felt-tipped pen, circular saw, screwgun, framing square, masonry hammer, claw hammer, line level, plumb bob.

Supplies: 2 × 4s, 10d nails, 2½" wallboard screws, mason's strings, masking tape.

How to Locate Post Footings

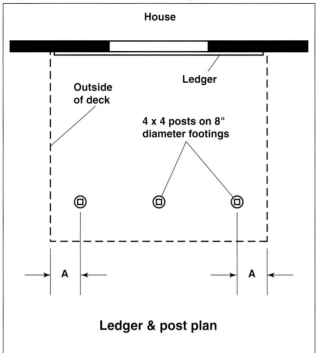

House

Ledger

Outside of deck

4 x 4 posts on 8" diameter footings

A

A

Ledger & post plan

1 Use the design plan (page 40) to find distance (A). Measure from the side of the deck to the center of each outside post. Use the elevation drawings (page 41) to find the height of each deck post.

2 Cut 2 × 4 stakes for batterboards, each about 8" longer than post height. Trim one end of each stake to a point, using a circular saw. Cut 2 × 4 crosspieces, each about 2 feet long.

3 Assemble batterboards by attaching crosspieces to stakes with 2½" wallboard screws. Crosspieces should be about 2" below tops of stakes.

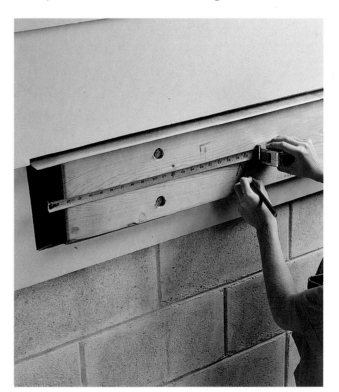

4 Transfer measurement A (step 1) to ledger, and mark reference points at each end of ledger. String lines will be stretched from these points on ledger. When measuring, remember to allow for outside joists and facing that will be butted to the ends of the ledger.

(continued next page)

5 Drive a batterboard 6" into the ground, about 2 feet past the post location. Crosspiece of batterboard should be parallel to the ledger.

6 Drive a 10d nail into bottom of ledger at reference point (step 4). Attach a mason's string to nail.

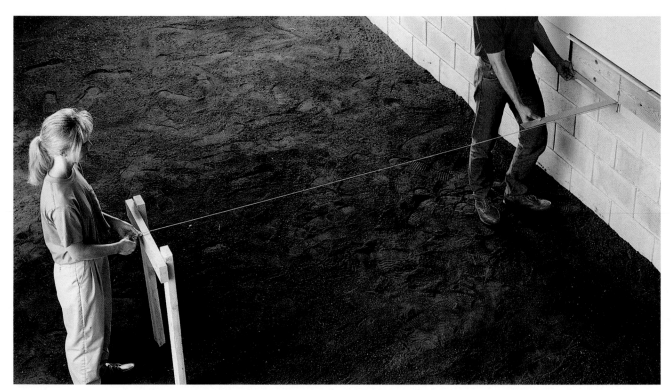

7 Extend the mason's string so that it is taut and perpendicular to the ledger. Use a framing square as a guide. Secure the string temporarily by wrapping it several times around the batterboard.

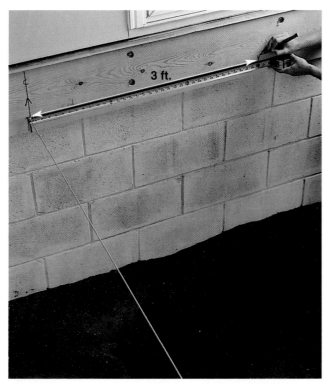

8 Check the mason's string for square using "3-4-5 carpenter's triangle." First, measure along the ledger 3 feet from the mason's string and mark a point, using a felt-tipped pen.

9 Measure mason's string 4 feet from edge of ledger, and mark with masking tape.

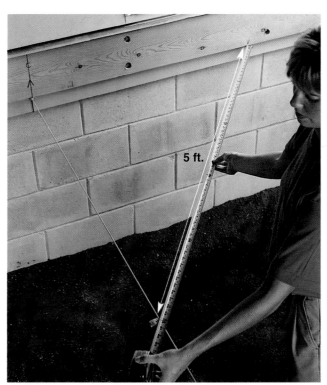

10 Measure distance between marks. If string is perpendicular to ledger, the distance will be exactly 5 feet. If necessary, move string left or right on batterboard until distance between marks is 5 feet.

11 Drive a 10d nail into top of batterboard at string location. Leave about 2" of nail exposed. Tie string to nail.

(continued next page)

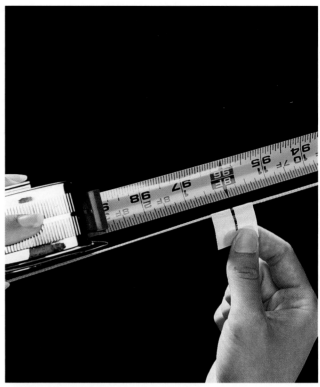

12 Hang a line level on the mason's string. Raise or lower string until it is level. Locate other outside post footing, repeating steps 5 to 12.

13 Measure along mason's strings from ledger to find centerpoint of posts. Mark centerpoints on stings, using masking tape.

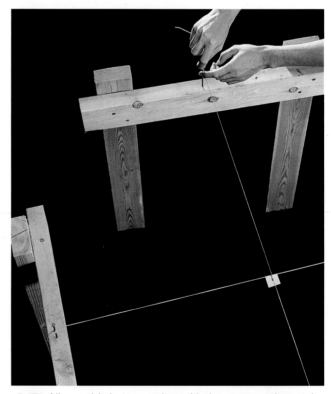

14 Drive additional batterboards into ground, about 2 feet outside mason's strings and lined up with post centerpoint marks (step 13).

15 Align a third cross string with the centerpoint marks on the first strings. Drive 10d nails in new batterboards, and tie off cross string on nails. Cross string should be close to, but not touching, the first strings.

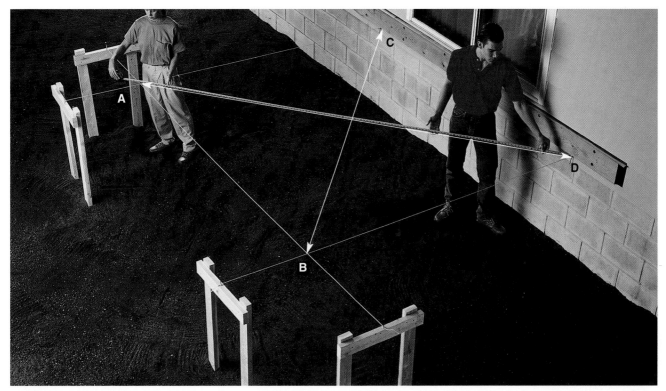

16 Check strings for square by measuring distances A-B and C-D. Measure diagonals A-D and B-C from edge of ledger to opposite corners. If strings are square, measurement A-B will be same as C-D, and diagonal A-D will be same as B-C. If necessary, adjust strings on batterboards until square.

17 Measure along the cross string and mark center-points of any posts that will be installed between the outside posts.

18 Use a plumb bob to mark post centerpoints on the ground, directly under the marks on the mason's strings. Drive a stake into ground at each point. Remove mason's strings before digging footings.

Digging & Pouring Footings

Concrete footings hold deck posts in place and support the weight of the deck. Check local codes to determine the size and depth of footings required for your area. In cold climates, footings must be deeper than the soil frost line.

To help protect posts from water damage, each footing should be poured so that it is 2" above ground level. Tube-shaped forms let you extend the footings above ground level.

It is easy and inexpensive to mix your own concrete by combining portland cement, sand, gravel, and water. See pages 22 to 23 for more information on buying and mixing concrete.

As an alternative to inserting J-bolts into wet concrete (see page 63), you can use masonry anchors, or install anchor bolts with an epoxy designed for deck footings and other masonry installations. The epoxy method provides you with more time to reset layout strings for locating bolt locations, and eliminates the problem of J-bolts tilting or sinking into concrete that is too loose. Most building centers sell threaded rod, washers, nuts, and epoxy syringes, but you also can buy these items separately at most hardware centers.

Before digging, consult local utilities for location of any underground electrical, telephone, or water lines that might interfere with footings.

Power augers quickly dig holes for post footings. They are available at rental centers. Some models can be operated by one person, while others require two people.

Everything You Need

Tools: power auger or clamshell posthole digger, tape measure, pruning saw, shovel, reciprocating saw or handsaw, torpedo level, hoe, trowel, shovel, old toothbrush, plumb bob, utility knife.

Materials: 8" concrete tube forms, portland cement, sand, gravel, J-bolts.

Supplies: wheelbarrow, scrap 2 × 4.

How to Dig & Pour Post Footings

1 Dig holes for post footings with a clamshell digger or power auger, centering the holes on the layout stakes. For holes deeper than 35", use a power auger.

2 Measure hole depth. Local building codes specify depth of footings. Cut away tree roots, if necessary, using a pruning saw.

3 Pour 2" to 3" of loose gravel in the bottom of each footing hole. Gravel will provide drainage under concrete footings.

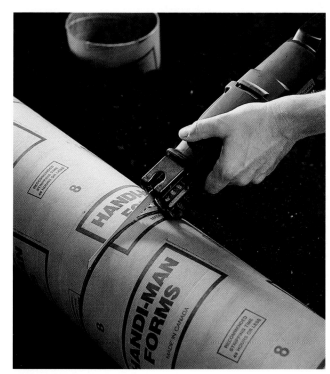

4 Add 2" to hole depth so that footings will be above ground level. Cut concrete tube forms to length, using a reciprocating saw or handsaw. Make sure cut is straight.

5 Insert tubes into footing holes, leaving about 2" of tube above ground level. Use a level to make sure tops of tubes are level. Pack soil around tubes to hold them in place.

(continued next page)

6 Mix dry ingredients for concrete in a wheelbarrow, using a hoe.

7 Form a hollow in center of dry concrete mixture. Slowly pour a small amount of water into hollow, and blend in dry mixture with a hoe.

8 Add more water gradually, mixing thoroughly until concrete is firm enough to hold its shape when sliced with a trowel.

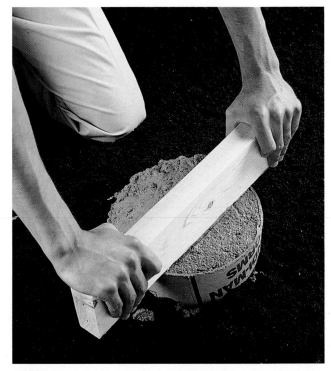

9 Pour concrete slowly into the tube form, guiding concrete from the wheelbarrow with a shovel. Fill about half of the form, using a long stick to tamp the concrete, filling any air gaps in the footing. Then finish pouring and tamping concrete into the form.

10 Level the concrete by pulling a 2 × 4 across the top of the tube form, using a sawing motion. Add concrete to any low spots. Retie the mason's strings on the batterboards, and recheck measurements.

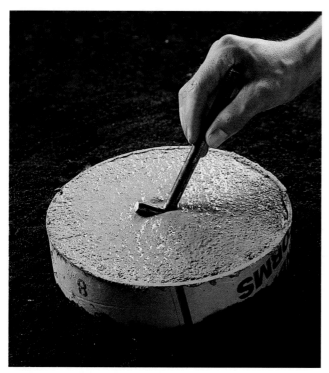

11 Insert a J-bolt at an angle into the wet concrete at center of the footing.

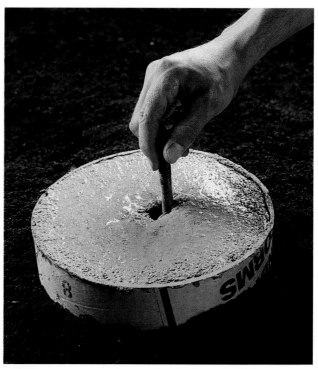

12 Lower the J-bolt slowly into the concrete, wiggling it slightly to eliminate any air gaps.

13 Set the J-bolt so ¾" to 1" is exposed above concrete. Brush away any wet concrete on bolt threads with an old toothbrush.

14 Use a plumb bob to make sure the J-bolt is positioned exactly at center of post location.

15 Use a torpedo level to make sure the J-bolt is plumb. If necessary, adjust the bolt and repack concrete. Let concrete cure, then cut away exposed portion of tube with a utility knife.

How to Install Anchor Bolts with Epoxy

1 After the concrete footing (see pages 61 to 62) has cured at least 48 hours and the bolt locations have been determined (see page 59), drill a hole for the threaded rod, using a hammer drill and masonry bit sized to match the diameter of rod. Make vertical holes, using a speed square to align the drill. Set the depth gauge of the drill so that ¾" to 1" of rod will protrude above the footing surface.

2 Use a shop vacuum to remove drilling debris. Clean the hole thoroughly, using a long, thin object, such as a narrow blade screwdriver, to loosen the debris. Otherwise the epoxy won't bond firmly with the concrete. Test fit the threaded rod to make certain it will insert to the proper depth.

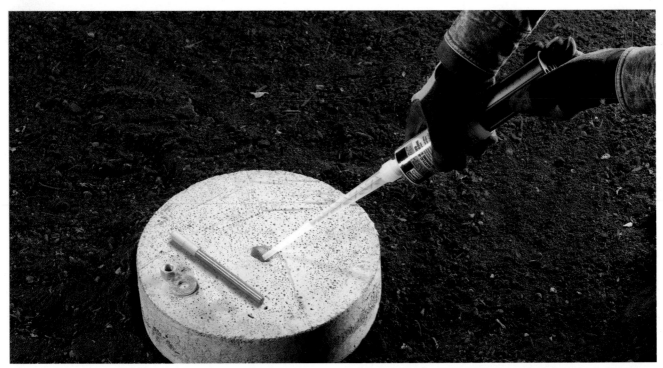

3 Wrap masking tape around the top ¾" to 1" of the threaded rod. This will help you insert it to the proper depth and protect the threads from epoxy. Inject epoxy into the hole, using the mixing syringe provided by the manufacturer. Use enough epoxy so a small amount is forced from the hole when the rod is fully inserted. Push the rod into the hole with a twisting motion as soon as the epoxy is injected because it begins to harden immediately.

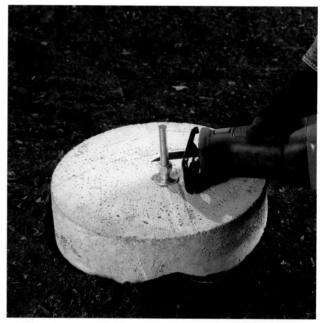

4 Make certain the threaded rod is fully inserted, checking the height of the rod above the footing surface. Let the epoxy cure for 16 to 24 hours (follow the manufacturer's instructions). Curing times are affected by moisture and temperature.

5 If you can't push the rod in far enough, don't try pulling it out. Wait until the epoxy cures, then install a nut on the rod past the point where you need to cut it. Using a hacksaw or reciprocating saw with a metal cutting blade, trim it to proper length above the footing surface. Remove the nut to rethread the cut end.

How to Dig & Pour a Stair Pad

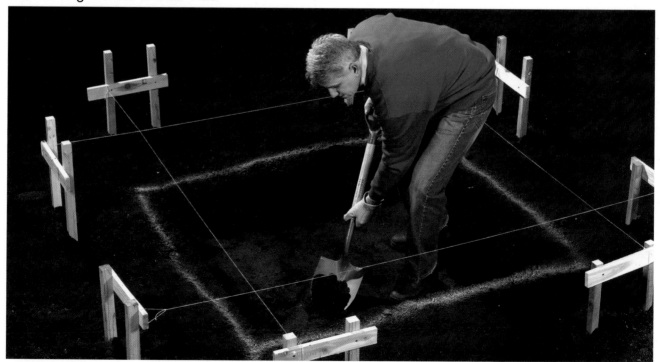

1 Using batterboards and mason's string, lay out the pad excavation area, adding at least 1½" on each side to allow for the 2 × 4 forms. Mark the excavation outline using spray paint or flour. Excavate the area to a depth that allows for a 4"-thick layer of compactable gravel and a 4"-thick concrete pad, with the surface of the pad 1" to 2" higher than ground level. (Check dimensions with your local building code.) The excavation area should be reasonably level.

(continued next page)

2 Build a form from 2 × 4s around the pad perimeter. Drive 12"-long, 1 × 3 stakes at each end of one side of the form, level the form at the proper height, then drive screws through the stakes into the form. Drive stakes for the opposite side, then level it with the first. (Use a straight board if the level isn't long enough to span the distance.) Square the form by measuring the diagonals and adjusting until they are equal. Drive stakes and attach the remaining sides of the form.

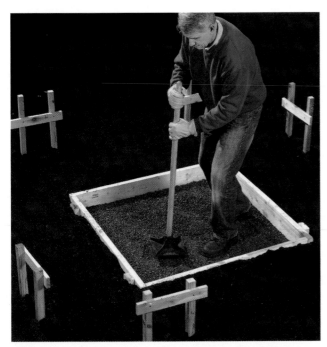

3 Tamp compactable gravel into a level 4"-thick layer in the bottom of the form. Coat the inside faces of the form with vegetable oil to make form removal easier.

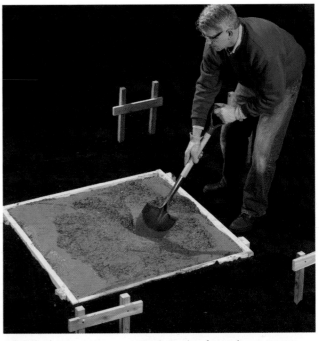

4 Mix and pour concrete into the form (see page 62). Tamp the concrete throughout the pad area to settle the concrete and remove air pockets. Pour and tamp enough concrete so that the form is slightly overfilled.

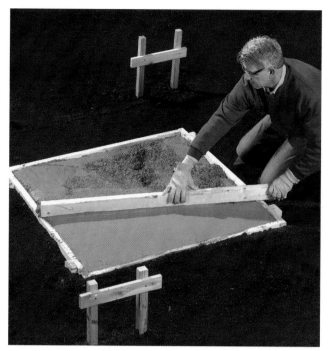

5 Screed the concrete surface with a straight 2 × 4 that is 2-ft. longer than the width of the form. Fill low spots with concrete and screed again as necessary.

6 Work the concrete surface (called floating) with a wood float just long enough to make it smooth and bring a thin film of water (called bleed water) to the surface. Don't float the surface too long after bleed water appears or the concrete will cure with a brittle surface that will deteriorate quickly.

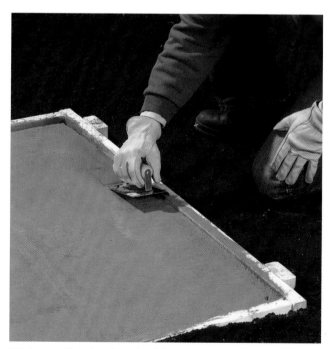

7 Immediately after the bleed water has evaporated, cut about 1" deep between the form and concrete with the point of a tuck-pointing trowel. Smooth and shape the perimeter edges of the pad with an edger. Lift the leading edge slightly as you move it so the edge doesn't dig into the concrete.

8 Brush the surface of the pad with a stiff bristle broom to provide a rougher surface for better traction. Cover the pad with a piece of 3-mil plastic sheeting and let the pad cure for at least a week. In hot weather, lift the plastic occasionally and mist the pad lightly with water so it doesn't dry too quickly. After curing, remove stakes and screws and pry off the form pieces. Backfill around the pad.

Setting Posts

Posts support the deck beams and transfer the weight of the deck to the concrete footings. For maximum strength, the posts must be plumb.

To prevent rot or insect damage, use pressure-treated lumber for posts, and make sure the factory-treated end faces down.

Use metal post anchors to attach the posts to the concrete footings. Post anchors have drainage holes and pedestals that raise the ends of the wood posts above the concrete footings.

Everything You Need

Tools: pencil, framing square, ratchet wrench, tape measure, power miter saw or circular saw, hammer, screwgun, level, combination square.

Materials: metal post anchors, nuts for J-bolts, lumber for posts, 6d galvanized common nails, 2" wallboard screws.

Supplies: long, straight 2 × 4; 1 × 4s; pointed 2 × 2 stakes.

How to Attach Post Anchors

1 Mark the top of each footing as a reference line for installing post anchors. Lay a long, straight 2 × 4 flat across two or three concrete footings, parallel to the ledger, with one edge tight against the J-bolts.

2 Draw a reference line across each concrete footing, using a edge of the 2 × 4 as a guide. Remove the 2 × 4.

3 Place a metal post anchor on each concrete footing, and center it over the J-bolt.

(continued next page)

How to Attach Post Anchors (continued)

4 Use a framing square to make sure the post anchor is positioned square to the reference line drawn on the footing.

5 Thread a nut over each J-bolt, and tighten it securely with a ratchet wrench.

How to Set Posts

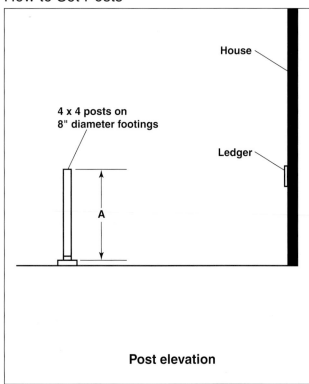

House

4 x 4 posts on
8" diameter footings

Ledger

A

Post elevation

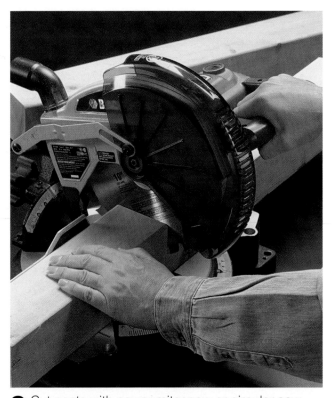

1 Use the elevation drawing from the design plan (page 41) to find the length of each post (A). Add 6" for a cutting margin.

2 Cut posts with power miter saw or circular saw. Make sure factory-treated ends of posts are square. If necessary, square them by trimming with a power miter saw or circular saw.

3 Place post in anchor, and tack into place with a single 6d galvanized common nail.

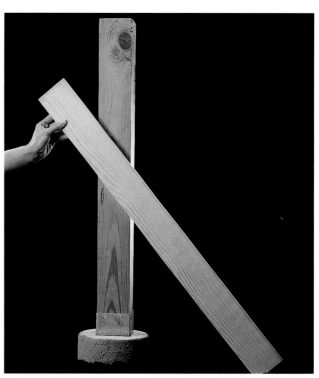

4 Brace post with a 1 × 4. Place the 1 × 4 flat across post, so that it crosses the post at a 45° angle about halfway up.

5 Attach the brace to the post temporarily with a single 2" wallboard screw.

6 Drive a pointed 2 × 2 stake into the ground next to the end of the brace.

(continued next page)

How to Set Posts (continued)

7 Use a level to make sure the post is plumb. Adjust the post, if necessary.

8 Attach the brace to the stake with two 2" wall-board screws.

9 Plumb and brace the post on the side perpendicular to the first brace.

10 Attach the post to the post anchor with 6d galvanized common nails.

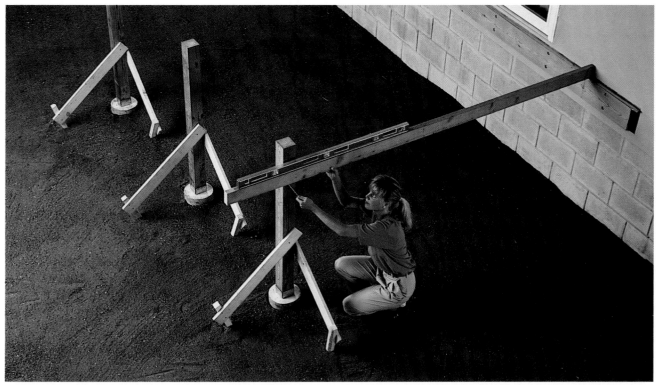

11 Position a straight 2 × 4 with one end on the ledger and the other end across the face of the post. Level the 2 × 4, then lower its post end ¼" for every 3 ft. between the ledger and the post (for water runoff). Draw a line on the post along the bottom of the 2 × 4. This line indicates the top of the joists.

12 From the line shown in step 11, measure down and mark the posts a distance equal to the width of the joists.

13 Use a square to draw a line completely around the post. This line indicates the top of the beam. From this line, repeat steps 12 and 13 to determine the bottom of the beam.

Installing a Beam

Use metal post-beam caps to secure deck beams to post tops. Post-beam caps ensure strong post to beam joints, and are required by many local building codes.

Everything You Need

Tools: tape measure, pencil, circular saw, paint brush, combination square, screwgun, drill, ⅜" auger bit, 1" spade bit, ratchet wrench, caulk gun, reciprocating saw or handsaw.

Materials: pressure-treated lumber, clear sealer-preservative, 2½" galvanized deck screws, 10d joist hanger nails, ⅜ × 8" carriage bolts with washers and nuts, ⅜ × 2" lag screws, silicone caulk.

Deck beams attach to the posts to help support the weight of the joists and decking. Installation methods depend on the deck design and local codes, so check with a building inspector to determine what is acceptable in your area.

In a saddle beam deck, the beam is attached directly on top of the posts. Metal fasteners, called post-beam caps, are used to align and strengthen the beam-to-post connection. The advantage is that the post bears the weight of the deck.

A notched-post deck requires 6 × 6 posts notched at the post top to accommodate the full size of the beam. The deck's weight is transferred to the posts, as in a post-and-beam deck.

A sandwich beam has two beam members that are sandwiched around posts. Because this method has less strength than a saddle beam design, local codes may restrict its use, or may require that the beam members be reinforced with joist ties (see page 19).

How to Prepare a Beam for Installation

Saddle type

Notched-post type

Sandwich type

Beam length can be found in the deck design plan (page 40). Three methods of beam installation are shown above. Check with a building inspector in your area to determine which methods are acceptable.

1 Measure and mark two straight pressure-treated boards to length. Cut boards with a circular saw. Seal cut ends with clear sealer-preservative.

2 Hold beam boards together. Measure and mark the post locations on the tops and sides of boards, using a combination square as a guide.

How to Install a Beam for a Saddle Beam Deck

1 Cut each post at the line indicating the bottom of the beam (page 75), using a reciprocating saw.

2 Attach post-beam caps to the top of posts. Fasten on opposite sides, using 10d joist hanger nails.

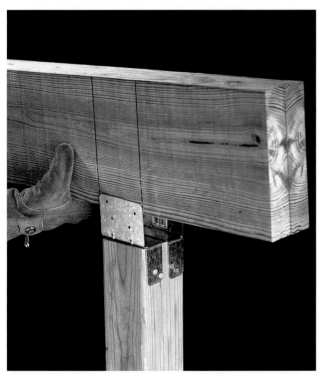

3 With someone's help, lift the beam into the post-beam caps. Make sure the crown side is up. Align the post location marks with the post-beam caps.

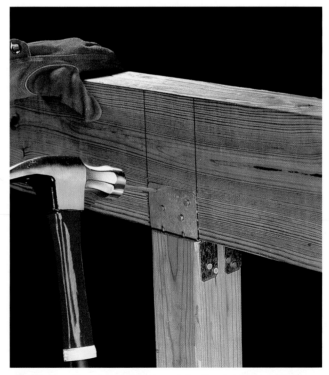

4 Fasten the post-beam cap to the beam on both sides, using 10d joist hanger nails.

How to Install a Beam for a Notched-Post Deck

1 Remove 6 × 6 posts from post anchors and cut to finished height. Measure and mark a 3" × 7½" notch at the top of each post. Trace the lines on all sides, using a framing square.

2 Use a circular saw to rough-cut the notches, then a reciprocating saw or hand saw to finish. Reattach posts to the post anchors (pages 71 to 72), with the notch-side facing away from the deck.

3 With someone's help, lift beam (crown side up) into the notches. Align beam and clamp to posts. Counterbore two ½"-deep holes, using a 1" spade bit, then drill ⅜" pilot holes through the beam and post, using a ⅜" auger bit.

4 Insert carriage bolts to each pilot hole. Add a washer and nut to the counterbore-side of each, and tighten using a ratchet. Seal both ends with silicone caulk. Apply self-sealing membrane to top surfaces of beam and posts if necessary (see page 17).

How to Install a Beam for a Sandwich Beam Deck

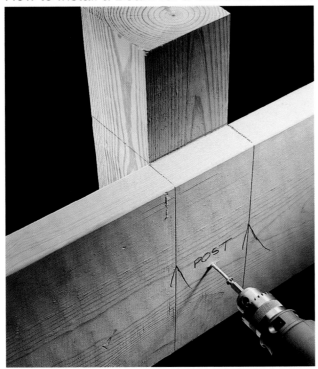

1 With the crown side up, place one beam member against the inner side of posts. Align post location marks on beam member with beam height marks on posts. Tack in position with 2½" deck screws. Repeat for second beam member on the outer side of posts.

2 On the inner beam member, counterbore two holes ½" deep, using 1" spade bit.

3 At the center of the counterbore holes, drill ⅜" pilot holes through the entire beam-post-beam assembly, using a ⅜" auger bit.

4 Thread a ⅜ × 8" carriage bolt through each pilot hole, with a washer and nut on the inner side with the counterbore. Tighten with a rachet wrench until the nut is snug and recessed in the counterbore hole. Reinforce beam members with joist ties (page 19).

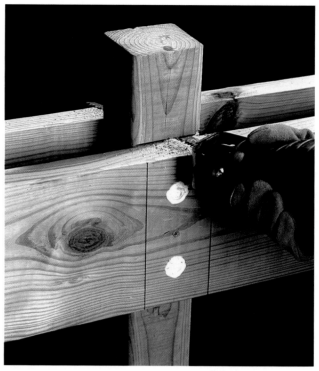

5 Seal around the nuts in the counterbore holes with silicone caulk.

6 Cut tops of posts flush with top edge of beam, using a reciprocating saw or handsaw. Seal cut ends of posts with clear sealer-preservative.

Reinforce elevated decks with beveled 4 × 4 Y-braces. For a solid beam (A), attach with lag screws to the sides of the post and the bottom of the beam. On a sandwich beam (B), use carriage bolts to mount the braces in between the two beam members.

Hanging Joists

Joists provide support for the decking boards. They are attached to the ledger and header joist with galvanized metal joist hangers, and are nailed to the top of the beam.

For strength and durability, use pressure-treated lumber for all joists. The exposed outside joists and header joist can be faced with redwood or cedar boards for a more attractive appearance.

Everything You Need

Tools: tape measure, pencil, hammer, combination square, circular saw, paintbrush, drill, twist bits (1/16", 1/4"), 1" spade bit.

Materials: pressure-treated lumber, clear sealer-preservative, 10d and 16d galvanized common nails, 10d joist hanger nails, joist angle brackets, galvanized metal joist hangers, 3/8 × 4" lag screws and 1" washers.

How to Hang Joists

Joist plan

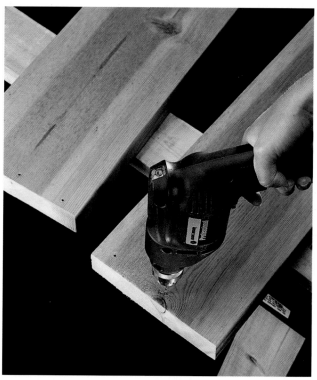

1 Use the deck plan (page 40) to find the spacing (A) between joists, and the length of inner joists (B), outside joists (C), and header joist (D). Measure and mark lumber for outside joists, using a combination square as a guide. Cut joists with a circular saw. Seal cut ends with clear sealer-preservative.

2 Drill three ⅟₁₆" pilot holes, spaced about 3" apart, through one end of each outside joist.

3 Fasten the outside joists in position at ends of ledger with 16d galvanized common nails driven into the ledger.

4 Attach the outside joists to the top of the beam by toenailing them with 10d galvanized common nails.

(continued next page)

How to Hang Joists (continued)

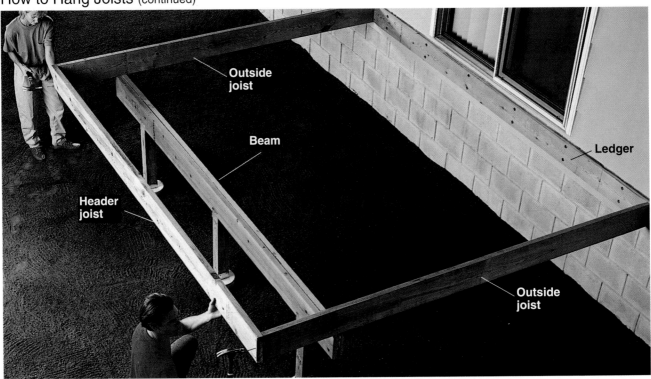

5 Measure and cut header joist. Seal cut ends with clear sealer-preservative. Drill 1/16" pilot holes at each end of header joist. Attach header to ends of outside joists with 16d galvanized common nails.

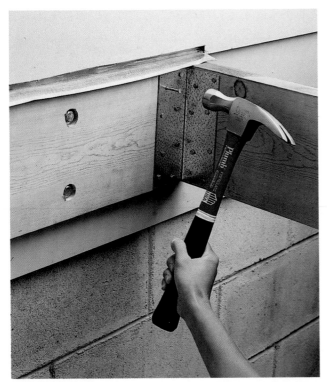

6 Strengthen each inside corner of the deck frame with an angle bracket. Attach the brackets with 10d joist hanger nails

7 Measure along ledger from edge of outside joist, and mark where joists will be attached to ledger.

8 Draw the outline of each joist on the ledger, using a combination square as a guide.

9 Measure along the beam from outside joist, and mark where joists will cross the beam. Draw the outlines across top of both beam boards.

10 Measure along the header joist from the outside joist, and mark where joists will be attached to header joist. Draw the outlines on the inside of the header, using a combination square as a guide.

11 Attach joist hangers to the ledger and to the header joist. Position each hanger so that one of the flanges is against the joist outline. Nail flanges to framing member with 10d galvanized common nails.

(continued next page)

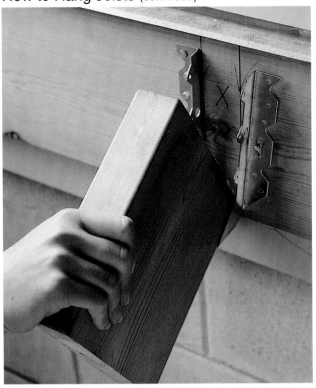

12 Cut a scrap board to use as a spacer. Hold spacer inside each joist hanger, then close the hanger around the spacer.

13 Nail the remaining side flange to the framing member with 10d joist hanger nails. Remove spacer.

14 Measure and mark lumber for joists, using a combination square as a guide. Cut joists with a circular saw.

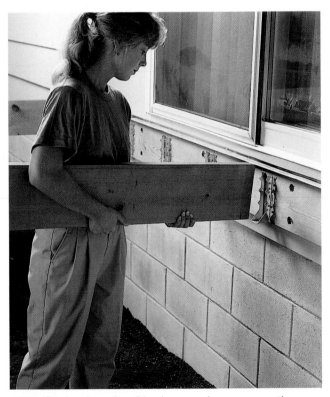

15 Seal cut ends with clear sealer-preservative. Place joists in hangers with crowned side up.

16 Attach the ledger joist hangers to the joists with 10d joist hanger nails. Drive nails into both sides of each joist.

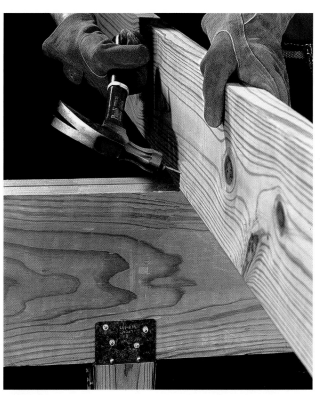

17 Align the joists with the outlines drawn on the top of the beam. Anchor the joists to the beam by toenailing from both sides with 10d galvanized nails.

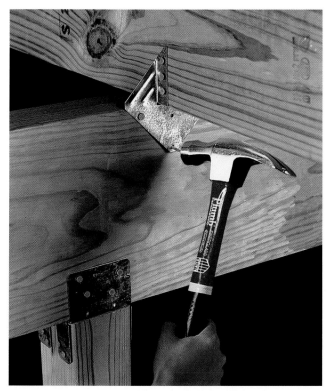

Alternate method: Fasten joists to beams using H-fit joist ties for strength and durability.

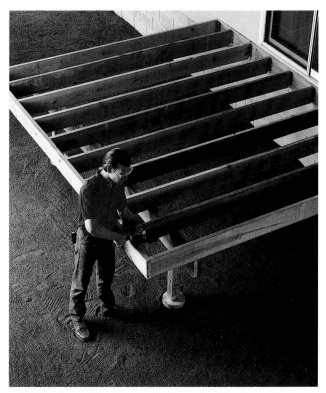

18 Attach the joists to the header joist hangers with 10d joist hanger nails. Drive nails into both sides of each joist.

Laying Decking

Buy decking boards that are long enough to span the width of the deck, if possible. If boards must be butted end-to-end, make sure to stagger the joints so they do not overlap from row to row. Predrill the ends of boards to prevent screws or nails from splitting the wood.

Install decking so that there is a ⅛" gap between boards to provide drainage. Boards naturally "cup" as they age (page 15). Lay boards with the bark side facing down, so that the cupped surface cannot hold standing water.

General installation instructions for alternative decking materials are shown here (see pages 90 to 93). Always follow the installation methods recommended by the manufacturer of the product you select.

Everything You Need

Tools: tape measure, circular saw, screwgun, hammer, drill, ⅛" twist bit, pry bar, chalk line, jig saw or handsaw.

Materials: decking boards, 2½" corrosion-resistant deck screws, galvanized common nails (8d, 10d), redwood or cedar facing boards.

How to Lay Decking

1 Position the first row of decking flush against the house. First decking board should be perfectly straight, and should be precut to proper length. Attach the first decking board by driving a pair of 2½" corrosion-resistant deck screws into each joist.

2 Position remaining decking boards so that ends overhang outside joists. Space boards about ⅛" apart. Attach boards to each joist with a pair of 2½" deck screws driven into each joist.

Alternate method: Attach decking boards with 10d galvanized common nails. Angle the nails toward each other to improve holding power.

(continued next page)

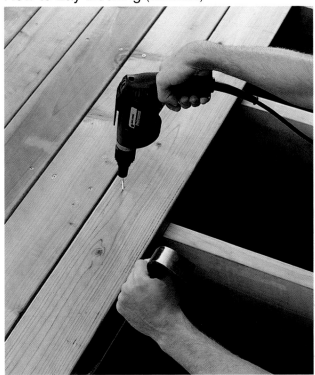

3 If boards are bowed, use a pry bar to lever them into position while fastening.

4 Drill ⅛" pilot holes in ends of boards before attaching them to outside joists. Pilot holes prevent screws from splitting decking boards at ends.

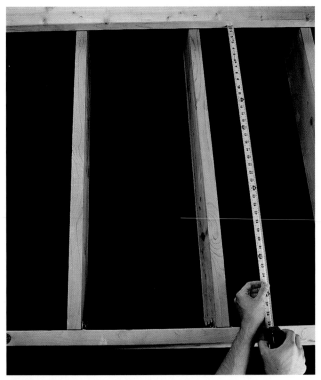

5 After every few rows of decking are installed, measure from edge of the decking board to edge of header joist. If measurements show that the last board will not fit flush against the edge of the deck, adjust board spacing.

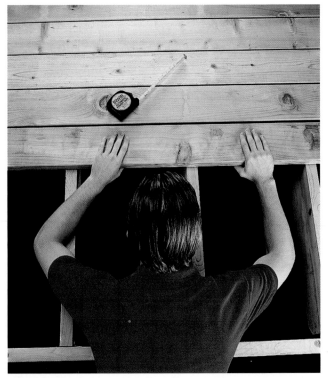

6 Adjust board spacing by changing the gaps between boards by a small amount over three or four rows of boards, Very small spacing changes will not be obvious to the eye.

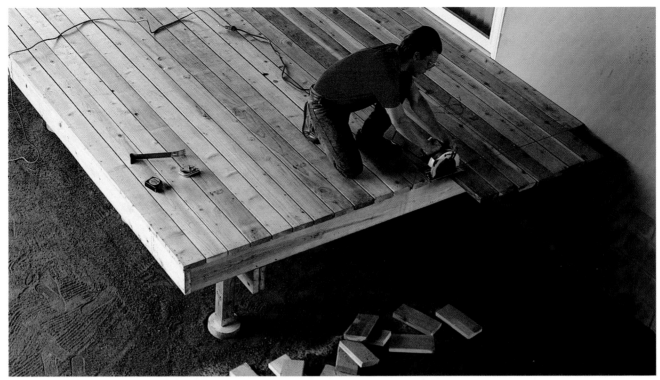

7 Use a chalk line to mark the edge of decking flush with the outside of deck. Cut off decking, using a circular saw. Set saw blade ⅛" deeper than thickness of decking so that saw will not cut side of deck. At areas where circular saw cannot reach, finish cutoff with a jig saw or handsaw.

8 For a more attractive appearance, face the deck with redwood or cedar facing boards. Miter-cut corners, and attach boards with deck screws or 8d galvanized nails.

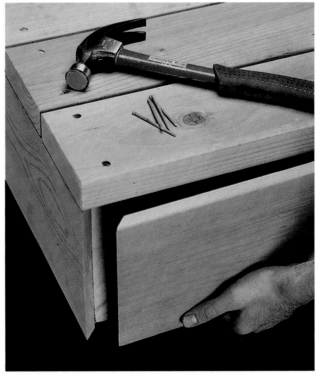

Alternate facing technique: Attach facing boards so that edges of decking overhang facing.

1 Lay composite decking as you would wood decking (pages 87 to 89). Position with the factory crown up so water will run off, and space rows ⅛" to ¼" apart for drainage.

2 Predrill pilot holes at ¾ the diameter of the fasteners, but do not countersink. Composite materials allow fasteners to set themselves. Use spiral shank nails, hot-dipped galvanized ceramic coated screws, or stainless steel nails or deck screws.

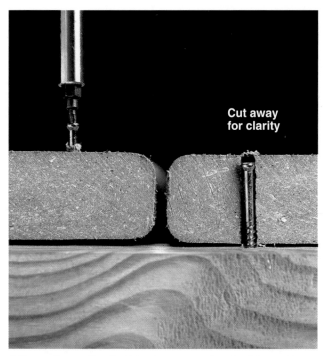

Cut away for clarity

Alternate method: Attach composite decking with self-tapping composite screws. These specially designed screws require no pilot holes. If the decking "mushrooms" over the screw head, use a hammer to tap back in place.

3 Lay remaining decking. For boards 16-ft. or shorter, leave a gap at deck ends and any butt joints, ¹⁄₁₆" for every 20°F difference between the temperature at the time of installation and the expected high temperature for the year.

How to Install Tongue-and-Groove Decking

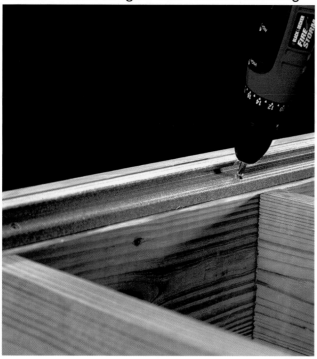

1 Position starter strip at far end of deck. Make sure it is straight and properly aligned. Attach with 2½" galvanized deck screws driven into the lower runner found under the lip of the starter strip.

2 Fit tongue of a deck board into groove of starter strip. There will be approximately a ¼" gap between the deck board and the starter strip. Fasten the deck board to the joists with 2½" galvanized deck screws, working from the middle out to the sides of the deck.

3 Continue to add decking. To lay deck boards end-to-end, leave a ⅛" gap between them, and make sure any butt joints are centered over a joist.

4 Place final deck board and attach with 2½" galvanized deck screws driven through top of the deck board into the joist. If necessary, rip final board to size, then support the board with a length of 1 × 1 and attach both to the joist. Attach facing boards to conceal exposed ends (pages 92 to 93).

How to Lay Decking with a T-clip System

1 Insert 2" galvanized deck screws into T-clips. Loosely attach one T-clip to the ledger at each joist location.

2 Position a deck board tight against the T-clips. Loosely attach T-clips against bottom lip on front side of deck board, just tight enough to keep the board in place. Fully tighten T-clips at back of board, against the house.

3 Push another deck board tightly against the front T-clips, attach T-clips at front of the new board, then fully tighten the previous set of T-clips. Add another deck board and repeat the process, to the end of the deck.

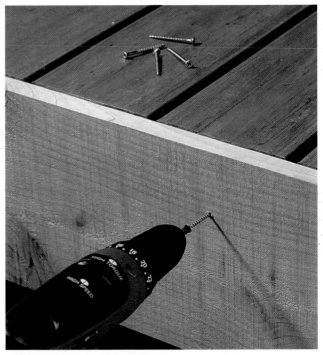

4 Cover exposed deck board ends. Miter-cut corners of the facing and drill pilot holes ¾ the diameter of the screws. Attach with 3" galvanized deck screws.

How to Install a Fiberglass Decking System

1 Place a length of retaining clips on top of the first joist. Center it on the joist and fasten with 2" galvanized deck screws. Attach lengths of retaining clips to the subsequent joists, so that the clips are perfectly aligned with the first length of clips, creating straight rows.

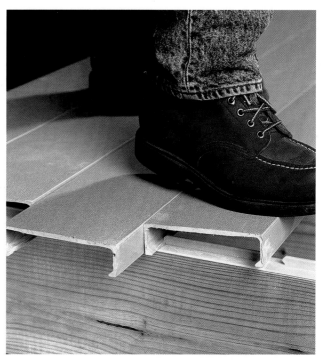

2 Place the open face of a decking board perpendicular to the joists, resting on top of a row of clips. Apply firm pressure to the top of the deck board until the decking snaps into place over the retaining clips. Work along the row, snapping the deck board in place. Attach the remaining deck boards in place, snapping each onto a row of retaining clips.

3 Cut the over-hanging ends of the decking boards flush with the outside joists, using a circular saw with a fresh carbide-tipped blade or a masonry cut-off disc.

4 Use 2" galvanized deck screws to attach the prefabricated facing, covering the exposed hollow ends and creating a decorative trim. Cover the screw heads with the screw caps.

Building Stairs

Building deck stairs requires four calculations.

Number of steps depends on the vertical drop of the deck. The vertical drop is the distance from the surface of the deck to the ground.

Rise is the vertical space between treads. Building codes require that the rise measurement be about 7".

Run is the depth of the treads. A convenient way to build deck stairs is to use a pair of 2 × 6s for each tread.

Span is figured by multiplying the run by the number of treads. The span lets you locate the end of the stairway, and position support posts.

Everything You Need

Tools: tape measure, pencil, framing square, level, plumb bob, clamshell posthole digger, wheelbarrow, hoe, circular saw, hammer, drill, ⅛" twist bit, 1" spade bit, ratchet wrench, caulk gun.

Materials: sand, portland cement, gravel, J-bolts, metal post anchors, 2 × 12 lumber, metal cleats, ¼" × 1¼" lag screws, joist angle brackets, 10d joist hanger nails, ⅜" × 4" lag screws and 1" washers, 2 × 6 lumber, 16d galvanized common nails, silicone caulk.

Supplies: long, straight 2 × 4; pointed stakes; masking tape.

Side stair elevation

Front stair elevation

A common deck stairway is made from two 2 × 12 stringers, and a series of 2 × 6 treads attached with metal cleats. Posts set 18" back from the end of the stairway help to anchor the stringers and the railings. Calculations needed to build stairs include the number of steps, the rise of each step, the run of each step, and the stairway span. Local codes may require a concrete pad at the foot of a stairway (see pages 65 to 67).

How to Find Measurements for Stairway Layout

Sample Measurements
(39" High Deck)

1. Find the number of steps: Measure vertical drop from deck surface to ground. Divide by 7. Round off to nearest whole number.	Vertical drop:		39"
	÷ 7 =		5.57"
	Number of steps:	=	= 6
2. Find step rise: Divide the vertical drop by the number of steps.	Vertical drop:		39"
	Number of steps:	÷	÷ 6
	Rise:	=	= 6.5"
3. Find step run: Typical treads made from two 2 × 6s have a run of 11¼". If your design is different, find run by measuring depth of tread, including any space between boards.	Run:		11¼"
4. Find stairway span: Multiply the run by the number of treads. (Number of treads is always one less than number of steps.)	Run:		11¼"
	Number of treads:	×	× 5
	Span:	=	= 56¼"

How to Build Deck Stairs

1 Use the stairway elevation drawings (page 95) to find measurements for stair stringers and posts. Use a pencil and framing square to outline where stair stringers will be attached to the side of the deck.

2 Locate the post footings so they are 18" back from the end of stairway span. Lay a straight 2 × 4 on the deck so that it is level and square to side of deck. Use a plumb bob to mark the ground at centerpoints of footings.

3 Dig holes and pour footings for posts (pages 60 to 65). Attach metal post anchors to footings and install 4 × 4 posts (pages 68 to 72).

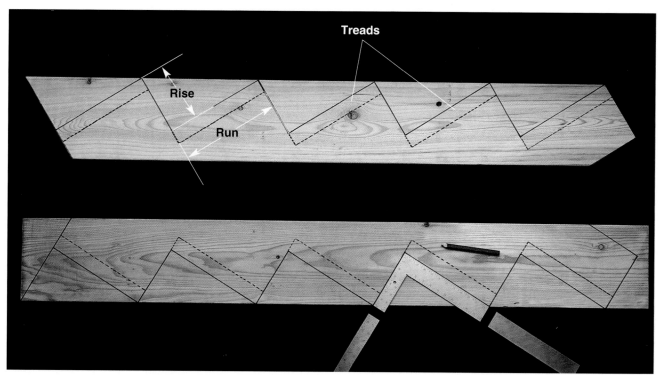

Treads

Rise

Run

4 Lay out stair stringers. Use tape to mark the rise measurement on one leg of a framing square, and the run measurement on the other leg. Beginning at one end of stringer, position the square with tape marks flush to edge of board, and outline the rise and run for each step. Then draw in the tread outline against the bottom of each run line. Use a circular saw to trim ends of stringers as shown.

5 Attach metal tread cleats flush with bottom of each tread outline, using ¼" × 1¼" lag screws. Drill ⅛" pilot holes to prevent the screws from splitting the wood.

6 Attach angle brackets to upper ends of stringers, using 10d joist hanger nails. Brackets should be flush with cut ends of stringers.

(continued next page)

How to Build Deck Stairs (continued)

7 Position the stair stringers against side of deck, over the stringer outlines. Align top point of stringer flush with the surface of the deck. Attach stringers by nailing the angle brackets to the deck with 10d joist hanger nails.

8 Drill two ¼" pilot holes through each stringer and into each adjacent post. Counterbore each hole to depth of ½", using a 1" spade bit. Attach stringers to posts with ⅜" × 4" lag screws and washers, using a ratchet wrench. Seal screw heads with silicone caulk.

9 Measure width of stair treads. Cut two 2 × 6s for each tread, using a circular saw.

10 For each step, position the front 2 × 6 on the tread cleat, so that the front edge is flush with the tread outline on the stringers.

11 Drill ⅛" pilot holes, then attach the front 2 × 6s to the cleats with ¼" × 1¼" lag screws.

12 Position the rear 2 × 6s on the cleats, allowing a small space between boards. Use a 16d nail as a spacing guide. Drill ⅛" pilot holes, and attach 2 × 6s to cleats with ¼" × 1¼" lag screws.

Stair Variations

Notched stringers precut from pressure-treated wood are available at building centers. Edges of cutout areas should be coated with sealer-preservative to prevent rot.

Installing a Deck Railing

Railings must be sturdy, and firmly attached to the framing members of the deck. Never attach railing posts to the surface decking. Check local building codes for guidelines regarding railing construction. Most codes require that railings be at least 36" above decking. Vertical balusters should be spaced no more than 4" apart. In some areas, a grippable handrail for any stairway over four treads may be required. Check with your local building inspector for the building codes in your area.

Everything You Need

Tools: tape measure, pencil, power miter saw, drill, twist bits (⅛", ¼"), 1" spade bit, combination square, awl, ratchet wrench, caulk gun, level, reciprocating saw or circular saw, jig saw with wood-cutting blade.

Materials: railing lumber (4 × 4s, 2 × 6s, 2 × 4s, 2 × 2s), clear sealer-preservative, ⅜ × 4" lag screws and 1" washers, silicone caulk, 2½" corrosion-resistant deck screws, 10d galvanized common nails.

How to Install a Deck Railing

Railing detail

1 Refer to the deck design plan (pages 38 to 41) for spacing (A) and length of railing posts and balusters. Posts should be spaced no more than 6 feet apart.

2 Measure and cut 4 × 4 posts, using a power miter saw or circular saw. Cut off tops of the posts square, and cut the bottoms at 45° angle. Seal cut ends of lumber with clear sealer-preservative.

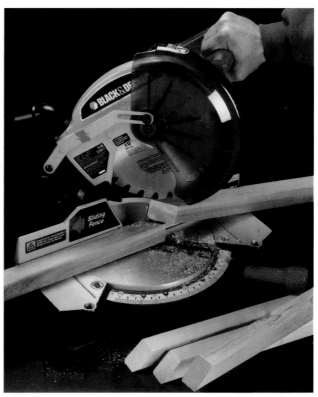

3 Measure and cut balusters for main deck, using a power miter saw or circular saw. Cut off tops of the balusters square, and cut bottoms at 45° angle. Seal cut ends of lumber with clear sealer-preservative.

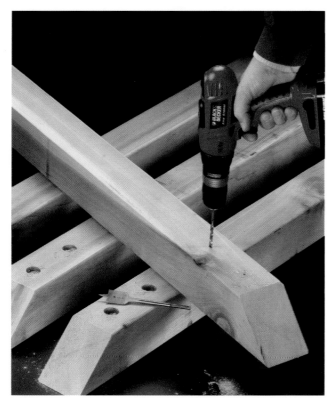

4 Drill two ¼" pilot holes through bottom end of each post, spaced 2" apart. Counterbore each pilot hole to ½" depth, using a 1" spade bit.

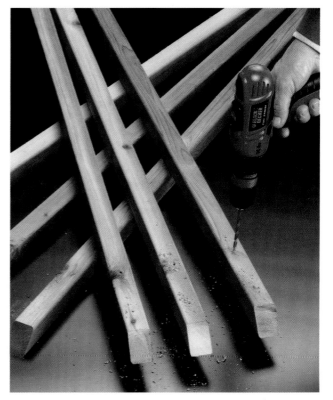

5 Drill two ⅛" pilot holes near bottom end of each baluster, spaced 4" apart. Drill two ⅛" pilot holes at top of each baluster, spaced 1½" apart.

(continued next page)

6 Measure and mark position of posts around the outside of the deck, using a combination square as a guide. Plan to install a post on outside edge of each stair stringer.

7 Position each post with beveled end flush with bottom of deck. Plumb post with a level. Insert a screwdriver or nail into pilot holes and mark side of deck.

8 Remove post and drill ¼" pilot holes into side of deck.

9 Attach railing posts to side of deck with ⅜" × 4" lag screws and washers, using a ratchet wrench or impact driver. Seal screw heads with silicone caulk.

10 Measure and cut 2 × 4 side rails. Position rails with edges flush to tops of posts, and attach to posts with 2½" corrosion-resistant deck screws.

11 Join 2 × 4s for long rails by cutting ends at 45° angles. Drill 1/16" pilot holes to prevent nails from splitting end grain, and attach rails with 10d galvanized nails. (Screws may split mitered ends.)

12 Attach ends of rails to stairway posts, flush with edges of posts, as shown. Drill 1/8" pilot holes, and attach rails with 2½" deck screws.

13 At stairway, measure from surface of decking to the top of the upper stairway post (A).

14 Transfer measurement A to lower stairway post, measuring from the edge of the stair stringer.

(continued next page)

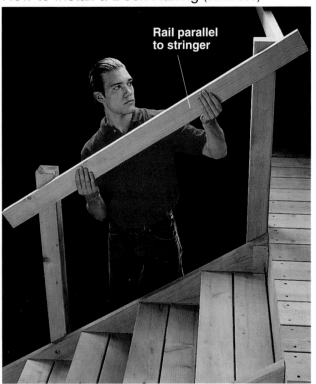

Rail parallel to stringer

15 Position 2 × 4 rail against inside of stairway posts. Align rail with top rear corner of top post and with the pencil mark on the lower post. Have a helper attach rail temporarily with 2½" deck screws.

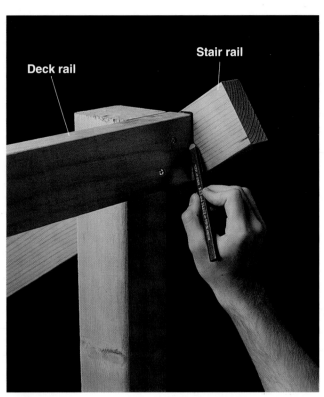

Deck rail   **Stair rail**

16 Mark the outline of the post and the deck rail on the back side of the stairway rail.

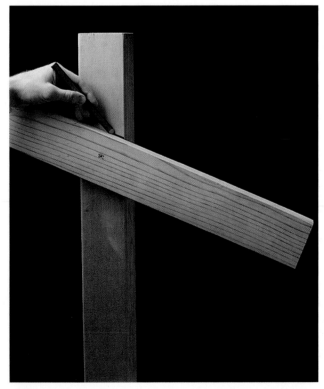

17 Mark the outline of the stairway rail on the lower stairway post.

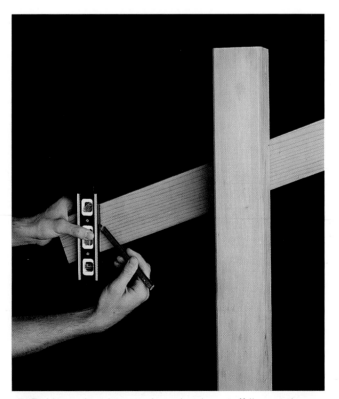

18 Use a level to mark a plumb cutoff line at the bottom end of the stairway rail. Remove the rail.

19 Extend the pencil lines across both sides of the stairway post, using a combination square as a guide.

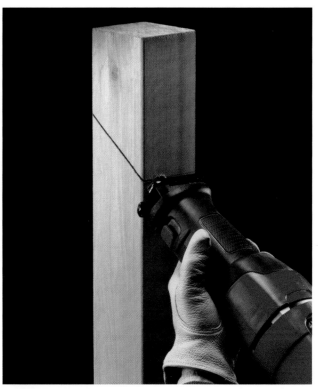

20 Cut off lower stairway post along diagonal cutoff line, using a reciprocating saw or circular saw.

21 Use a jig saw to cut the stairway rail along the marked outlines.

22 Position the stairway rail flush against top edge of posts. Drill ⅛" pilot holes, then attach rail to posts with 2½" deck screws.

(continued next page)

23 Use a spacer block to ensure equal spacing between balusters. Beginning next to a plumb railing post, position each baluster tight against spacer block, with top of baluster flush to top of rail. Attach each baluster with 2½" deck screws.

24 For stairway, position baluster against stringer and rail, and adjust for plumb. Draw diagonal cutoff line on top of baluster, using top of stair rail as a guide. Cut baluster on marked line, using power miter saw. Seal ends with clear sealer-preservative.

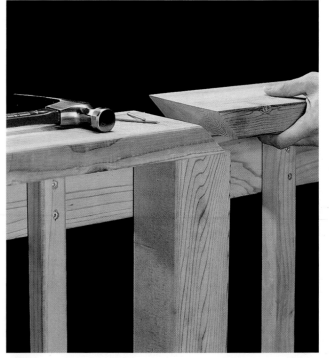

25 Beginning next to upper stairway post, position each baluster tight against spacer block, with top flush to top of stair rail. Attach baluster with 2½" deck screws.

26 Position 2 × 6 cap so edge is flush with inside edge of rail. Drill ⅛" pilot holes, and attach cap to rail with 2½" deck screws driven every 12". Also drive screws into each post and into every third baluster. For long caps, bevel ends at 45°. Drill ¹⁄₁₆" pilot holes, and attach at post using 10d nails.

27 At corners, miter ends of railing cap at 45°. Drill ⅛" pilot holes, and attach cap to post with 2½" deck screws.

28 At top of stairs, cut cap so that it is flush with stairway rail. Drill ⅛" pilot holes and attach cap with 2½" deck screws.

29 Measure and cut cap for stairway rail. Mark outline of post on side of cap, and bevel-cut the ends of the cap.

30 Position cap over the stairway rail and balusters so that edge of cap is flush with inside edge of rail. Drill ⅛" pilot holes, and attach cap to rail with 2½" deck screws driven every 12". Also drive screws through cap into stair post and into every third baluster.

Open space below a deck can be covered with a *skirt* to improve the appearance of the deck. A 2 × 4 framework built between the bottom of the deck and the ground supports the skirting materials. Common choices for skirting materials include lap siding (above) and lattice panels (page 111).

Enclosing the Underside of a Deck

When enclosing the underside of a deck, you have two broad choices: give the space a functional use, or hide it with a decorative screen. The option you choose depends largely on the site. If your deck is fairly tall and the ground beneath it is flat, you can turn the space into a functional patio or storage area. But if the area beneath the deck is narrow or steeply sloped, your best option is to make the skirt area more attractive by screening it with landscape plants or wood panels, or by blanketing the soil with a ground cover, such as decorative gravel.

To inhibit weed growth on bare ground under a deck, cover the earth with a layer of landscape fabric before finishing the area.

Everything You Need

Tools: pencil, plumb bob, hammer, drill, level, circular saw with carbide blade, maul.

Materials: pressure treated lumber, lattice panels, landscape fabric, corrosion-resistant deck screws (1½", 3"), ½" rebar, galvanized metal plates.

Options for Finishing the Underside of a Deck

A sheltered, shady patio covered with decking boards or brick pavers can be installed if the ground under the deck is flat. In this example, the expansive area under a large overhead deck is transformed into usable space by laying a ground-level deck platform with built-in benches.

Storage space can be created by walling-in the skirt area with siding materials and installing an access door. This space is ideal for storing yard-care tools and materials, gardening supplies, or children's outdoor toys.

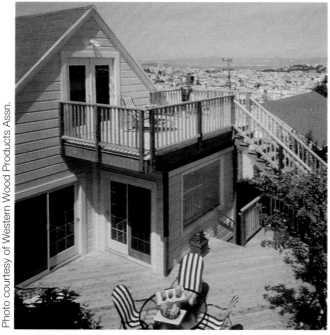

Photo courtesy of Western Wood Products Assn.

Photo courtesy of Lindal Cedar Homes, Inc., Seattle, WA

Enclosed porch can be created by laying a water-proof material over the decking surface, finishing the floor area under the deck, then building finished walls around the skirt area, complete with doors and windows. In this example, the area under a small balcony deck has been transformed into a weathertight entry porch.

Ground covers, such as bark chips, gravel, or shrubs, ease the visual transition between the deck and surrounding landscape. Before laying bark or gravel, cover the ground with landscape fabric to inhibit the growth of weeds. For the deck shown above, bark chips and shrubs complement the wood used in the deck and house.

How to Build a Skirt Frame on Uneven Ground

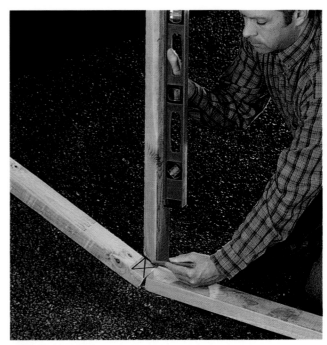

1 Cut 2 × 4 sole plates to follow the slope of the ground. Position them directly below the inside edge of the outside deck joist, using a plumb bob as a guide. Lay out stud locations on the outside joist, spaced every 2 ft., and use the plumb bob to mark corresponding locations on the sole plate. Studs will extend from the sole plate to a point about 4" up from the bottom edge of the joists.

2 Mark bevel angles for the bottoms of the studs by holding each stud in a plumb position, with the top against the inside face of the rim joist and the bottom against the inside edge of the sole plate. Scribe a cutting line on the stud, following the edge of the sole plate. Measure the angle with a speed square (page 169), then set the blade of your circular saw to match.

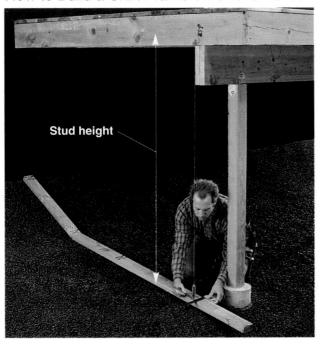

3 Cut studs to length (step 1), then attach the studs to the sole plates with 3" deck screws driven through the bottoms of the sole plates. Attach 1 × 4 braces across the studs near the top to maintain the proper spacing.

4 Position the frame against the inside face of the rim joist. To reduce the likelihood of rot, use temporary 2 × 4 spacers to elevate the frame slightly off the ground. Check for plumb, then attach the frame to the rim joist with 3" deck screws.

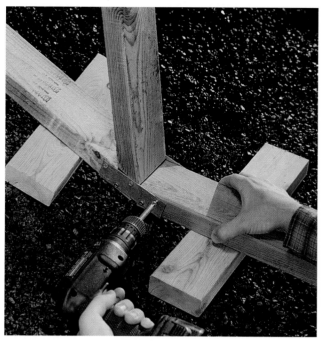

5 Secure sole plate joints with galvanized metal plates attached with deck screws.

6 Check to make sure the frame is plumb, then drill ½"-diameter holes through the sole plate between each pair of studs. Drive 1-ft.-long lengths of ½"-diameter steel rebar through the holes and into the ground.

7 Remove the scrap 2 × 4 blocks under the sole plate, then cut skirting materials to fit over the frame. (We used ⅜"-thick cedar lattice panels.) Attach the materials to the frame with 1½" deck screws. Joints between the panels should be aligned over a frame stud.

Finishing a New Deck

Finish a deck with clear sealer-preservative or staining sealer. Sealer-preservatives protect wood from water and rot, and are often used on cedar or redwood because they preserve the original color of the wood. If you want the wood to look weathered, wait several months before applying sealer-preservative.

Staining sealers, sometimes called toners, are often applied to pressure-treated lumber to give it the look of redwood or cedar. Staining sealers are available in a variety of colors.

For best protection, use finishing products with an alkyd base. Apply fresh finish each year.

Everything You Need

Tools: orbital sander, sandpaper, shop vacuum, pressure sprayer, eye protection, paint brush.

Materials: clear sealer-preservative or staining sealer.

Use an orbital sander to smooth out any rough areas before applying finish to decking boards, railings, or stair treads.

How to Finish a Redwood or Cedar Deck

1 Test wood surface by sprinkling water on it. If wood absorbs water quickly, it is ready to be sealed. If wood does not absorb water, let it dry for several weeks before sealing.

2 Sand rough areas and vacuum deck. Apply clear sealer to all wood surfaces, using a pressure sprayer. If possible, apply sealer to underside of decking and to joist, beams, and posts.

3 Use a paint brush to work sealer into cracks and narrow areas that could trap water.

How to Finish a Pressure-treated Deck

 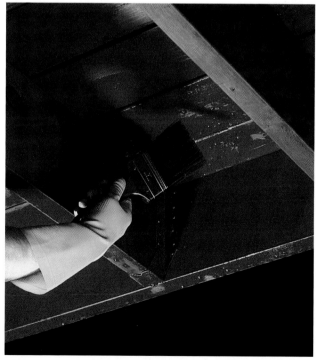

1 Sand rough areas and vacuum the deck. Apply a staining sealer (toner) to all deck wood, using a pressure sprayer.

2 Use a paint brush to smooth out drips and runs. Porous wood may require a second coat of staining sealer for even coverage.

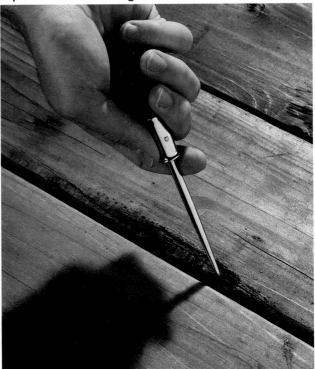

Use an awl or screwdriver to check deck for soft, rotted wood. Replace or reinforce damaged wood (pages 116 to 119).

Inspect hidden areas regularly for signs of rotted or damaged wood. Apply a fresh coat of finish yearly.

Maintaining a Deck

Inspect your deck once each year. Replace loose or rusting hardware or fasteners, and apply fresh finish to prevent water damage.

Look carefully for areas that show signs of damage. Replace or reinforce damaged wood as soon as possible (pages 116 to 119).

Restore an older, weathered deck to the original wood color with a deck-brightening solution. Brighteners are available at any home improvement store.

Everything You Need

Tools: flashlight, awl or screwdriver, screwgun, putty knife, scrub brush, rubber gloves, eye protection, pressure sprayer.

Materials: 2½" corrosion-resistant deck screws, deck brightener.

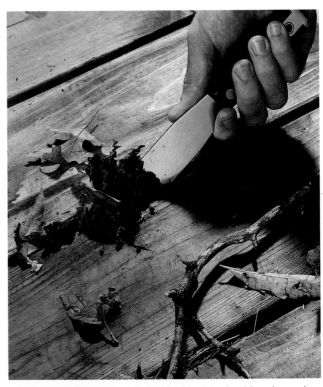

Clean debris from cracks between decking boards with a putty knife. Debris traps moisture, and can cause wood to rot.

Drive new fasteners to secure loose decking to joists. If using the old nail or screw holes, new fasteners should be slightly longer than the originals.

1 Mix deck-brightening solution as directed by manufacturer. Apply solution with pressure sprayer. Let solution set for 10 minutes.

2 Scrub deck thoroughly with a stiff scrub brush. Wear rubber gloves and eye protection.

3 Rinse deck with clear water. If necessary, apply a second coat of brightener to extremely dirty or stained areas. Rinse and let dry. Apply a fresh coat of sealer or stain (pages 112 to 113).

Repairing a Deck

Replace or reinforce damaged deck wood as soon as possible. Wood rot can spread and weaken solid wood.

After replacing or reinforcing the rotted wood, clean the entire deck and apply a fresh coat of clear sealer-preservative or staining sealer. Apply a fresh coat of finish each year to prevent future water damage. If you need to repair more than a few small areas, it is probably time to replace the entire deck.

Everything You Need

Tools: cat's paw or flat pry bar, screwgun, awl or screwdriver, hammer, chisel, eye protection, pressure-sprayer, circular saw, scrub brush, paint brush, hydraulic jack, drill or hammer drill, ⅝" masonry bit, level, ratchet wrench.

Materials: sealer-preservative or staining sealer, galvanized nails (6d, 10d), deck lumber, baking soda, corrosion-resistant deck screws, ⅝" masonry anchor, ⅜" lag screw.

Supplies: rubber gloves, bucket, concrete block, scrap plywood.

How to Repair Damaged Decking & Joists

1 Remove nails or screws from the damaged decking board, using a cat's paw or screwgun. Remove the damaged board.

2 Inspect the underlying joists for signs of rotted wood. Joists with discolored, soft areas should be repaired and reinforced.

3 Use a hammer and chisel to remove any rotted portions of joist.

4 Apply a thick coat of sealer-preservative to damaged joist. Let dry, then apply a second coat of sealer. Cut a reinforcing joist (sister joist) from pressure-treated lumber.

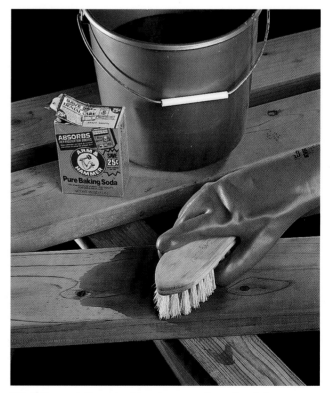

5 Treat all sides of sister joist with clear sealer-preservative, and let dry. Position sister joist tightly against the damaged joist, and attach with 10d nails driven every 2 feet.

6 Attach sister joist to ledger and header joist by toenailing with 10d nails. Cut replacement decking boards from matching lumber, using a circular saw.

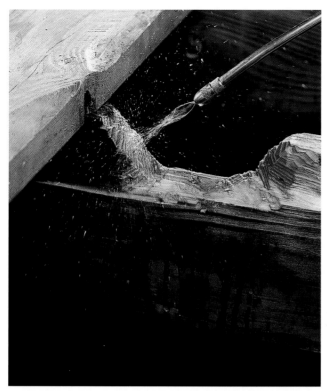

7 If the existing decking is gray, "weather" the new decking by scrubbing with a solution made from 1 cup baking soda and 1 gallon warm water. Rinse and let dry.

(continued next page)

How to Repair Damaged Decking & Joists (continued)

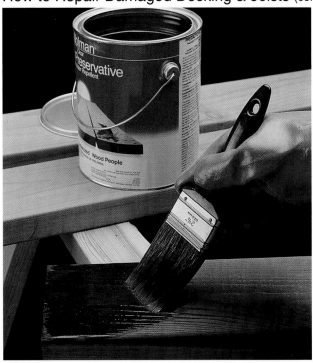

8 Apply a coat of sealer-preservative or staining sealer to all sides of the new decking boards.

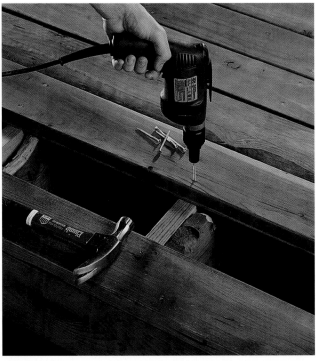

9 Position the new decking and attach to joists with galvanized deck screws or nails. Make sure space between boards matches that of existing decking.

How to Replace a Post on an Older Deck

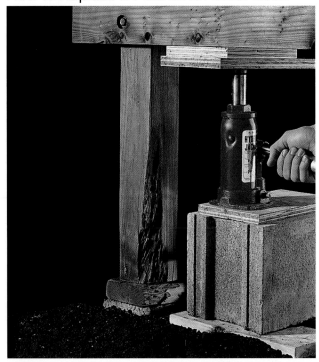

1 Build a support, using plywood scraps, a concrete block, and a hydraulic jack. Place 1½" layer of plywood between head of jack and beam. Apply just enough pressure to lift the beam slightly.

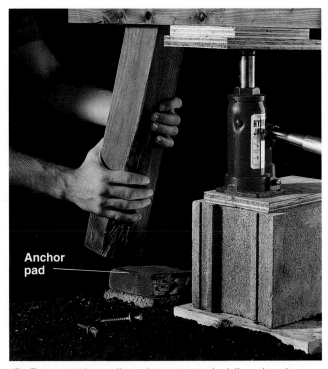

Anchor pad

2 Remove the nails or lag screws holding the damaged post to the anchor pad and to the beam. Remove the damaged post and the wood anchor pad on the concrete pier.

3 Drill a hole in the middle of the concrete pier, using a hammer drill and a ⅝" masonry bit. Insert ⅝" masonry anchor into hole.

4 Position galvanized post anchor on pier block, and thread a ⅜" lag screw with washer through the hole in the anchor and into the masonry anchor. Tighten the screw with a ratchet wrench.

5 Cut new post from pressure-treated lumber, and treat cut ends with sealer-preservative. Position post and make sure it is plumb.

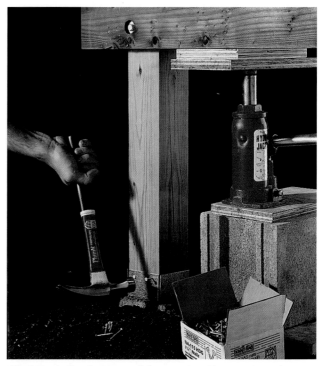

6 Attach the bottom of the post to the post anchor, using 10d or 16d joist hanger nails. Attach the post to the beam by redriving the lag screws, using a ratchet wrench. Release the pressure on the jack and remove the support.

Advanced Techniques

Advanced Deck Features

On the following pages you will see illustrations of several decks, each containing several advanced features that are usually found only on elaborate decks designed and built by professionals.

Incorporating these features into a deck you design and build yourself is not as difficult as you might imagine. First, you'll need a good understanding of basic deck-building skills, as demonstrated in the previous chapter.

Once you are confident of your basic skills, you will need to learn a few special construction methods. These techniques are highlighted on the following few pages. The remainder of this chapter presents step-by-step instructions for these construction methods.

Hot tubs installed on a deck must have extra beams and closely spaced joists to support the extra weight. See pages 176 to 179.

Stairway railings must be installed on any stairway with more than two steps, and should have grippable handrails. See pages 188 to 189.

Raised platforms are often used to partially enclose a hot tub. See pages 176 to 179.

Horizontal railings blend well with modern house styles. The railing can be built by framing posts into the deck structure, then mortising the rails into the posts for improved strength. See page 185.

Low-profile decks feature beams that rest directly on concrete footings instead of posts. See pages 130 to 133.

Insets are an effective way to build a deck around your favorite landscape features. See pages 172 to 175.

Curved railings rely on the use of geometry and special layout and construction techniques to create the curved top rail and cap rail. See pages 190 to 193.

Curved decks are usually built by cutting joists to a circular outline, then attaching a curved rim joist. See pages 166 to 171.

Wall-style railings make a deck more private and allow it to visually blend in with the house. See pages 186 to 187.

Multilevel decks can share the same row of posts along the overlapping sides. See pages 134 to 141.

Vertical railings use balusters attached to rails that are mortised into the posts, providing greater strength and a more finished appearance. See page 184.

Landings are required whenever a deck stairway has 12 or more steps. See pages 142 to 151.

Decorative treatments like lattice panels can conceal the area below a deck. See pages 108 to 111.

Deck layout traditionally is done with batterboards and strings, but some situations require other layout methods. For angled decks, the board template method (left) described on pages 162 to 163 is easier than batterboards. For a very high deck or one built on a steep slope (right), the layout is often done by constructing the outer framework first, then elevating it with a temporary wall to find the exact location for footings and posts (pages 152 to 157).

Advanced Construction Tips

The step-by-step overview shown on pages 44 to 45 outlines the basic steps of deck construction, but more complicated decks require special materials and techniques, like those shown here. If you're building an angled deck, for instance, it is easier to do the basic on-site layout using a board template rather than strings and batterboards. And for a deck with many angles, a speed square is very helpful for marking and cutting lumber.

Whenever possible, build your deck so the beams rest on top of the posts—an arrangement that is stronger than attaching beam timbers to the sides of posts with lag screws.

Post cross-bracing helps stabilize a deck platform, and may be required for raised four-post decks and for stairway landings. For best results, install braces diagonally between support posts.

Cross blocks

Cross blocks between joists help stabilize decks that have very long joist spans. Cross braces are also recommended when constructing a curved deck.

Post-beam caps allow you to rest beams on top of posts. Some local codes require that, wherever possible, beams rest on top of posts, attached with post-beam caps. Two types of post-beam caps are widely available: a single piece cap (left) for use when the beam is the same width as the posts, and an adjustable two-piece cap (right) that can be used when the beam and the posts are different widths.

Post anchors elevate the bottoms of posts above footings, helping prevent rot. The post rests on a metal pedestal that fits over a J-bolt embedded in the footing. Once the post is set in place, a nut is screwed onto the J-bolt, the metal flange is bent up against the post, and the post anchor is secured to the post with nails.

How to Build a Beam Using Dimensional Lumber

1 Cut the timbers to size. Sight along the boards to check for crowning, then position the timbers so any crowns are facing the same direction. Nail the timbers together at the ends, using galvanized 16d nails.

2 Turn the beam on edge, and where the timbers are not flush, toenail the higher board down into the lower one so the edges are forced into alignment. If necessary, use clamps to draw the boards into position. Facenail the timbers together, using rows of 16d nails spaced about 16" apart.

3 Attach post-beam caps to the outside posts, but leave the caps loose on inside posts. Position the beam in the caps, with the crowned edge up. Check for gaps at the inside posts, and shim under the post-beam caps, if necessary. Secure the beam to the caps and posts with 10d joist hanger nails.

Beams for a low-profile deck often rest directly on concrete footings, with no posts. Because low-profile decks may require 2 × 8 or 2 × 6 joists, an intermediate beam may be required to provide adequate support for these narrower joists. At each end of the last beam, the outside timber must be 1½" longer than the inside timber, creating a recess where the end of the rim joist will fit.

Building Low-profile Decks

Building a deck that sits very close to the ground generally is easier than constructing a very high deck, but low-profile situations do require some design modifications. If the deck is extremely low (8" to 12" high), it is best to rest the beams directly on the concrete footings, since posts are not practical. The joists usually are hung on the faces of the beams rather than resting on top of the beams; cantilever designs are rarely used. Since the ledger is mounted so low on the house, it may need to be anchored to the foundation wall rather than to the rim joist (right).

A deck that is more than 12" above the ground should have at least one step, either box-frame style, or suspended from the deck.

Masonry sleeves are used to attach a ledger to a masonry foundation. Drill 3"-deep guide holes for the sleeves, using a ⅝" masonry bit, then drive sleeves for ⅜"-diameter lag screws into the holes. Position the ledger, then attach it with lag screws driven through the ledgers and into the masonry sleeves.

Support Options

Direct-bearing hardware is used to secure beams when the deck is very low to the ground. Carefully set the footing forms so the tops are at the planned height, then pour concrete and set the hardware into the wet concrete. Use layout strings to ensure that the hardware is aligned correctly.

Posts and post-beam caps can be used if the full deck height is more than 18". Posts less than 9" tall are prone to splitting.

Step Options

Box-frame steps are simple platforms constructed from dimensional lumber and covered with decking boards. Box-frame steps are best suited to mild climates where there is little chance the step will be heaved by frost. See page 133.

Suspended steps are hung from the underside of the deck. The steps are constructed with joists attached to the lower portions of the deck joists. Suspended steps are a good option in cold-weather climates, where box-frame steps would be susceptible to frost heave. However, this method cannot be used if the step joists run perpendicular to the deck joists. See page 133.

How to Build a Low-profile Deck

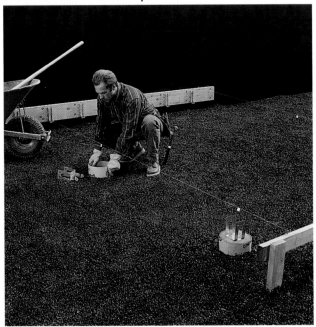

1 Install the ledger, then lay out and dig footings. If beams will rest directly on footings, use tube forms. Raise the tubes to the proper height and check them for plumb as you pour the concrete. Smooth off the surfaces of the footings, and insert direct-bearing hardware while the concrete is still wet, using layout strings to ensure that the hardware is aligned correctly.

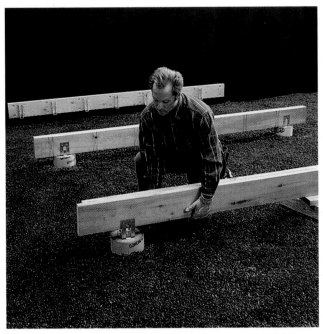

2 Construct beams (page 129), then set the beams into the direct-bearing hardware. Drill pilot holes and use 3½" lag bolts to secure the beam to the hardware. Mark joist locations on the faces of the beams, then install joist hangers.

3 Cut and install all joists, attaching them with joist-hanger nails. Complete your deck, using standard deck-building techniques. Install a box-frame or suspended step, if desired (page opposite).

How to Build a Box-frame Step

1 Construct a rectangular frame for the step, using dimension lumber (2 × 6 lumber is standard), joining the pieces with deck screws. The step must be at least 36" wide and 9" deep. Cut cross blocks and install them inside the frame, spaced every 16".

2 Dig a flat-bottomed trench where the step will rest, about 4" deep. Fill the trench with compactible gravel, and pack with a tamper. Set the step in position, then measure and attach deck boards to form the tread of the step.

How to Build a Suspended Step

1 Screw 2 × 4 furring strips against one side of the deck joists where the step joists will be installed. These strips provide an offset so the step joists will not conflict with the joist hangers attached to the beam. Use a reciprocating saw to make 1½"-wide notches in the rim joist adjacent to the furring strips. NOTE: To maintain adequate structural strength, notches in the joists should be no more than 1½" deep.

2 Measure and cut step joists, allowing about 3 ft. of nailing surface inside the deck frame, and 9" or more of exposed tread. Make sure the step joists are level with one another, then attach them to the deck joists, using deck screws. Cut and attach deck boards to the tread area of the step.

Constructing Multilevel Decks

A multilevel deck has obvious advantages, but many do-it-yourselfers are wary of building such a deck, feeling that it is too complex. In reality, however, a multilevel deck is nothing more than two or more adjacent deck platforms set at different heights. You can build a multilevel deck with the same simple construction techniques used to build a standard deck—with one exception: For efficiency, multilevel decks usually are designed so the platforms share a single support beam on the side where they meet. For this reason, it is essential that the shared posts and beams be sturdy enough to carry the load of both platforms.

Except for the shared beam, the separate platforms on a multilevel deck are independent and can use different construction methods. For example, the upper level might use a post and beam design with decking boards installed perpendicular to the joists, while the lower level might use a curved cantilever design with decking laid at an angle. If your time and budget are limited, you can build your deck in phases, completing one platform at a time, at your convenience.

Remember to include railings (pages 180 to 195) and stairs (pages 142 to 151) where needed. Any deck platform more than 30" above the ground—or above a lower deck platform—requires a railing.

Different support methods can be used in the same multilevel deck. In the deck shown here, the top platform is supported by a beam resting on top of posts, while the lower platform is supported by 2 × 12 beam timbers sandwiched around the posts. The opposite side of the lower platform might use yet another support method, such as a set-back beam supporting cantilevered joists.

Design Options

The shared beam method has one beam supporting both platforms where they overlap. The upper platform rests directly on the beam, while the lower hangs from the face of the beam. This method is an economical choice, since only one beam is required, and it is well suited for relatively flat building sites where the deck levels are close together. See pages 136 to 137.

The shared post method has two beams supported by the same row of posts. The top platform is supported by a beam resting on top of the posts, while the beam for the lower platform is built from 2 × 12 timbers sandwiched around the posts. This method often is used when there is a considerable drop between levels. It also is a good choice if you want to complete your deck in phases, delaying construction of the lower platform until a later date. See pages 138 to 139.

The support-wall method features a top platform supported by a stud wall that rests on the lower platform, directly over the beam and posts. Unlike the methods listed above, the support-wall method requires that the lower deck platform be built first. This method is a good choice when you want to use decorative wall materials, such as cedar siding, to cover the gap between the two platforms. The support-wall method also works well if you want to complete your deck in phases, delaying construction of the upper level. See pages 140 to 141.

How to Use the Shared Beam Method

Joist location

Final cut-off

Beam location

1 After laying out and installing the ledger and all posts and footings, mark the posts to indicate where the beam will rest. Use a straight 2 × 4 and level to establish a point that is level with the top of the ledger, then measure down a distance equal to the height of the joists plus the height of the beam. Cut off the posts at this point, using a reciprocating saw.

2 Position a post-beam cap on each post. Construct a beam from 2 × 10 or 2 × 12 dimension lumber (page 129), then position the beam in the post-beam caps. If the beam is crowned, install it so the crowned side is up; if there is a gap between the middle cap and the beam, shim under the gap. Secure the post-beam caps to the posts and beam with galvanized deck screws.

3 Lay out joist locations for the upper platform on the ledger and on the top of the beam, then use a carpenter's square to transfer joist marks for the lower platform onto the face of the beam. Attach joist hangers at the joist layout lines on the ledger.

4 Measure, cut, and install joists for the upper platform, leaving a 1½" setback to allow for the thickness of the rim joist. At the beam, secure the joists by toenailing with 16d galvanized nails.

5 Attach joist hangers for the lower platform along the face of the beam, using a scrap piece of lumber as a spacer. Cut and install the joists for the lower platform.

6 Cut rim joists for both the upper and lower platforms, and attach them to the ends of the joists by endnailing with 16d nails. Complete the deck, using standard deck-building techniques.

How to Use the Shared Post Method

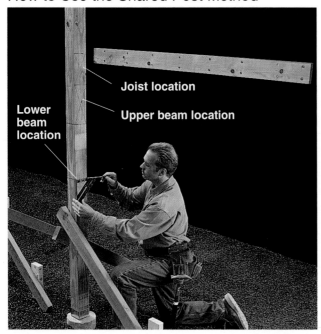

Joist location

Upper beam location

Lower beam location

1 After laying out the deck and installing the ledger and all footings and posts, mark the posts to indicate where both beams will rest. Begin by finding a point level with the top edge of the ledger (page 136), then measure down and mark cutting lines where the bottom of the top beam will rest. For the lower beam, measure down and mark a point on the posts where the top edge of the beam will be positioned.

2 Use a reciprocating saw to cut off the posts at the lines marking the bottom edge of the top beam. Construct the top beam and install it, using post-beam caps (page 129).

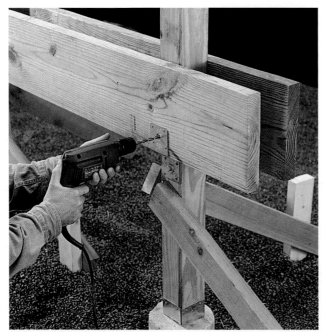

3 Align bearing surfaces of joist ties with the line indicating the bottom of the lower beam on each post. Drill pilot holes and attach with ⅜ × 3" lag screws. Install beam members and drive lag screws through the joist ties, beams, and into posts. Also drive lag screws 1½" from the top edge of each beam to secure to posts.

4 Lay out and mark the joist locations on the ledger and on the top edges of both the upper and lower beam, using a carpenter's square as a guide.

5 Cut and install the joists for the lower platform, toenailing them to the beams with 16d galvanized nails. Cut rim joists for the lower platform and endnail them to the ends of the joists. Cut and install the joists and rim joist for the upper platform.

6 Attach nailing blocks to the sides of the posts where necessary to provide surfaces for attaching decking boards. Complete the deck, using standard deck-building techniques.

Framing option: If you plan to finish the gap between the upper and lower platform with a decorative wall treatment (pages 186 to 187), install nailing strips between the platforms to provide surfaces for attaching siding materials. Nailing strips and posts should be spaced so the intervals are no more than 16".

How to Use the Support-wall Method

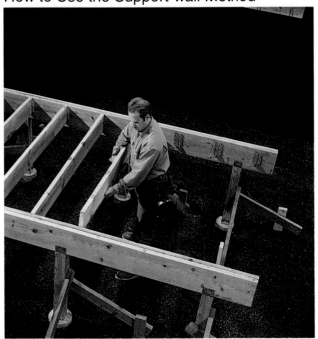

1 Lay out and install the ledger and all posts and footings, then frame the lower platform, using standard deck-building techniques.

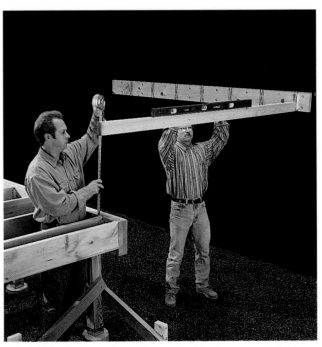

2 Use a straight 2 × 4 and level to establish a reference point level with the bottom of the ledger, then find the total height for the support wall by measuring the vertical distance to the top of the lower platform. Cut the wall studs 3" less than this total height, to allow for the thickness of the top and bottom plates.

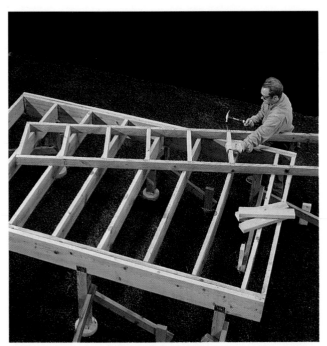

3 Cut 2 × 4 top and bottom plates to cover the full width of the upper platform, then lay out the stud locations on the plates, 16" on center. Cut studs to length, then assemble the support wall by endnailing the plates to the studs, using galvanized 16d nails.

4 Set a long "sway" brace diagonally across the stud wall, and nail it near one corner only. Square the wall by measuring the diagonals and adjusting until both diagonal measurements are the same. When the wall is square, nail the brace at the other corner, and to each stud. Cut off the ends of the brace flush with the plates.

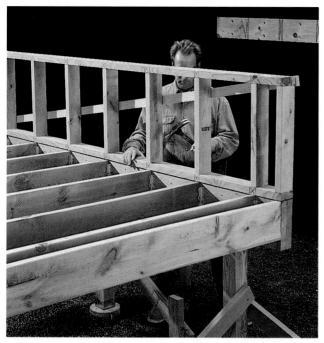

5 Raise the support wall into position, aligning it with the edge of the beam and the end of the deck. Nail the sole plate to the beam with 16d galvanized nails driven on both sides of each stud.

6 Adjust the wall so it is plumb, then brace it in position by nailing a 1 × 4 across the end stud and outside joist.

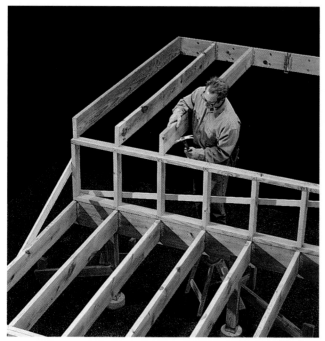

7 Lay out joist locations for the upper platform, and install joist hangers on the ledger. Cut joists so they are 1½" shorter than the distance from the ledger to the front edge of the wall. Install the joists by toenailing them to the top plate with 16d nails. Remove the braces.

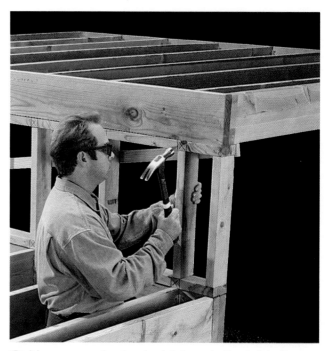

8 Measure and cut a rim joist, and attach it to the ends of the joists by endnailing with 16d nails. Also toenail the rim joist to the top plate of the support wall. Complete the deck, using standard deck-building techniques. To cover the support wall with siding, see pages 186 to 187.

Building Stairways with Landings

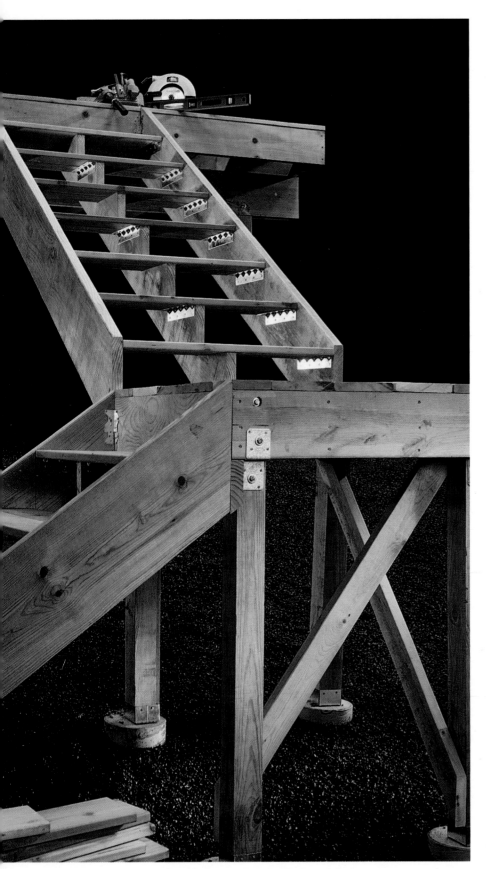

A landing functions essentially as a large step that interrupts a tall stairway. For the builder, the landing provides a convenient spot from which to change the direction of the stairway. For the homeowner, the landing provides a spot to catch your breath momentarily while climbing.

Designing and building a stairway with a landing can be one of the most challenging elements of a deck project. Precision is crucial, since building codes have very exact standards for stairway construction. To ensure that the steps for both the top and bottom staircases have the same vertical rise and tread depth, the landing must be set at the right position and height.

Even for professional builders, designing a stairway layout is a process of trial and revision. Begin by creating a preliminary layout that fits your situation, but as you plan and diagram the project, be prepared to revise the layout to satisfy code requirements and the demands of your building site. Measure your site carefully, and work out all the details on paper before you begin any work. Accuracy and meticulous planning will help ensure that your steps are level and uniform in size.

Remember that local building codes may require handrails for any stairway with three or more risers, and a concrete pad at the foot of the stairway.

Building a stairway with a landing is a six-stage project:

- Creating a preliminary layout (page 146)
- Creating a final layout (page 147)
- Building a stairway landing (pages 147 to 148)
- Laying out stringers (page 149)
- Building the lower staircase (page 150)
- Building the upper staircase (page 151)

Stairway Design Options

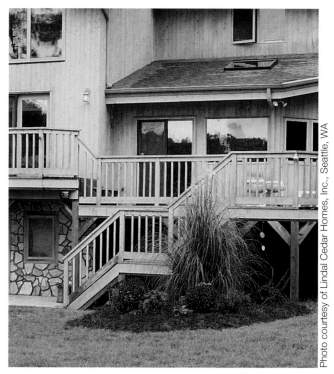

Straight layout with no landing may be unavoidable if space on the building site is limited. In this example, the straight stairway layout provides a direct, quick path from a balcony deck to a ground-level platform deck below.

Straight layout with landing is relatively easy to plan and build, but requires more yard space than other stairway designs.

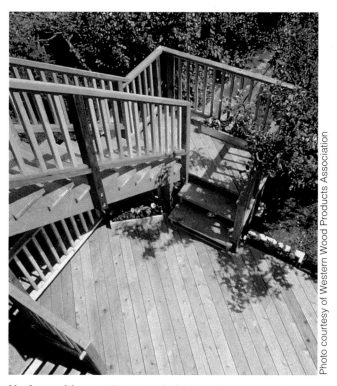

L-shaped layout is used when the building site requires that the stairway change directions.

U-shaped layout is a good choice when space is limited. In the situation shown above, a U-shaped stairway is the most efficient way to connect deck platforms separated by a long vertical rise.

Anatomy of a Stair with Landing

Deck

Rise

Run

Landing

Vertical drop

Span A

Span B

Stairway Basics

The goal of any stairway is to allow people to move easily and safely from one level to another. When designing a deck stairway, the builder must consider the **vertical drop**—the vertical distance from the surface of the deck to the ending point; and the **span**—the horizontal distance from the starting point to the end of the stairway.

During the planning stage, the vertical drop is divided into a series of equal-size steps, called **rises**. Similarly, the horizontal span is divided into a series of equal-size **runs**. On a stairway with a landing, there are two span measurements to consider: the distance from the deck to the edge of the landing, and from the landing to the end point on the ground. In general, the combined horizontal span of the staircases, not counting the landing, should be 40% to 60% more than the total vertical drop.

For safety and comfort, the components of a stairway must be built according to clearly pre-scribed guidelines, as listed at right.

The challenge when planning a stairway is adjusting the preliminary layout and the step dimensions as needed to ensure that the stairway fits the building site and is comfortable to use.

Rises must be no less than 4" and no more than 8" high.

Runs, the horizontal depth of each step, must be at least 9". The number of runs in a staircase is always one less than the number of rises.

Combined sum of the step rise and run should be about 18" to 20". Steps built to this guideline are the most comfortable to use.

Variation between the largest and smallest rise or run measurement can be no more than ⅜".

Stair width must be at least 36", so two people can comfortably pass one another on the stairway.

Stringers should be spaced no more than 36" apart. For added support, a center stringer is recommended for any staircase with more than three steps.

Landings serve as oversized steps; their height must be set as precisely as the risers for the other steps in the stairway. Landings should be at least 36" square, or as wide as the staircase itself. U-shaped stairways should have oversized land-ings, at least 1 ft. wider than the combined width of the two staircases. Landings very often require reinforcement with diagonal cross braces between the support posts.

Concrete footings should support all stringers resting on the ground.

Construction Details for Stairways

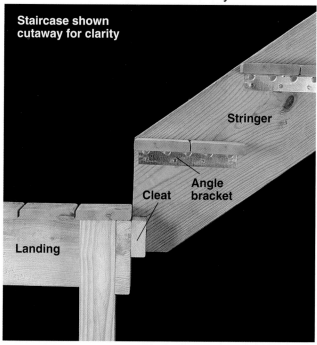

Stringers for the top staircase rest on a 2 × 4 cleat attached to the side of the landing. The stringers are notched to fit around the cleat. On the outside stringers, metal cleats support the treads.

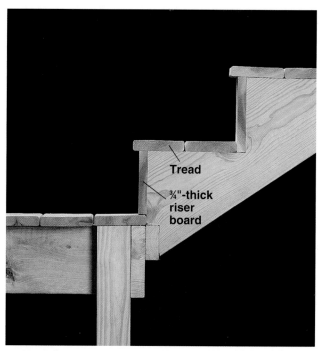

Steps may be boxed in the riser boards, and may have treads that overhang the front edge of the step for a more finished look. Treads should overhang the riser boards by no more than 1".

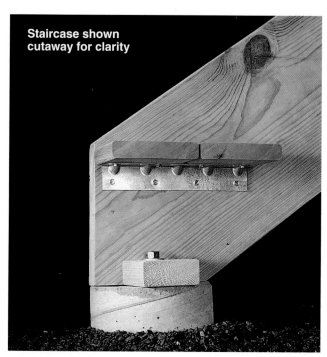

Concrete footings support the stringers for the lower staircase. J-bolts are inserted into the footings while the concrete is still wet. After the footings dry, wooden cleats are attached to the bolt to create surfaces for anchoring the stringers. After the staircase is positioned, the stringers are nailed or screwed to the cleats.

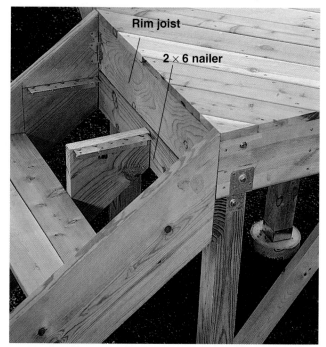

Center stringers are recommended for any staircase that has more than 3 steps or is more than 36" wide. Center stringers are supported by a 2 × 6 nailer attached to the bottom of the rim joist with metal straps. The bottom edge of the nailer is beveled to match the angle of the stringers. The center stringer is attached by driving deck screws through the back of the nailer and into the stringer.

How to Create a Preliminary Layout

1 Evaluate your building site and try to visualize which stairway design best fits your needs (page 143). When creating a preliminary layout, it is generally best to position the landing so the upper and lower staircases will be of equal length. Select a general design idea.

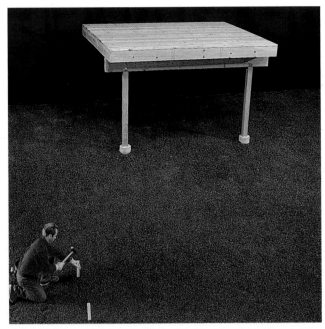

2 Establish a rough starting point for the stairway on the deck, and an ending point on the ground that conforms with your design. Mark the starting point on the rim joist, and mark the ending point with two stakes, spaced to equal the planned width of your stairway. This is a rough layout only; later calculations will give you the precise measurements.

3 To determine the vertical drop of the stairway, extend a straight 2 × 4 from the starting point on the deck to a spot level with the deck directly over the ending point on the ground. Measure the distance to the ground; this measurement is the total vertical drop. NOTE: If the ending point is more than 10 ft. from the starting point, use a mason's string and line level to establish a reference point from which to measure.

Span for upper staircase

Span for lower staircase

4 Measure the horizontal span for each staircase. First, use batterboards to establish level layout strings representing the edges of the staircases. Find the span for the upper staircase by measuring from a point directly below the edge of the deck out to the edge of the landing. Measure the span for the lower staircase from the landing to the endpoint.

How to Create a Final Layout—an Example

A) Total vertical drop = 115"
115" ÷ 7 = 16.43, or 16 rises
(8 rises per staircase)

Vertical drop

B) 115" ÷ 16 = 7.187,
or 7³⁄₁₆" per rise

C) Span 1 (80") + span 2 (80") = 160"
160" ÷ 14 runs (7 per staircase) =
11.42", or about 11⁷⁄₁₆" per tread run

Span 1

Span 2

1 Find the total number of step rises you will need by dividing the vertical drop by 7, rounding off fractions. (A, example above). Next, determine the exact height for each step rise by dividing the vertical drop by the number of rises (B).

2 Find the horizontal run for each step by adding the spans of both staircases (not including the landing), then dividing by the number of runs (C). Remember that the number of runs in a staircase is always one less than the number of rises.

3 If the layout does not conform with the guidelines on page 144, adjust the stairway starting point, ending point, or landing, then recalculate the measurements. After finding all dimensions, return to your building site and adjust the layout according to your final plan.

How to Build a Stairway Landing

1 Begin construction by building the landing. On a flat surface, build the landing frame from 2 × 6 lumber. Join the corners with 3" deck screws, then check for square by measuring diagonals. Adjust the frame until the diagonals are equal, then tack braces across the corners to hold the frame square.

2 Using your plan drawing, find the exact position of the landing on the ground, then set the frame in position and adjust it for level. Drive stakes to mark locations for the landing posts, using a plumb bob as a guide. Install the footings and posts for the landing.

(continued next page)

How to Build a Stairway Landing (continued)

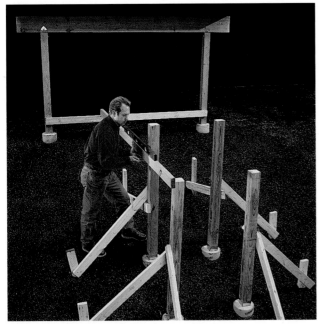

3 From the top of the deck, measure down a distance equal to the vertical drop for the upper staircase. Attach a 2 × 4 reference board across the deck posts at this height. Position a straightedge on the reference board and against the landing posts so it is level, and mark the posts at this height. Measure down a distance equal to the thickness of the decking boards, and mark reference lines to indicate where the top of the landing frame will rest.

4 Attach the landing frame to the posts at the reference lines. Make sure the landing is level, then secure it with joist ties attached to the posts with ⅝" × 3" lag screws. Cut off the posts flush with the top of the landing frame, using a reciprocating saw.

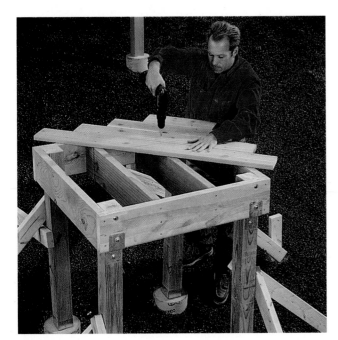

5 Remove the diagonal braces from the top of the landing frame, then cut and install joists. (For a diagonal decking pattern, space the joists every 12".) Attach the decking boards, and trim them to the edge of the frame.

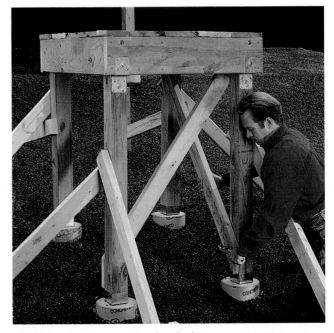

6 For extra support and to help prevent sway, create permanent cross braces by attaching 2 × 4 boards diagonally from the bottoms of the posts to the inside of the landing frame. Brace at least two sides of the landing. Remove the temporary braces and stakes holding the posts.

Tips for Laying Out Stairway Stringers

Upper staircase

(A) Outside stringers for upper staircase

(B) Middle stringer for upper staircase

Lower staircase

(C) Middle stringer for lower staircase

(D) Outside stringers for lower staircase

Lay out stringers on 2 × 12 lumber using a carpenter's square. Trim off the waste sections with a circular saw, finishing the notched cuts with a handsaw—in the illustrations above, the waste sections are left unshaded. In standard deck construction, the outside stringers are fitted with metal tread supports that are attached to the inside faces of the stringers. The middle stringer in each flight of stairs is notched to create surfaces that support the stair treads—when cut, these surfaces must align with the tops of the metal tread supports. For the upper staircase stringers, notches are cut at the bottom, front edges to fit over a 2 × 4 cleat that is attached to the landing (see page 145). The top of each notch should lie below the nose of the bottom tread by a distance equal to one rise plus the thickness of a decking board.

How to Build the Lower Staircase

1 Lay out and cut all stringers for both the upper and lower staircases (page 149). For the center stringers only, cut notches where the treads will rest. Start the notches with a circular saw, then finish the cuts with a handsaw. Measure and cut all tread boards.

2 Use ¾"-long lag screws to attach angle brackets to the stringers where the treads will rest, then turn the stringers upside down and attach the treads with lag screws. Gap between tread boards should be no more than ⅜".

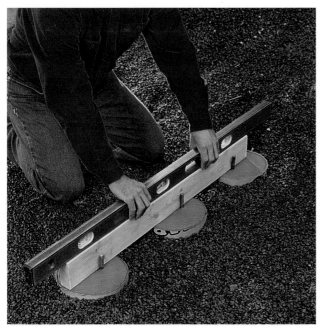

3 Dig and pour a concrete footing to support each stringer. Make sure the footings are level and are the proper height to the landing. Install a metal J-bolt in each footing while the concrete is wet, positioning the bolts so they will be offset about 2" from the stringers. After the concrete dries, cut 2 × 4 footing cleats, drill holes in them, and attach them to the J-bolts with nuts (see construction details, page 145).

4 Attach a 2 × 6 nailer to the landing to support the center stringer (page 145), then set the staircase in place, making sure the outside stringers are flush with the top of the decking. Use corner brackets and joist-hanger nails to anchor the stringers to the rim joist and nailer. Attach the bottoms of the stringers by nailing them to the footing cleats.

How to Build the Upper Staircase

1 Measure and cut a 2 × 4 cleat to match the width of the upper staircase, including the stringers. Use lag screws to attach the cleat to the rim joist on the landing, flush with the tops of the joists. Notch the bottoms of all stringers to fit around the cleat (page 145), and attach angle brackets on the stringers to support the treads.

2 To support the center stringer at the top of the staircase, measure and cut a 2 × 6 nailer equal to the width of the staircase. Attach the nailer to the rim joist with metal straps and screws.

3 Position the stringers so they rest on the landing cleat. Make sure the stringers are level and properly spaced, then toenail the bottoms of the stringers into the cleat, using galvanized 16d nails. At the top of the staircase, use angle brackets to attach the outside stringers to the rim joist and the middle stringer to the nailer.

4 Measure, cut, and position tread boards over the angle brackets, then attach them from below, using ¾"-long lag screws. The gap between tread boards should be no more than ⅜". After completing the stairway, install railings (pages 188 to 189).

Building Decks on Steep Slopes

Constructing a deck on a steep slope can be a complicated job if you use standard deck-building techniques. Establishing a layout for posts and footings is difficult on steeply pitched terrain, and construction can be demanding when one end of the deck is far above your head.

Professional deck contractors adapt to steep slope situations by using a temporary post-and-beam support structure, and by slightly altering the construction sequence. Rather than beginning with post-footing layout, experienced builders begin by constructing the outer frame and raising it onto a temporary support structure. Once the elevated frame is in position, the locations of the permanent posts and footings can be determined.

In most instances, you will need helpers when building a deck on a steep slope. To raise and position the deck frame on temporary supports, for example, you will need the help of three or four other people.

On some building sites, a deck may be at a considerable height above the ground. Always exercise caution when working at heights on a ladder or scaffold (page opposite).

The directions on the following pages show the construction of a deck featuring a corner-post design, but the technique can easily be adapted to cantilevered decks.

Positioning and measuring posts on a steep slope is much easier if the deck frame is already in position, resting on temporary supports.

Safety Tips for Building Decks on Slopes

Stepladders should be used in the open position only if the ground is level. On uneven ground you can use a closed stepladder by building a support ledger from 2 × 6 scraps (inset) and clamping it to a post. Lean the closed ladder against the ledger, and level the base of the ladder, if necessary (below). Never climb onto the top step of the ladder.

Extension ladders should be leveled and braced. Install sturdy blocking under ladder legs if the ground is uneven or soft, and drive a stake behind each ladder foot to keep it from slipping. Never exceed the weight limit printed on the ladder.

Scaffolding can be rented from rental centers or paint supply stores. When working at heights, scaffolding offers a safer, more stable working surface. Place blocking under the legs of the scaffolding, and level it by screwing the threaded legs in or out.

How to Build a Deck on a Steep Slope

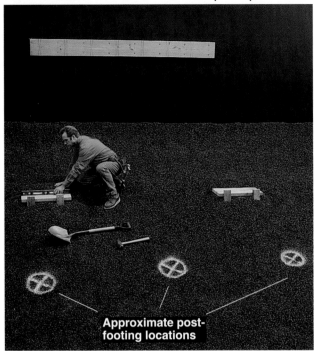

Approximate post-footing locations

1 After installing the ledger, use spray paint or stakes to mark the approximate locations for the post footings, according to your deck plans. Lay two 2 × 12 scraps on the ground to support temporary posts. Level the scraps, and anchor them with stakes. The bases for the temporary posts should be at least 2 ft. away from post-footing locations.

2 Construct two temporary posts by facenailing pairs of long 2 × 4s together. Erect each post by positioning it on the base and attaching a diagonal 2 × 4 brace. Toenail the post to the base.

3 Attach a second diagonal brace to each post, running at right angles to the first brace. Adjust the posts until they are plumb, then secure them in place by driving stakes into the ground and screwing the diagonal braces to the stakes.

4 Mark a cutoff line on each post by holding a long, straight 2 × 4 against the bottom of the ledger and the face of the post, then marking the post along the bottom edge of the 2 × 4. Cut off the posts at this height, using a reciprocating saw.

5 Construct a temporary support beam at least 2 ft. longer than the width of your deck by facenailing a pair of 2 × 4s together. Center the beam on top of the posts, and toenail it in place.

6 Build the outer frame of your deck according to your construction plans, and attach joist hangers to the inside of the frame, spaced 16" on center. With several helpers, lift the frame onto the temporary sup-ports and carefully move it into position against the ledger. NOTE: On very large or high decks, you may need to build the frame piece by piece on top of the temporary supports.

(continued next page)

7 Endnail the side joists to the ends of the ledger, then reinforce the joint by installing angle brackets in the inside corners of the frame.

8 Check to make sure the frame is square by measuring the diagonals. If the measurements are not the same, adjust the frame on the temporary beam until it is square. Also check the frame to make sure it is level; if necessary, shim between the temporary beam and the side joists to level the frame. Toenail the frame to the temporary beam.

9 Use a plumb bob suspended from the deck frame to stake the exact locations for post footings on the ground. NOTE: Make sure the footing stakes correspond to the exact center of the posts, as indicated by your deck plans.

10 Dig and pour footings for each post. While the concrete is still wet, insert J-bolts for post anchors, using a plumb bob to ensure that the bolts are at the exact center of the post locations. Let the concrete dry completely before continuing.

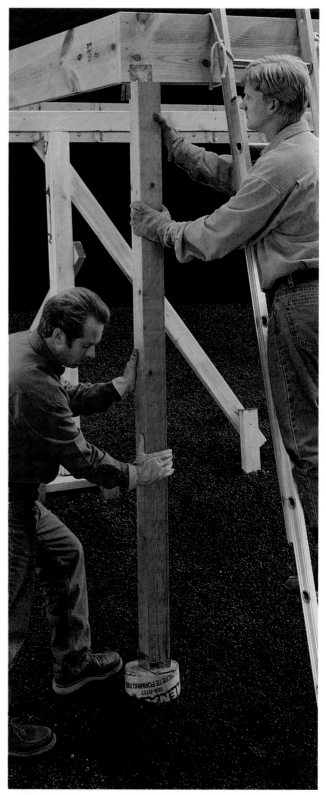

11 Check once more to make sure the deck frame is square and level, and adjust if necessary. Attach post anchors to the footings, then measure from the anchors to the bottom edge of the deck beam to determine the length for each post. NOTE: If your deck uses a cantilever design, make sure to allow for the height of the beam when cutting the posts.

12 Cut posts and attach them to the beam and footing with post-beam caps and post anchors (page 129). Brace the posts by attaching 2 × 4 boards diagonally from the bottom of the post to the inside surface of the deck frame (page 148). Remove the temporary supports, then complete the project using standard deck-building techniques.

Joists on a cantilevered deck can be easily marked for angled cuts by snapping a chalk line between two points on adjacent sides of the deck corner. Marking and cutting joists in this fashion is easier than measuring and cutting the joists individually. To help hold the joists in place while marking, tack a brace across the ends. Mark joist locations on the brace for reference.

Working with Angles

Decks with geometric shapes and angled sides have much more visual interest than basic square or rectangular decks. Most homes and yards are configured with predictable 90° angles and straight sides, so an angled deck offers a pleasing visual surprise.

Contrary to popular belief, elaborate angled decks are relatively easy to plan and build, if you follow the lead of professional designers. As professionals know, most polygon-shaped decks are nothing more than basic square or rectangular shapes with one or more corners removed. An octagonal island deck, for example, is simply a square with all four corners omitted.

Seen in this light, complicated multilevel decks with many sides become easier to visualize and design.

For visual balance and ease of construction, use 45° angles when designing an angled, geometric deck. In this way, the joinery requires only common cutting angles (90°, 45°, or 22½°), and you can use skewed 45° joist hangers, readily available at home centers. You can, of course, build a deck using irregular angles, but computing the cutting angles on such a deck is much more difficult, and you may need to special-order joist hangers and other hardware.

Design Options for Angled Decks

Cantilever design is the easiest and least expensive to build, since it requires the fewest posts. But the length of the angled side is limited by code regulations that restrict the amount of joist overhang. And since the joists rest on top of the beam, cantilever designs are not suited for a deck with a very low profile. On cantilever designs, the joists along the angled side are beveled at 45° at the ends and are attached to the rim joist by endnailing. See page 161.

Corner-post design is a good choice for large decks with long angled sides. It also works well for low-profile decks, since the joists are mounted to the inside faces of the beams. Many builders use a single beveled post to support the angled corners on this type of deck, but our method calls for two posts and footings at each of these corners, making the design easier to construct and more versatile. On a corner-post deck, the joists on the angled side are square-cut, and are attached to the beam with skewed 45° joist hangers. See page 162.

Multilevel design features an upper platform built using the corner-post method (above), but adds a lower platform (see pages 134 to 135). The lower level is supported by a second angled beam, created by sandwiching timbers around the same posts that support the upper platform. On the lower platform, the joists rest on top of the beam and are beveled on the back ends so they are flush with the edge of the beam. See page 165.

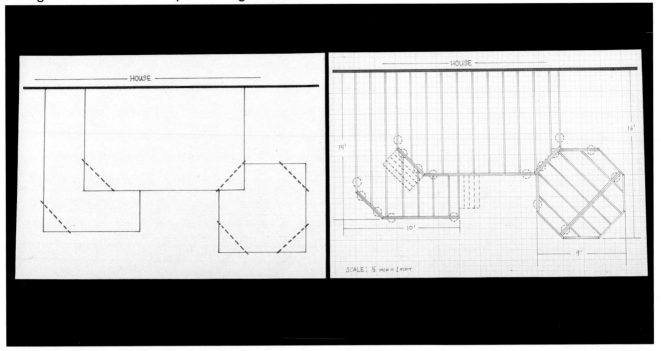

Draw squares and rectangles to create the basic deck platforms, then form angles by eliminating one or more corners. Using this method, you can design an almost infinite variety of single- and multilevel geometric decks. To ensure 45° angles, make sure the sides of the removed corners are the same length.

Use skewed 45° joist hangers to install joists when the beams are not parallel to the ledger. When mounted with skewed hangers, joists can be square-cut at the ends. Skewed 45° joist hangers are available at building centers in both left- and right- hand skews. However, if your deck joists angle away from the beam at angles other than 45°, you will need to special order skewed joist hangers to fit your situation, or use skewable joist hangers (page 20).

How to Build an Angled Deck Using the Cantilever Design

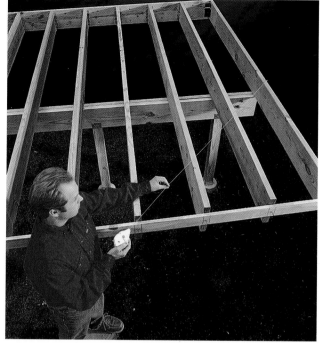

1 Lay out and begin construction, using standard deck-building techniques. After installing the joists, mark cutting lines on the angled side by snapping a chalk line across the tops of the joists. Make sure the chalk line is angled 45° to the edge of the deck.

2 At the outside joists, use a speed square to change the 45° chalk line to a line angled at 22½° in the opposite direction. When joined to a rim joist that is also cut to 22½°, the corner will form the correct angle.

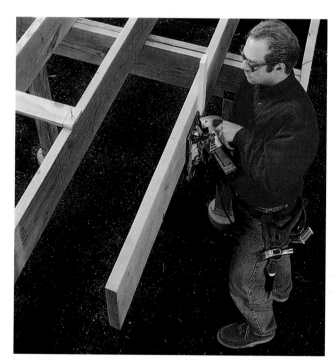

3 Use a combination square to extend the angle marks down the faces of the joists. Bevel-cut the deck joists with a circular saw, using a clamped board as a guide for the saw foot. Interior joists should be beveled to 45°; outside joists, to 22½°.

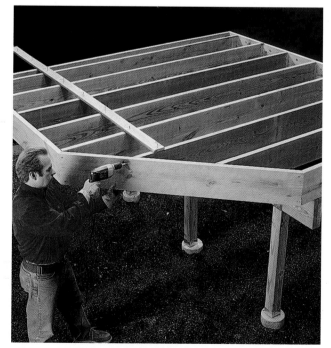

4 Cut and install the rim joists. At the angled corners, bevel-cut the ends of the rim joists at 22½°. Endnail the rim joists in place, and reinforce the inside corners with adjustable angle brackets attached with joist-hanger nails (page 165). Finish the deck, using standard deck-building techniques.

How to Build an Angled Deck Using the Corner-post Design

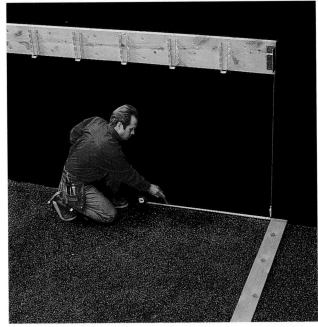

1 Use boards to create a rectangular template of the deck. To ensure that the template is square, use the 3-4-5 triangle method: From the corner directly below the ledger, measure 3 ft. along the foundation, and mark a point. Measure out along the template board 4 ft., and mark a second point. Measure diagonally between the two points. This measurement should be 5 ft.; if not, adjust the template to square it.

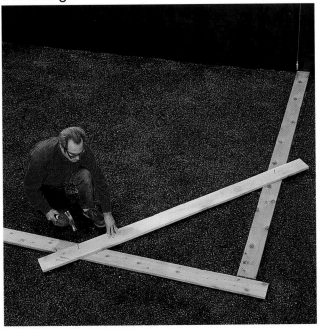

2 Indicate each angled edge by positioning a board diagonally across the corner of the template. To ensure that the angles measure 45°, make sure the perpendicular legs of the triangle have exactly the same measurement. Nail the boards together where they overlap.

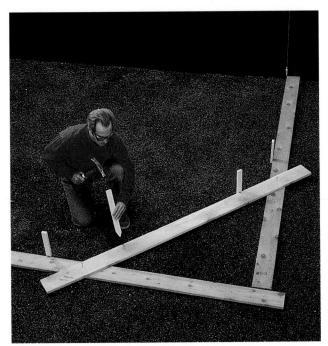

3 Mark locations for post footings with stakes or spray paint. At each 45° corner, mark locations for two posts, positioned about 1 ft. on each side of the corner. Temporarily move the board template, then dig and pour concrete footings.

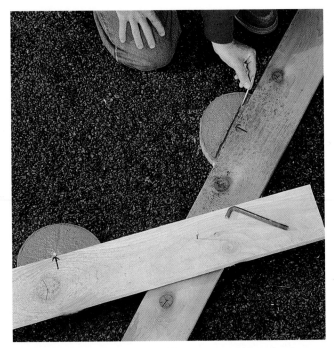

4 While the concrete is still wet, reposition the template and check to make sure it is square to the ledger. Use a nail to scratch a reference line across the concrete next to the template boards, then insert J-bolts in the wet concrete. Let the concrete dry completely.

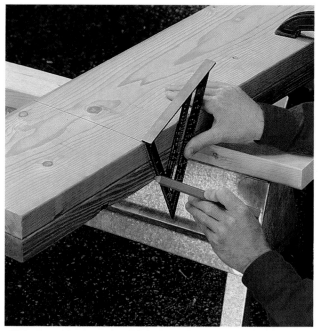

5 Attach metal post anchors to the J-bolts, centering them on the reference lines scratched in the concrete. The front and back edges of the anchors should be parallel to the reference line.

6 Measure and cut beam timbers to size. On ends that will form angled corners, use a speed square to mark 22½° angles on the tops of the timbers, then use a combination square to extend cutting lines down the face of the boards. Use a circular saw set for a 22½° bevel to cut off the timbers, then join them together with 16d nails.

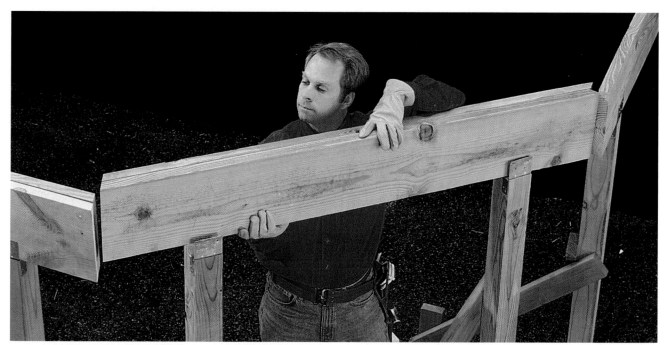

7 Set posts into the post anchors, then use a mason's string and line level to mark cutoff lines on the posts at a point level with the bottom of the ledger. Cut off the posts, using a reciprocating saw. Attach post-beam caps to the posts, then set the beams into place. Secure beam corners together with adjustable angle brackets attached to the inside of each corner with joist-hanger nails (page 165).

(continued next page)

How to Build an Angled Deck Using the Corner-post Design (continued)

8 Measure and mark joist locations on the ledger and beams. If your joists are spaced 16" on center along the ledger, they will be spaced 22⅝" apart measured along the angled beam. If they are spaced 24" on center at the ledger, the joists will be spaced 33⁵⁄₁₆" apart along the angled beam.

9 Attach joist hangers at the layout marks on the ledger and beam. Use skewed 45° joist hangers on the angled beam.

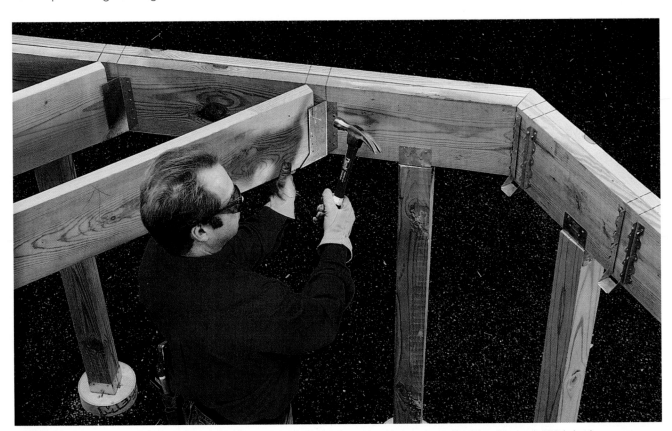

10 Cut and install joists, securing them with joist-hanger nails. Joists installed in skewed 45° joist hangers can be square-cut; they need not be beveled to match the angle of the beam. Complete the deck, using standard deck-building techniques.

Corner-post Variation: Adding a Second Platform

1 After installing the beam and joists for the top deck platform, mark the posts to indicate where the beam for the lower platform will be attached. Remember that the joists for the lower deck platform will rest on top of the beam (page 135). To help measure for beam length, clamp scrap pieces of 2 × 4 to the front and back faces of the posts over the layout marks. At corners, the ends of the 2 × 4s should touch.

2 Determine the length for each beam timber by measuring from the point where the 2 × 4 blocks touch. Remember that this measurement represents the short side of the bevel-cut timbers.

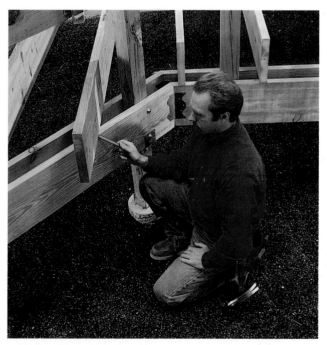

3 Lay out and cut beam timbers to length. At angled ends, cut the timbers with a 22½° bevel (page 163). Position and attach the beams to the posts, using 3" lag screws and joist ties. Reinforce angled corners with adjustable angle brackets attached with joist-hanger nails (photo, step 4). Install the remaining posts for the lower platform.

4 Measure and cut joists for the lower platform, attaching them to the beam by toenailing with 16d nails. Where joists rest on the angled beam, position the joists so they overhang the beam, then scribe cutting lines along the back edge of the beam. Bevel-cut the joists to this angle. Cut and install rim joists, then complete the deck, using standard deck-building techniques.

Creating Curves

By their nature, curved shapes lend a feeling of tranquility to a landscape. A deck with curved sides tends to encourage quiet relaxation. A curved deck can also provide an effective visual transition between the sharp architectural angles of the house and the more sweeping natural lines of the surrounding landscape.

Curved decks nearly always use a cantilevered design (page 36), in which the curved portion of the deck overhangs a beam that is set back from the edge of the deck. This set-back distance generally should be no more than one-third of the total length of the deck joists, but longer cantilevers are possible if you use a combination of thicker joists, closer joist spacing, and stronger wood species, such as southern yellow pine.

Accurate planning is essential when building a curved deck. Building inspectors carefully scrutinize plans for cantilevered decks, so you will need precisely drawn construction plans and a complete materials list when you apply for a building permit. Detailed plans will also help you define and visualize how you will use the deck, and they can help you save money by determining exact lengths for joists and decking boards.

If your curved deck will be high enough to require a railing, we recommend a design that incorporates a circular curve rather than an elliptical or irregular curve. Adding a curved railing (pages 190 to 193) is much easier if the deck curve is based on a circular shape.

A curved deck is created by cutting joists to match the curved profile, then attaching a curved rim joist, which can be shaped in one of two ways (page opposite). Braces attached to the tops of the joists hold them in place as the rim joist is installed.

Design Options for Curved Decks

Circular designs are the best choice for curved decks that require railings. However, circular curves require a fairly long cantilever, a limitation that may limit the overall size of your deck. Circular decks are laid out using simple geometry and a long compass tool, called a *trammel,* which you can make yourself. See page 193.

Irregular or elliptical curves should be used only on relatively low decks, since railings are quite difficult to construct for this kind of curve. These designs also work well for large decks, since the amount of over-hang on the cantilever is relatively short compared to that for a circular curve.

Construction Options

Kerfed rim joist is formed by making a series of thin vertical cuts (kerfs) across the inside face of the board, making it flexible enough to wrap around the curve. A kerfed rim joist made from 2"-thick dimension lumber is sufficiently strong, but if you are kerfing a 1"-thick redwood or cedar fascia board, it should be backed with a laminated rim joist (photo, right). See page 170.

Laminated rim joist is made by bending several layers of flexible ¼"- or ⅜"-thick exterior-grade plywood around the curve, joining each layer to the preceding layer with glue and screws. A laminated rim joist can stand alone, or it can provide backing for a more decorative fascia, such as a kerfed redwood or cedar board. See page 171.

How to Lay Out a Curved Deck

1 Install posts and beam for a cantilevered deck. Cut joists slightly longer than their final length, and attach them to the ledger and the beam. Add cross-blocking between the two outside joists to ensure that they remain plumb.

2 Mark the joist spacing on a 1 × 4 brace, and tack it across the tops of the joists at the point where the deck curve will begin. Measure the distance between the inside edges of the outer joists at each end of the beam, then divide this measurement in half to determine the radius of the circular curve. Mark the 1 × 4 brace to indicate the midpoint of the curve.

3 Build a trammel by anchoring one end of a long, straight 1 × 2 to the centerpoint of the curve, using a nail. (If the centerpoint lies between joists, attach a 1 × 4 brace across the joists to provide an anchor.) Measure out along the arm of the trammel a distance equal to the curve radius, and drill a hole. Insert a pencil in the hole, and pivot the trammel around the centerpoint, marking the joists for angled cuts.

VARIATION: For elliptical or irregular curves, temporarily nail vertical anchor boards to the outside joists at the start of the curve. Position a long strip of flexible material, such as hardboard or paneling, inside the anchor boards, then push the strip to create the desired bow. Drive nails into the joists to hold it in position, then scribe cutting lines on the tops of the joists.

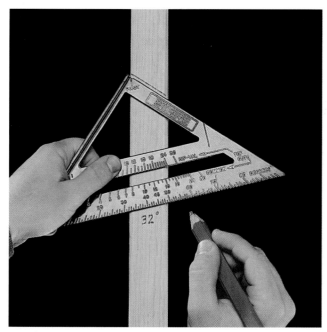

4 Use a speed square or protractor to determine the bevel angles you will use to cut the joists. Position the square so the top is aligned with the layout mark on the joist, then find the degree measurement by following the edge of the joist down from the pivot point and reading where it intersects the degree scale on the square.

5 Use a combination square to extend the cutting lines down the front and back faces of the joists. At the outside joists where the curve begins, mark square cutting lines at the point where the circular curve touches the inside edge of the joists.

6 Cut off each joist with a circular saw set to the proper bevel. Clamp a straightedge to the joist to provide a guide for the foot of the saw. On the outside joists where the curve begins, make 90° cuts.

7 Where the bevel angle is beyond the range of your circular saw, use a reciprocating saw to cut off the joists.

How to Construct a Kerfed Rim Joist for a Curved Deck

1 Mark the inside face of the rim joist lumber with a series of parallel lines, 1" apart. Using a circular saw or radial-arm saw set to a blade depth equal to ¾ of the rim joist thickness (1⅛", for 2"-thick lumber), make crosscut kerfs at each line. Soak the rim joist in water for about 2 hours to make it easier to bend.

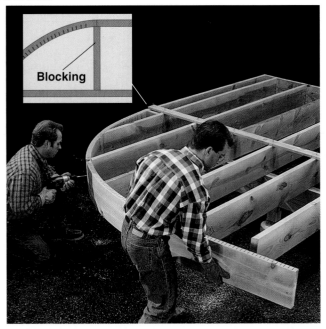

2 Install a cross block between the first two joists on each side of the curve, positioned so half the block is covered by the square-cut outside joist (inset). While it is still damp, attach the rim joist by butting it against the end joist and attaching it to the cross block with 3" deck screws. Bend the rim joist so it is flush against the ends of the joists, and attach with two or three 3" deck screws driven at each joist.

3 Where butt joints are necessary, mark and cut the rim joist so the joint will fall at the center of a joist. To avoid chipping, cut off the rim joist at one of the saw kerfs.

4 Complete the installation by butting the end of the rim joist against the outside joist and attaching it to the cross block. Use bar clamps to hold the rim joist in position as you screw it to the blocking. NOTE: If the rim joist flattens near the sides of the deck, install additional cross-blocking, cut to the contour of the curve, to hold the rim joist in proper position.

How to Construct a Curved Rim Joist with Laminated Plywood

1 Install blocking between the first two joists on each side of the deck (step 2, previous page). Cut four strips of ¼"-thick exterior plywood the same width as the joists. Butt the first strip against the outside joist and attach it to the blocking with 1½" deck screws. Bend the strip around the joists and attach with deck screws. If necessary, install additional blocking to keep the plywood in the proper curve. If butt joints are necessary, make sure they fall at the center of joists.

2 Attach the remaining strips of plywood one at a time, attaching them to previous layers with 1" deck screws and exterior wood glue. Make sure butt joints are staggered so they do not overlap previous joints. For the last layer, use a finish strip of ⅜" cedar plywood. Where the finish strip butts against the outside joists, bevel-cut the ends at 10° to ensure a tight fit.

How to Install Decking on a Curved Deck

1 Install decking for the square portion of the deck, then test-fit decking boards on the curved portion. If necessary, you can make minor adjustments in the spacing to avoid cutting very narrow decking boards at the end of the curve. When satisfied with the layout, scribe cutting lines on the underside of the decking boards, following the edge of the rim joist.

2 Remove the scribed decking boards, and cut along the cutting lines with a jig saw. Install the decking boards with deck screws, and smooth the cut edges of the decking boards with a belt sander, if necessary.

Framing for Insets

If your planned deck site has a tree, boulder, or other large obstacle, you may be better off building around it rather than removing it. Although framing around a landscape feature makes construction more difficult, the benefits usually make the effort worthwhile. A deck with an attractive tree set into it, for example, is much more appealing than a stark, exposed deck built on a site that has been leveled by a bulldozer.

The same methods used to frame around a pre-existing obstacle also can be used to create a decorative or functional inset feature, such as a planter box, child's sandbox, or brick barbecue. On a larger scale, the same framing techniques can be used to enclose a hot tub or above-ground pool.

A framed opening can also provide access to a utility fixture, such as a water faucet, electrical outlet, or central air-conditioning compressor. Covering a framed opening with a removable hatch (page 175) preserves the smooth, finished look of your deck.

Large insets that interrupt joists can compromise the strength of your deck. For this reason, inset openings require modified framing to ensure adequate strength. Double joists on either side of the opening bear the weight of double headers, which in turn support the interrupted joists. Always consult your building inspector for specifics when constructing a deck with a large inset.

Inset framing makes it possible to save mature trees when building a deck. Keeping trees and other landscape features intact helps preserve the value and appearance of your property. Check with a tree nursery for an adequate opening size for any tree you want to contain within an inset.

172

Applications for Framed Insets

Trees inset into a deck should have plenty of room around them to allow for growth and wind sway. In this deck, the planter boxes have been positioned around the inset opening to lend a more natural appearance.

Fire pits can be inset into decks, if you are careful to use fireproof masonry materials and follow local code guidelines. This redwood deck has been framed around a brick fire pit that rests on a concrete slab.

Built-in planters can be inset so they are flush with the deck, or they can be built with raised timber sides for more visual impact (above). The same technique can be used to inset a sandbox in a deck.

Hot tubs are often built into a deck. In some situations, the hot tub is supported by the deck structure and is partially enclosed by a secondary platform (pages 176 to 179). Or, the hot tub can be fully inset into the deck, supported by a concrete pad on the ground.

How to Frame for an Inset

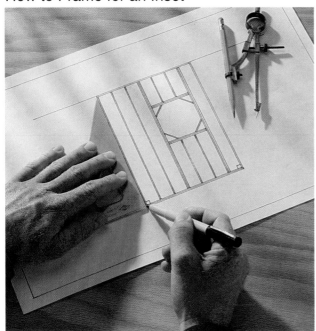

1 Modify your deck plan, if necessary, to provide the proper support for the interrupted joists in the inset opening. If the inset will interrupt one or two joists, frame both sides of the opening with double joists. If the opening is larger, you may need to install additional beams and posts around the opening to provide adequate support. Consult your building inspector for specific requirements for your situation.

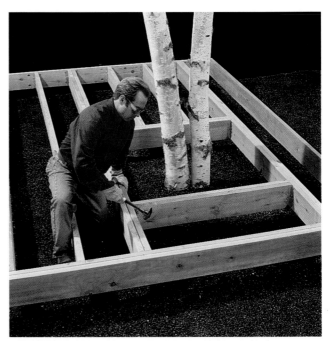

2 Rough-frame the opening by using double joist hangers to install double joists on each side of the inset, and double headers between these joists. Install the interrupted joists between the double headers and the rim joist and ledger.

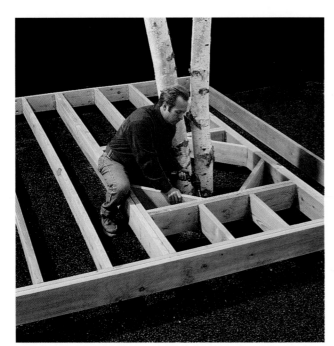

3 Where needed, cut and install angled nailing blocks between the joists and headers to provide additional support for the decking boards. When trimmed, decking boards may overhang support members by as much as 4" around an inset opening.

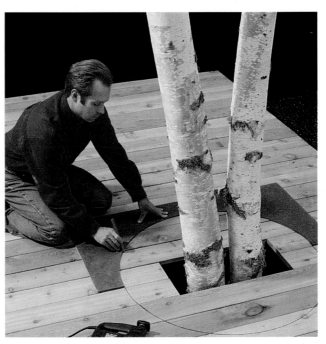

4 Lay the decking boards so the ends overhang the rough opening. Make a cardboard template to draw a cutting line on the deck boards. (When framing for a tree, check with a tree nursery for adequate opening size to provide space for growth.) Cut the decking boards along the marked line, using a jig saw.

Framing Variations

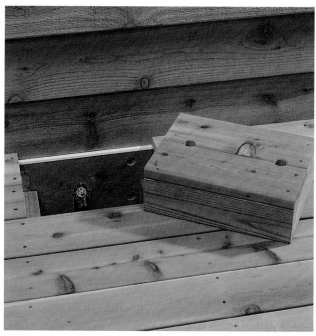

Inset box can be used as a planter for flowers or herbs. Build the box from ¾"-thick exterior-grade plywood, and attach it to the framing members with deck screws. A deep box can be supported by landscape timbers. Line the inside of the box with layers of building paper, then drill ½"-wide holes in the bottom of the box to provide drainage. To keep soil from washing out through drainage holes, line the box with landscape fabric.

Access hatch made from decking can hide a utility feature, such as a water faucet or air-conditioner compressor. Install cleats along the inside of the framed opening to support the hatch. Construct the hatch from decking boards mounted on a 2 x 4 frame. Finger holes drilled in the hatch make removal easier.

Hot Tub Variation

Hot tub inset completely into a deck requires a concrete pad to support the weight. The surface decking is flush with the lip of the tub, but does not bear any of the tub's weight. For this reason, the deck height must be carefully planned when laying out the posts, beams, and joists.

Framing for a Hot Tub

Building a hot tub into a deck is usually done in one of two ways. If you design your deck at exactly the right height, you can create a full inset by resting the hot tub on a concrete pad and building the deck around it (page 175).

But on a low-profile deck, or a tall deck, the most practical solution is to mount the hot tub on the surface of the deck and build a secondary platform around it, creating a partial inset. As shown on the following pages, the structural design of the deck must be modified to ensure that it can support the added weight of a hot tub filled with water. Make sure your deck plans are approved by the building inspector before you begin work.

Installing a hot tub usually requires the installation of new plumbing and electrical lines. When planning the installation, make sure to consider the location of plumbing pipes, electrical cables, switches, and access panels. For convenience, arrange to have the rough-in work for these utilities done before you install the decking boards.

How to Frame for a Hot Tub

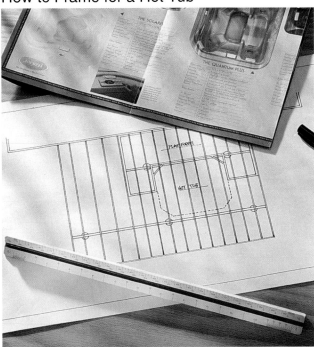

1 Plan posts and beams to support the maximum anticipated load, including the weight of the hot tub filled with water. In most cases, this means altering your deck plan to include extra beams and posts directly under the hot tub.

2 Lay out and install the ledger, footings, posts, and support beams, according to your deck plans. Lay out joist locations on the ledger and beams, and install the joists, following local code requirements. Many building codes require joists spaced no more than 12" on center if the deck will support a hot tub. If your hot tub requires new plumbing or electrical lines, have the preliminary rough-in work done before continuing with deck construction.

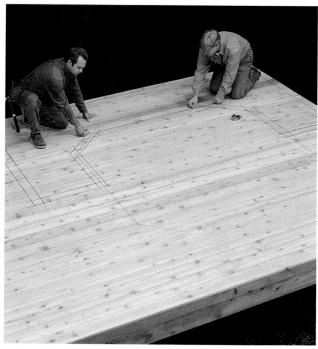

3 Install the decking boards, then snap chalk lines to outline the position of the hot tub and the raised platform that will enclose the hot tub.

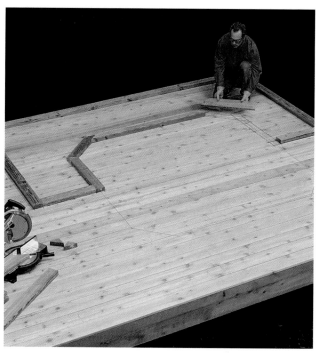

4 Lay out and cut 2 × 4 sole plates and top plates for the stud walls on the raised platform.

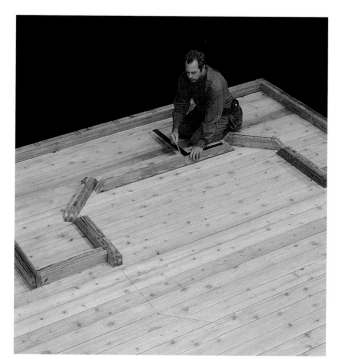

5 Mark stud locations on the top and bottom plates. Studs should be positioned every 16" (measured on center), and at the ends of each plate.

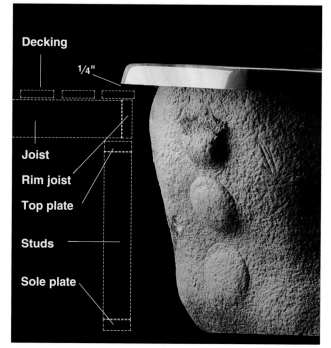

Decking

1/4"

Joist

Rim joist

Top plate

Studs

Sole plate

6 Measure the height of the hot tub to determine the required height of the studs in the platform walls. Remember to include the thickness of both wall plates, the joists that will rest on the walls, and the decking material on the platform. The surface of the finished platform should be 1/4" below the lip of the hot tub.

(continued next page)

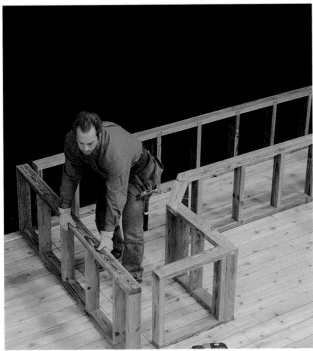

7 Construct the stud walls by screwing the plates to the studs. Position the walls upright on the deck over the outline marks, and anchor them to the deck with 2½" deck screws.

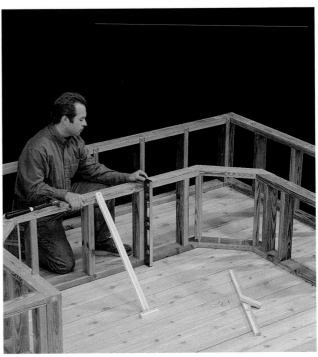

8 At corners, join the studs together with 3" deck screws. Check the walls for plumb, and brace them in position.

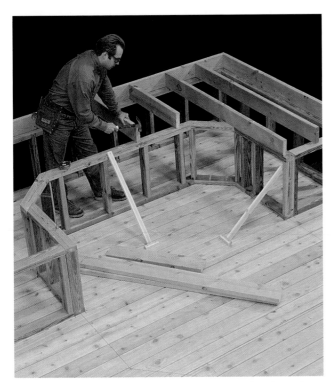

9 Toenail a 2 × 6 rim joist along the back edge of the platform, then cut and install 2 × 6 joists across the top of the stud walls at 16" intervals, toenailing them to the top plates. The ends of the joists should be set back 1½" from the edges of the top plates to allow for the rim joist.

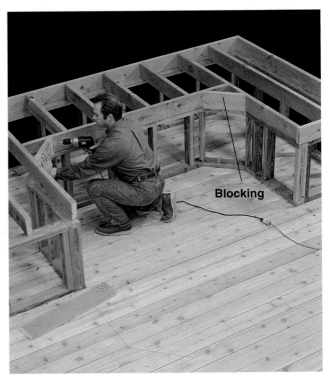

10 Cut 2 × 6 rim joists to length, and endnail them to the joists with 16d nails. At angled wall segments, cut diagonal blocking and attach it between the rim joist and adjoining joists with deck screws.

Blocking

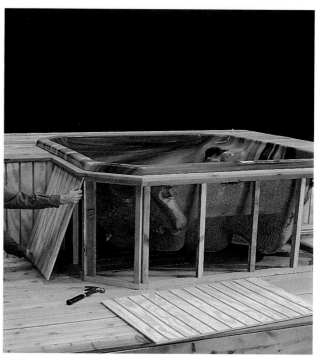

11 Cut decking boards, and attach them to the platform joists with 2½" deck screws. If your hot tub requires cutouts for plumbing or electrical lines, do this work now.

12 Set the hot tub in place, then build 2 × 2 stud walls around the exposed sides of the tub. Measure, cut, and install siding materials on the exposed walls.

13 Build platform steps (page 131) to provide access to the platform, using siding materials to box in the risers. Where required by code, install railings around the elevated platform (pages 180 to 187).

Railings are required for safety on most decks, but they also contribute to the overall visual appeal. Curved railings like the one shown here are usually built with the vertical baluster style. See pages 190 to 193.

Building Railings

Railings are the crowning touch for a deck project. Required by code for any deck more than 30" high, railings serve a practical function by making your deck safe. But railings also serve an ornamental function, by helping to create the style and mood of a deck.

There are numerous designs used for deck railings, but most are variations of the styles you will learn how to build on the following pages. (See

pages 100 to 107 for another common variation.) The key to successful railing construction is to have detailed plans. When drawing up railing plans, exercise the same care used when creating your deck plans.

Railing construction is governed by specific code requirements. See pages 32 to 33 for basic code guidelines, and consult your local building inspector when designing a deck railing.

Railing Options

Vertical baluster railing is a popular style because it complements most house styles. To improve the strength and appearance of the railing, the advanced variation shown here uses a "false mortise" design. The 2 × 2 balusters are mounted on 2 × 2 horizontal rails that slide into mortises notched into the posts. See page 184.

Horizontal railing visually complements modern ranch-style houses with predominantly horizontal lines. For improved strength and a more attractive appearance, the style shown here features 1 × 4 rails set on edge into dadoes cut in the faces of the posts. A cap rail running over all posts and top rails helps unify and strengthen the railing. See page 185.

Wall-style railing is framed with short 2 × 4 stud walls attached flush with the edges of the deck. The stud walls and rim joists are then covered with siding materials, usually chosen to match the siding on the house. A wall-style railing creates a more private space and visually draws the deck into the home, providing a unified appearance. See pages 186 to 187.

Stairway railings are required for any stairway with more than two steps. They are usually designed to match the style used on the deck railing. See pages 188 to 189.

Railing Design Variations

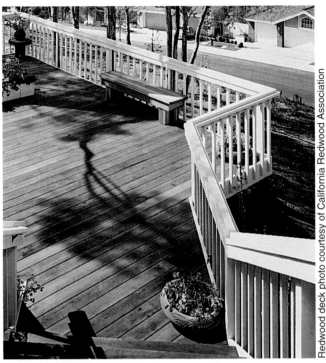

Unique railing patterns give your deck a custom-designed look. The railing shown here was built with 2 × 2s joined with lap joints. You can use any pattern you choose; however, the design must comply with code requirements. To ensure the safety of children, railings must be constructed so a sphere 4" in diameter cannot fit through any portion of the railing.

Painted railings create an elegant contrast to the natural wood colors found in the decking boards and stairway treads. When painted to match or complement house trim, painted railings help establish consistency of style.

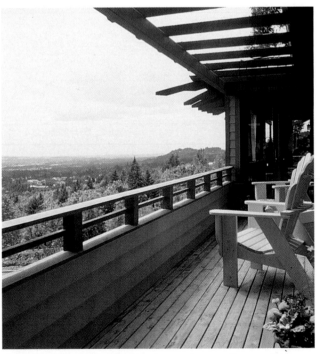

Cables threaded through deck posts create a modern-looking, unobtrusive railing that does not hinder your view. Turnbuckles installed near the edge of the deck can be adjusted to keep the cables taut.

Wall-style railing with horizontal top rails provides a secure barrier for a deck high above the ground, but does not completely obstruct the view.

Railing Construction Tips

Railing posts can be surface-mounted to the edges of rim joists (left), but to improve strength and preserve the smooth lines of the deck, posts can be mounted inside the deck frame (right). Attach the posts with lag screws driven through the deck framing, then cut and endnail extra blocking between joists to reinforce the posts and to provide a nailing surface for attaching decking boards. To ensure sturdiness, posts should be spaced no more than 5 ft. apart.

Specialty railing hardware and wood products make construction easier and can be used to create a railing with a more customized appearance. Common specialty products include rail brackets (A), post caps (B), milled balusters (C), prenotched posts (D), and grippable stairway rails (E).

How to Build a Vertical Baluster Railing

1 Cut 4 × 4 railing posts to size (at least 36", plus the height of the deck rim joists). Lay out and mark partial dadoes 1½" wide and 2½" long where the horizontal 2 × 2 rails will fit. Use a circular saw set to ½" blade depth to make a series of cuts from the edge of the post to the end of layout marks, then use a chisel to clean out the dadoes and square them off. On corner posts, cut dadoes on adjoining sides of the post.

2 Attach the posts inside the rim joists (page 183). To find the length for the rails, measure between the bases of the posts, then add 1" for the ½" dadoes on each post. Measure and cut all balusters. Install the surface boards before continuing with railing construction.

3 Assemble the rails and balusters on a flat surface. Position the balusters at regular intervals (no more than 4" apart), and secure them by driving 2½" deck screws through the rails. A spacing block cut to match the desired gap can make this work easier.

4 Slide the assembled railings into the post dadoes, and toenail them in position with galvanized casing nails. Cut plugs to fit the exposed dadoes, and glue them in place. The resulting joint should resemble a mortise-and-tenon.

5 Measure and cut the 2 × 6 cap rails, then secure them by driving 2" deck screws up through the top rail. At corners, miter-cut the cap rails to form miter joints.

How to Build a Horizontal Railing

1 Cut all 4 × 4 posts to length, then clamp them together to lay out 3½"-wide × ¾"-deep dadoes for the horizontal rails. Cut the dadoes by making a series of parallel cuts, about ¼" apart, between the layout marks. For corner posts, cut dadoes on adjacent faces of the post.

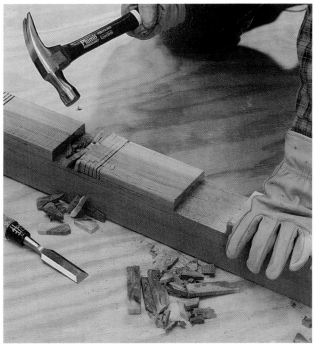

2 Knock out the waste wood between the layout marks, using a hammer, then use a chisel to smooth the bottom of each dado. Attach the posts inside the rim joists (page 183). Install decking before continuing with railing construction.

3 Determine the length of 1 × 4 rails by measuring between the bases of the posts. Cut rails to length, then nail them in place using 8d splitless cedar siding nails. At corners, bevel-cut the ends of the rails to form miter joints. If the rails butt together, the joint should fall at the center of a post.

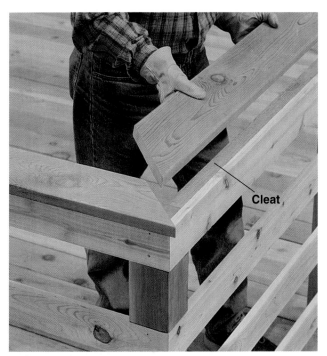

Cleat

4 Measure and cut 2 × 2 cleats and attach them between the posts, flush with the top rail, using galvanized casing nails. Then, measure and cut cap rails, and position and attach them by driving 2" deck screws up through the cleats. At corners, miter-cut the ends of the cap rails.

Building Stair Railings

For safety and convenience, any stairway that has more than two risers or is more than 30" above the ground, should have a railing. The stair railing is generally designed to match the look of the main deck railing.

The dado techniques used to attach deck rails to posts (page 185) are difficult to accomplish with the angled rails on a stairway. Instead, stairway rails can be attached with L-brackets or by toenailing them into the posts.

The sequence shown here demonstrates how to build a horizontal stair railing. A vertical baluster stair railing is built in much the same way, except that it has only two rails, with a series of angle-cut balusters attached between them.

Grippable handrails are required for stairways with more than two risers. The handrail should be shaped so the grippable portion is between 1¼" and 2" in diameter, and should be angled into posts at the ends. The top of the handrail should be 34" to 38" above the stair treads, measured from the nose of a step.

posts
joists
cular
cuts
the w
squa
railin

How to Build a Horizontal Stair Railing

1 Use a combination square to mark the face of the top stairway post, where the railings will fit. For most horizontal stairway designs, the top stairway rail should start level with the second deck rail. Mark the other stairway posts at the same level.

2 Position a rail board against the faces of the posts, with the bottom edge against the stringer, then scribe angled cutting lines across the rail along the inside edges of the posts. Cut the rail at these lines, then cut the remaining rails to match.

1 O
p

3 B
h
and a
top p

3 Secure the rails to the posts with galvanized metal L-brackets attached to the inside of the rails.

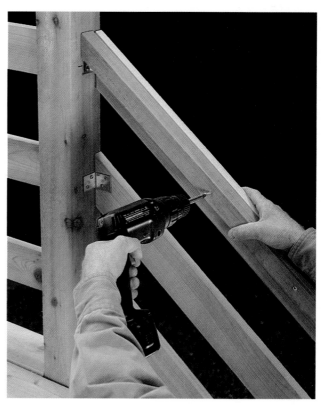

4 Measure and cut a 2 × 2 cleat, and attach it flush with the top inside edge of the top rail, using 2" deck screws. Anchor the cleat to the posts by toe-nailing with galvanized casing nails.

5 Measure and cut the cap rail to fit over the top rail and cleat. At the bottom of the railing, cut the post at an angle and attach the cap rail so it overhangs the post slightly. Secure the cap rail by driving 2" deck screws up through the cleat.

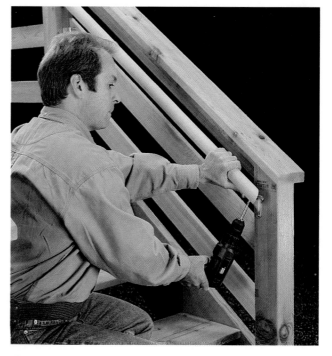

6 Measure and cut a grippable handrail, attaching it to the posts with mounting brackets. Miter-cut the ends, and create a return back to the post by cutting another mitered section of handrail and nailing it in place between the handrail and post (page opposite).

Building Curved Railings

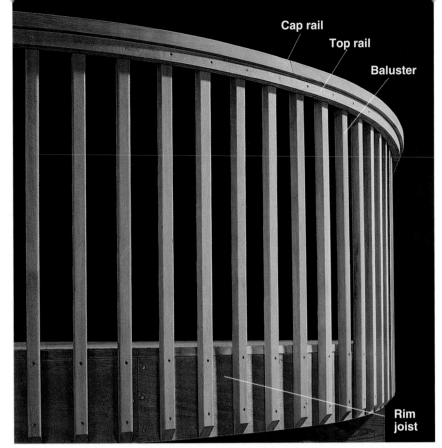

Laying out and constructing a curved railing requires a basic understanding of geometry and the ability to make detailed drawings using a compass, protractor, and a special measuring tool called a *scale ruler*.

The method for constructing a curved cap rail shown on the following pages works only for symmetrical, circular curves—quarter circles, half circles, or full circles. If your deck has irregular or elliptical curves, creating a cap rail is very difficult. For these curves, it is best to limit the railing design to include only balusters and a laminated top rail.

Components of a curved railing include: vertical balusters attached to the curved rim joist, a top rail built from laminated layers of plywood, and a curved cap rail. The cap rail is constructed by laying out mitered sections of 2 × 12 lumber, marking a curved shape, and cutting it out with a jig saw.

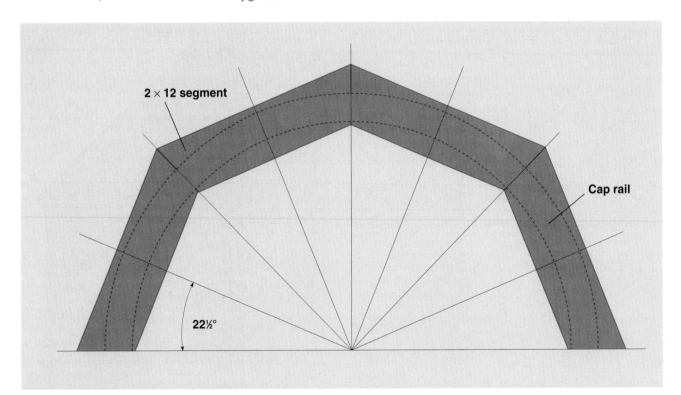

Curved cap rail is created from mitered segments of 2 × 12 lumber. After positioning the 2 × 12 segments end to end, the shape of the 6"-wide cap rail is outlined on the pieces. For a semicircle with a radius of up to 7 ft., four 2 × 12 segments will be needed, with ends mitered at 22½°. For a semicircle with a larger radius, you will need eight segments, with ends mitered at 11¼°.

How to Build a Curved Railing

1 To create a curved top rail, use exterior glue to laminate four 1½"-wide strips of ⅜"-thick cedar plywood together, using the curved rim joist of the deck as a bending form. First, cover the rim joist with kraft paper for protection. Then, begin wrapping strips of plywood around the rim joist. Clamp each strip in position, starting at one end of the curve. The strips should differ in length to ensure that butt joints will be staggered from layer to layer.

2 Continue working your way around the rim joist, toward the other end. Make sure to apply clamps on both sides of the butt joints where plywood strips meet. Cut the last strips slightly overlong, then trim the laminated rail to the correct length after the glue has set. For extra strength, drive 1" deck screws through the rail at 12" intervals after all strips are glued together. Unclamp the rail, and sand the top and bottom edges smooth.

3 Install prenotched 4 × 4 posts (page 183) at the square corners of the deck. Then, cut 2 × 2 balusters to length, beveling the bottom ends at 45°. Attach the balusters to the rim joist with 2½" deck screws, using a spacer to maintain even intervals. Clamp the curved top rail to the tops of the balusters and posts, then attach it with deck screws.

4 After the top rail and balusters are in place, attach 2 × 2 top rails to the balusters in the straight sections of the deck. The ends of the straight top rails should be flush against the ends of the curved top rail. Now, measure the distance between the inside faces of the balusters at each end of the curve. Divide this distance in half to find the required radius for the curved cap rail.

(continued next page)

5 Using a scale of 1" equals 1 ft., make a diagram of the deck. (A scale ruler makes this job easier.) First, draw the arc of the deck with a compass, using the radius measurement found in step 4. Divide the curved portion of the deck into an even number of equal sections by using a protractor to draw radius lines from the center of the curve. For a semicircular curve, it is usually sufficient to draw eight radius lines, angled at 22½° to one another. (For a deck with a radius of more than 7 ft., you may need to divide the semicircle into 16 portions, with radius lines angled at 11¼°.)

6 From the point where one of the radius lines intersects the curved outline of the deck, use the scale ruler to mark points 5½" above and 5½" below the intersection. From these points, use a protractor to draw perpendicular lines to the adjoining radius lines. The polygon outlined by the perpendicular lines and the adjoining radius lines represents the shape and size for all of the 2 × 12 segments that will be used to construct the cap rail.

7 Draw a pair of parallel arcs 5½" apart, representing the curved cap railing, inside the outline for the 2 × 12 segments. Shade the portion of the drawing that lies between the straight parallel lines and the two adjacent radius lines. This area represents the shape and size for each of the angled 2 × 12 segments. Measure the angle of the miter at the ends of the board; in this example, the segments are mitered at 22½°.

8 Measure the length of the long edge; this number is the overall length for each of the 2 × 12 segments you will be cutting. Using this highlighted area, determine how many segments you will need to complete the curve. For a semicircular curve with radius up to 7 ft., four segments are required, with ends mitered at 22½°. For curves with a larger radius, you will need eight segments, with ends mitered at 11¼°.

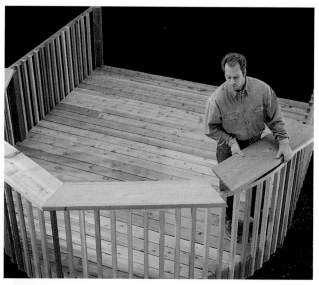

9 Measure and mark 2 × 12 lumber for the cap rail segments, with ends angled inward at 22½° from perpendicular. Set the blade on your circular saw or tablesaw to a 15° bevel, then make compound miter cuts along the marked lines. When cut to compound miters, the segments will form overlapping *scarf* joints that are less likely to reveal gaps between the boards.

10 Arrange the cap rail segments over the curved deck railing, and adjust the pieces, if necessary, so they are centered over the top rail. When you are satisfied with the layout, temporarily attach the segments in place by driving 2" deck screws up through the curved top rail. Measure and install the 2 × 6 cap railing for the straight portion of the railing.

11 Temporarily nail or clamp a long sturdy board between the railings at the start of the curve. Build a long compass, called a *trammel*, by nailing one end of a long 1 × 2 to a 1 ft.-long piece of 1 × 4. Measure from the nail out along the arm of the trammel, and drill holes at the desired radius measurements; for our application, there will be two holes, 5½" apart, representing the width of the finished cap rail. Attach the 1 × 4 base of the trammel to the temporary board so the nail point is at the centerpoint of the deck rail curve, then insert a pencil through one of the holes in the trammel arm. Pivot the arm of the trammel around the cap rail, scribing a cutting line. Move the pencil to the other hole, and scribe a second line.

12 Remove the trammel, and unscrew the cap rail segments. Use a jig saw to cut along the scribed lines, then reposition the curved cap rail pieces over the top rail. Secure the cap rail by applying exterior adhesive to the joints and driving 2½" deck screws up through the top rail. Remove saw marks by belt sanding.

Decorative Pipe Railings

How to Build Decorative Pipe Railing

Use ¾" copper tubing available in the plumbing section of building centers for decorative balusters in a railing. Over time, the copper is affected by the climate and develops an attractive patina. Metal balusters coated in colors also are available from some manufacturers. If you can't find them at your local building center, manufacturers and suppliers can be found on the Internet.

1 Layout and attach railing posts as you would for traditional railings (see pages 100 to 102). Measure and cut pairs of 2 × 4 rails to fit between post faces or in notches cut in the post faces.

2 On one edge of an 8-ft. 2 × 4, layout and mark hole locations every 4½", beginning at the centerpoint and working towards the ends. Use this board as a story pole to create consistent spacing between balusters. Clamp the story pole to each rail pair, aligning the centerpoint of the rails with that of the story pole. If the hole locations fall within 1½" of the ends, adjust the rails as necessary. Transfer marks to the rails using a speed square.

3 Drill a ¾"-diameter hole ¾" deep at each location, using a portable drill guide and Forstner bit.

4 Apply a small amount of silicone caulk in each hole in the bottom rail and insert a baluster. The caulk prevents moisture penetration.

5 Lay a 1 × 4 under the baluster ends to hold them up uniformly. Brace the bottom end so it won't move, then fit the top rail over the baluster ends. A helper will make this much easier. Set the assembly upright, and hammer against a scrap block placed on the top rail to fully seat the balusters in both rails.

6 For stair rails, mark hole locations that are 5½" apart on center. Turn the top rail 180° and flip it upside down before clamping the rails together. Begin marking at the centerpoint of the rails. Drill holes for the balusters with the clamped rail pair resting on the stair treads. Use a level to set the proper angle for the drill guide if necessary.

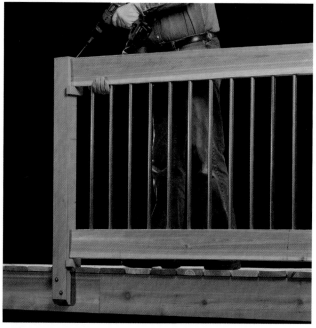

7 Install each rail assembly between the appropriate posts, using 2½" deck screws. Attach cap rails following the methods shown on pages 106 to 107.

Deck Plans

An alternative to developing and drawing your own deck plans is to use an existing plan and drawings. You save the significant amount of time it takes to create quality plan drawings and you can be reasonably certain that the plans cover all necessary details. The only drawback is in finding a plan that meets your needs and fits the requirements of your house.

The ten deck plans on the following pages cover the most popular and versatile styles. Any one of them should provide you with the basic plan you need. There also are plans for common deck furnishings: benches, planters, and an arbor. Information on installing deck lighting also is provided. These accessories are designed to complement any deck plan and provide you with options to help you build a deck that matches your needs, both functionally and aesthetically.

These step-by-step plans should provide you with everything you need to know to build the deck or furnishings presented, including lumber lists and detailed drawings. It is still up to you to evaluate the labor and costs involved. The cost of a deck can vary widely, depending on its size, the materials used, and your location.

The plans in this book should conform to the building code in your area, but you'll still need to get approval from your local building inspector and make any required changes. Before setting an appointment with a building inspector, make copies of your plan (call the inspector to find out how many copies are required).

Although the plans presented in this book offer a wide selection of styles and placements, it's possible that you'll want to modify a plan to fit your house or yard, or just to suit your tastes. Use the information on pages 30 to 41 to ensure that the changes in size, shape, or height you make to a plan will produce a safe and secure deck. Footings, joist spans, beam sizes, post sizes or spacing, and stair and railing requirements may be affected by the changes.

When working with a plan, become familiar with common symbols and conventions before beginning the project. As you prepare to cut lumber, take the time to confirm the exact measurements of all the cuts. If you aren't certain how to accomplish a particular step, review the required building techniques shown in previous sections of this book.

NOTICE TO READERS

Any deck building plan, including its detailed construction diagrams, will provide the information necessary for a successful deck project. However, no plan or set of diagrams can cover every aspect of the work you will encounter, especially those details specific to your building site and conditions. Make certain you have adequate general construction experience and skills before beginning a deck project, or have someone who does work with you.

Rectangular Deck

Extend your living space and increase your home's value.

Here's a deck that's classic in its simplicity. Moderately sized and easy to build, this rectangular deck won't cost you an arm and a leg—in either time or money. The framing and decking plans are quite straightforward, and you can likely build the entire deck in just two or three weekends, even with limited carpentry and building experience. Within just a few weeks time, you can transform your yard into a congenial gathering place for cooking, entertaining and just plain relaxing; a place where you, your family, and your friends can enjoy the fresh air in convenience and comfort.

Cutaway View

Lumber List			
Qty.	Size	Material	Part
4	2 × 8" × 12'	Trtd. lumber	Ledger (A), Beam bds (C), Rim joist (E)
1	4 × 4" × 8'	Trtd. lumber	Deck posts (B)
10	2 × 8" × 10'	Trtd. lumber	End joists (D), Joists (F)
25	2 × 6" × 12'	Cedar	Decking (G), Rail cap (N)
7	4 × 4" × 8'	Cedar	Stair posts (H), Rail post (K)

Lumber List			
Qty.	Size	Material	Part
2	2 × 12" × 8'	Cedar	Stringers (I)
5	2 × 6" × 6'	Cedar	Treads (J)
32	2 × 2" × 8'	Cedar	Balusters (L)
2	2 × 4" × 12'	Cedar	Top rail (M)
2	2 × 4" × 10'	Cedar	Top rail (M)

Supplies: 8"-diameter footing forms (5); J-bolts (5); 4 × 4" metal post anchors (5); 4 × 4" metal post-beam caps (3); 2 × 8" joist hangers (16); 1½ × 6" angle brackets (6); 1½ × 10" angle brackets (10); 3" galvanized deck screws;16d galvanized nails; 2½" galvanized deck screws; 2½" galvanized screws; ⅜ × 4" lag screws and washers (20); ⅜ × 5" lag screws and washers (22); ¼ × 1¼" lag screws and washers (80); flashing (12 ft.); exterior silicone caulk (3 tubes); concrete as needed.

Framing Plan

Elevation

N · M

K K · L

36"

42"

7¼" · C

B

H · I

L

J

D

62" · 35" · 23"

120"

After outlining the position of the ledger and cutting the siding with a circular saw, use a chisel to finish the corners of the cutout.

Directions: Rectangular Deck

Attach the Ledger

1 Draw a level outline on the siding to show where the ledger and the end joists will fit against the house. Install the ledger so that the surface of the decking boards will be 1" below the indoor floor level. This height difference prevents rainwater or melted snow from seeping into the house.

2 Cut out the siding along the outline with a circular saw. To prevent the blade from cutting the sheathing that lies underneath the siding, set the blade depth to the same thickness as the siding. Finish the cutout with a chisel *(photo A),* holding the beveled side in to ensure a straight cut.

Check the strings for square, by measuring from corner to corner. If the measurements are not equal, adjust the strings on the batterboards. When the diagonal measurements are equal, the outline is square.

Drop a plumb bob from the centerpoint of each footing to transfer the location to the ground. Mark the footing locations with stakes.

3 Cut galvanized flashing to the length of the cutout, using metal snips. Slide the flashing up under the siding at the top of the cutout.

4 Measure and cut the ledger (A) from pressure-treated lumber. Center the ledger end to end in the cutout, with space at each end for the end joist.

5 Brace the ledger in position under the flashing. Tack the ledger into place with galvanized deck screws.

6 Drill pairs of ¼" pilot holes at 16" intervals through the ledger and into the house header joist. Counterbore each pilot hole ½", using a 1" spade bit. Attach the ledger to the wall with ⅜ × 4" lag screws and washers, using a ratchet wrench.

7 Apply a thick bead of silicone caulk between siding and flashing. Also seal the lag screw heads and the cracks at the ends of the ledger.

Pour the Footings

1 Referring to the measurements shown in the *Framing Plan,* page 200, mark the centerlines of the two outer footings on the ledger and drive nails at these locations.

2 Set up temporary batterboards and stretch a mason's string out from the ledger at each location. Make sure the strings are perpendicular to the ledger, and measure along the strings to find the centerpoints of the posts.

3 Set up additional batterboards and stretch another string parallel to the ledger across the post centerpoints.

4 Check the mason's strings for square *(photo B),* by measuring diagonally from corner to corner and adjusting the strings so that the measurements are equal.

5 Measure along the cross string and mark the center

post location with a piece of tape.

6 Use a plumb bob to transfer the footing centerpoints to the ground, and drive a stake to mark each point *(photo C).*

7 Remove the mason's strings and dig the post footings, using a clamshell digger or power auger. Pour 2" to 3" of loose gravel into each hole for drainage. NOTE: When measuring the footing size and depth, make sure you comply with your local building code, which may require flaring the base.

8 Cut the footing forms to length, using a reciprocating saw or handsaw, and insert them into the footing holes, leaving 2" above ground level. Pack soil around the forms for support, and fill the forms with concrete, tamping with a long stick or rod to eliminate any air pockets.

9 Screed the tops flush

D

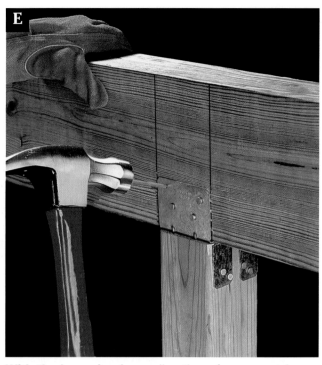

E

After the posts have been set in place and braced plumb, use a straight 2 × 4 and a level to mark the top of the beam on each post.

With the beam in place, align the reference marks with the post-beam caps, drill pilot holes, and fasten using 10d joist hanger nails.

with a straight 2 × 4. Insert a J-bolt into each footing, set so ¾" to 1" of thread is exposed. Retie the mason's strings and position the J-bolts at the exact center of the posts, using a plumb bob as a guide. Clean the bolt threads before concrete sets.

Set the Posts

1 Lay a long, straight 2 × 4 flat across the footings, parallel to the ledger. With one edge tight against the J-bolts, draw a reference line across each footing.
2 Place a metal post anchor on each footing, centering it over the J-bolt and squaring it with the reference line. Attach the post anchors by threading a nut over each bolt and tightening with a ratchet wrench.
3 Cut the posts to length, adding approximately 6" for final trimming. Place the posts in the anchors and tack into place with one nail.

4 With a level as a guide, use braces and stakes to plumb the posts. Finish nailing the posts to the anchors.
5 Determine the height of the beam by extending a straight 2 × 4 from the bottom edge of the ledger across the face of a post. Level the 2 × 4, and draw a line on the post *(photo D)*.
6 From that line, measure 7¼" down the post and mark the bottom of the beam. Using a level, transfer this line to the remaining posts.
7 Use a combination square to extend the level line completely around each post. Cut the posts to this finished height, using a reciprocating saw or hand saw.

Install the Beam

1 Cut the beam boards (C) several inches longer than necessary, to allow for final trimming.
2 Join the beam boards

together with 2½" galvanized deck screws. Mark the post locations on the top edges and sides, using a combination square as a guide.
3 Attach the post-beam caps to the tops of the posts. Position the caps on the post tops, and attach using 10d joist hanger nails.
4 Lift the beam into the post-beam caps, with the crown up. Align the post reference lines on the beam with the post-beam caps. NOTE: You should have at least two helpers when installing boards of this size and length, at this height.
5 Fasten the post-beam caps to the beam on both sides using 10d joist hanger nails *(photo E)*.

Install the Frame

1 Measure and cut the end joists to length using a circular saw.

Cut the rim joist to length, and attach to the ends of end joists with 16d galvanized nails.

2 Attach end joists to the ends of the ledger with 10d common nails.

3 Measure and cut the rim joist (E) to length with a circular saw. Fasten to end joists with 16d galvanized nails *(photo F).*

4 Square up the frame by measuring corner to corner and adjusting until measurements are equal. Toenail the end joists in place on top of the beam, and trim the beam to length.

5 Reinforce each inside corner of the frame with an angle bracket fastened with 10d joist hanger nails.

Install the Joists

1 Mark the outlines of the inner joists (F) on the ledger, beam, and rim joist (see *Framing Plan,* page 200), using a tape measure and a combination square.

2 Attach joist hangers to the ledger and rim joist with 10d joist hanger nails, using a scrap 2 × 8 as a spacer to achieve the correct spread for each hanger.

3 Measure, mark and cut lumber for inner joists, using a circular saw. Place the joists in the hangers with crown side up *(photo G),* and attach at both ends with 10d joist hanger nails. Be sure to use all the holes in the hangers.

4 Align the joists with the marks on top of the beam, and toenail in place.

Lay the Decking

1 Cut the first decking board (G) to length, position it against the house, and attach by driving a pair of 2½" galvanized deck screws into each joist.

2 Position the remaining decking boards with the ends overhanging the end joists. Leave a ⅛" gap between boards to provide for drainage, and attach the boards to each joist with a pair of deck screws.

3 Every few rows of decking, measure from the edge of the decking to the outside edge of the deck. If the measurement can be divided evenly by 5⅝, the last board will fit flush with the outside edge of the deck as intended. If the measurement shows that the last board will not fit flush, adjust the spacing as you install the remaining rows of boards.

4 If your decking overhangs the end joists, snap a chalk line to mark the outside edge of the deck and cut flush with a circular saw. If needed, finish the cut with a jig saw or handsaw where a circular saw can't reach.

Build the Stairway

1 Refer to the *Framing Plan,* page 200, for the position of the stairway footings.

2 Locate the footings by extending a 2 × 4 from the deck, dropping a plumb bob *(photo H),* and marking the centerpoints with stakes.

3 Dig post holes with a clamshell digger or an auger, and pour the stair-

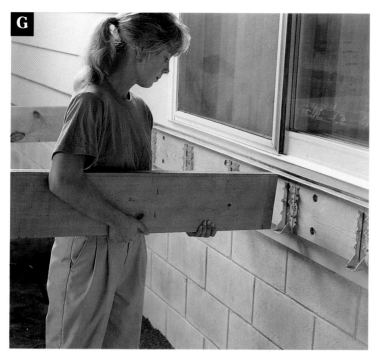

Install joists in hangers with crown side up.

Install the Railing

1 Cut posts (K) and balusters (L) to length (see *Railing Detail,* page 207) with a power miter saw or circular saw. Cut the top ends square, and the bottom ends at a 45° angle.

2 Mark and drill two ¼" pilot holes at the bottom end of each post. Holes should be spaced 4" apart and counterbored ½", with a 1" spade bit.

3 Drill two ⅛" pilot holes, 4" apart, near the bottom of each baluster. At the top of each baluster, drill a pair of ⅛" pilot holes spaced 1½" apart.

4 Using a combination square, mark the locations of the posts on the outside of the deck. NOTE: Position corner posts so there is no more than 4" clearance between them.

5 Clamp each post in place. Keep the beveled end flush with the bottom of the deck, and make sure the post is

way footings using the same method as for the deck footings.

4 Attach metal post anchors to the footings, and install posts (H), leaving them long for final trimming.

5 Cut the stair stringers (I) to length and use a framing square to mark the rise and run for each step (see *Stairway Detail,* page 206). Draw the tread outline on each run. Cut the angles at the end of the stringers with a circular saw. (For more information on building stairways, see pages 94 to 99.)

6 Position a 1½ × 10" angle bracket flush with the bottom of each tread line. Attach the brackets with 1¼" lag screws.

7 Fasten angle brackets to the upper ends of the stringers, using 1¼" lag screws; keep the brackets flush with cut ends on stringers. Position the top ends of the stringers on the side of the deck, making sure the top point of the stringer and the surface of the deck are flush.

8 Attach the stringers by driving 10d joist hanger nails through the angle brackets into the end joist, and by drilling ¼" pilot holes from inside the rim joist into the stringers and fastening with ⅜ × 4" lag screws.

9 To connect the stringers to the stair posts, drill two ¼" pilot holes **(photo I)** and counterbore the pilot holes ½" deep with a 1" spade bit. Use a ratchet wrench to fasten the stringers to the posts with 4" lag screws and washers.

10 Measure the length of the stair treads (J) and cut two 2 × 6 boards for each tread. For each tread, position the front board on the angle bracket so the front edge is flush with the tread outline on the stringers. Attach the tread to the brackets with ¼ × 1¼" lag screws.

11 Place the rear 2 × 6 on each tread bracket, keeping a ⅛" space between the boards. Attach with 1¼" lag screws.

12 Attach the treads for the lowest step by driving deck screws through the stringers.

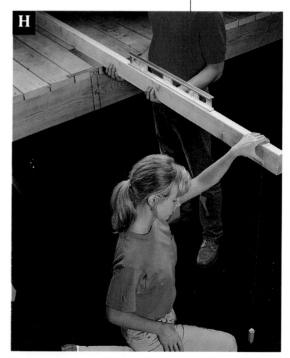

To locate the stairway footings, refer to the measurements in the *Framing Plan,* and extend a straight 2 × 4 perpendicularly from the deck. Use a plumb bob to transfer centerpoints to the ground.

Stairway Detail

I

After attaching the stringers to the deck, fasten them to the posts. Drill and counterbore two pilot holes through the stringers into the posts, and attach with lag screws.

plumb. Use an awl to mark pilot hole locations on the side of the deck. Remove posts and drill ¼" pilot holes at marks. Attach the railing posts to the side of the deck with ⅜ × 5" lag screws and washers.

6 Cut top rails (M) to length, with 45° miters on the ends that meet at the corners. Attach to posts with 2½" deck screws, keeping the top edge of the rail flush with the top of the posts. Join rails by cutting 45° bevels at ends.

7 Temporarily attach stairway top rails **(photo J)** with 3" galvanized screws. Mark the outline of the deck railing post and top rail on the back side of the stairway

Railing Detail

Position the stairway top rail in place against the posts. Attach temporarily and mark for cutting to size.

top rail. Mark the position of the top rail on the stairway post. Use a level to mark a plumb cutoff line at the lower end of the rail. Remove the rail.

8 Cut the stairway post to finished height along the diagonal mark, and cut the stairway rail along outlines. Reposition the stairway rail and attach with deck screws.

9 Attach the balusters between the railing posts at equal intervals of 4" or less. Use deck screws, and keep the top ends of balusters flush with the top rail. On the stairway, position the balusters against the stringer and top rail, and check for plumb. Draw a diagonal cut line at top of baluster and trim to final height with a power miter saw.

10 Confirm measurements, and cut rail cap sections (N) to length. Position sections so that the inside edge overhangs the inside edge of the rail by ¼". Attach cap to rail with deck screws. At corners, miter the ends 45° and attach caps to posts *(photo K)*.

11 Cut the cap for stairway rail to length. Mark angle of deck railing post on side of cap and bevel-cut the ends of the cap. Attach cap to top rail and post with deck screws. NOTE: Local building codes may require a grippable handrail for any stairway over four treads. Check with your building inspector.

Position the rail cap over the posts and balusters. Make sure mitered corners are tight, and attach with deck screws.

High Rectangular Deck

Simplicity, security, and convenience are the hallmarks of this elevated deck.

This simple rectangular deck provides a secure, convenient outdoor living space. The absence of a stairway prevents children from wandering away or unexpected visitors from wandering in. It also makes the deck easier to build.

Imagine how handy it will be to have this additional living area only a step away from your dining room or living room, with no more need to walk downstairs for outdoor entertaining, dining or relaxing.

And if you'd like to add a stairway, just refer to the helpful instructions in the final chapter of this book.

Cutaway View

Lumber List			
Qty.	Size	Material	Part
2	2 × 12" × 20'	Trtd. lumber	Beam boards (C)
2	2 × 10" × 18'	Trtd. lumber	Ledger (A), Rim joist (F)
15	2 × 10" × 14'	Trtd. lumber	Joists (G), End joists (E)
3	6 × 6" × 10'	Trtd. lumber	Deck posts (B)
2	4 × 4" × 8'	Trtd. lumber	Braces (D)

Lumber List			
Qty.	Size	Material	Part
32	2 × 6" × 18'	Cedar	Decking (H), Top rail (J)
2	2 × 6" × 16'	Cedar	Top rail (J)
50	2 × 2" × 8'	Cedar	Balusters (I)

Supplies: 12"-diameter footing forms (3); J-bolts (3); 6 × 6" metal post anchors (3); 2 × 10" joist hangers (26); galvanized deck screws (3", 2½" and 1¼"); joist hanger nails; ⅜ × 4" lag screws and washers (28); ¼ × 5" lag screws and washers (16); ⁵⁄₁₆ × 7" carriage bolts, washers, and nuts (6); 16d galvanized nails; metal flashing (18 ft.); silicone caulk (3 tubes); concrete as required.

Framing Plan

213" [17'-9"]

1½"   1½"

10½" 16" 16" 16" 16" 16" 16" 16" 16" 16" 16" 16" 16" 10½"

A

E

142" [11'-10"]

168" [14'-0"]

18"   90"   90"   18"

B   C   G   26"

F

216" [18'-0"]

Railing Detail

1½"

J

36"

H   I

43¾"

1½"

9¼"

E

1½"

Face Board Detail

E

⅛"

H   5½"

⅛"

3⅞"

2¾"

F

2¾"   4"   4"

1½"   1½"

Elevation

216" [18'-0"]

J

I

36"

1½"

9¼"

11¼"

C

F

30"

D

B

110" [9'-2"]

18"

90"

90"

18"

℄

℄

℄

Directions: High Rectangular Deck

Attach the Ledger

1 Draw a level outline on the siding to show where the ledger and the end joists will fit against the house. Install the ledger so that the surface of the decking boards will be 1" below the indoor floor level *(photo A)*. This height difference prevents rainwater or melted snow from seeping into the house.

2 Cut out the siding along the outline with a circular saw. To avoid cutting the sheathing that lies underneath the siding, set the blade depth to the same thickness as the siding. Finish the cutout with a chisel, holding the beveled side in to ensure a straight cut.

3 Cut galvanized flashing to

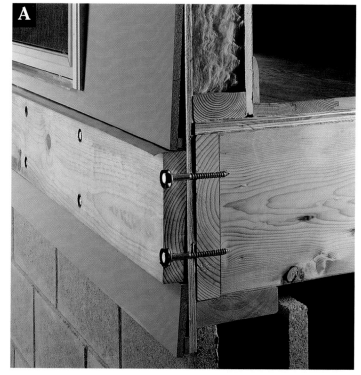

A

The ledger is anchored through the sheathing to the rim joist of the house with ⅜ × 4" lag screws. Metal flashing protects against water seepage.

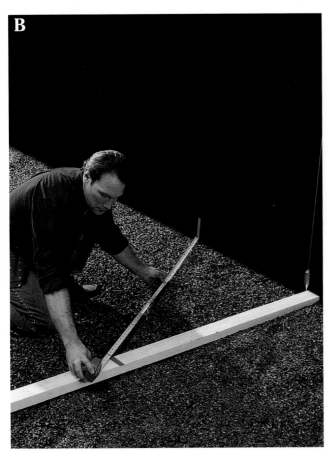

B

To make measurements easier, drop a plumb bob from the ledger to ground level, and use the 3-4-5 triangle method to check for square.

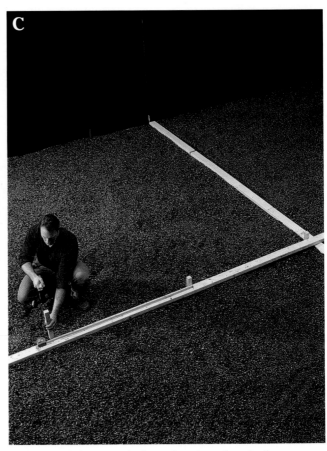

C

Use a template made from 2 × 4s to locate the post footings on the ground, then mark the footings with stakes.

the length of the cutout, using metal snips. Slide the flashing up under the siding at the top of the cutout.

4 Measure and cut the ledger (A) from pressure-treated lumber. Center the ledger end to end in the cutout, with space at each end for the end joist.

5 Brace the ledger into position under the flashing. Tack the ledger into place with galvanized nails.

6 Drill pairs of ¼" pilot holes at 16" intervals through the ledger and into the house header joist. Counterbore each pilot hole ½", using a 1" spade bit. Attach the ledger with 4" lag screws and washers, using a ratchet wrench.

7 Apply silicone caulk

between the siding and flashing. Also seal the lag screw heads and the cracks at the ends of the ledger.

Pour the Footings

1 To establish a reference point for locating the footings, drop a plumb bob from the ends of the ledger down to the ground.

2 Position a straight 14 ft.-long 2 × 4 perpendicular to the house at the point where the plumb bob meets the ground. NOTE: If you are building on a steep slope or uneven ground, the mason's string method of locating footing positions will work better (see *Locating Post Footings,* pages 54 to 59).

3 Check for square, using the 3-4-5 triangle method.

From the 2 × 4, measure 3 ft. along the wall and make a mark. Next, measure 4 ft. out from the house and make a mark on the 2 × 4. The diagonal line between the marks will measure 5 ft. *(photo B)* when the board is accurately square to the house. Adjust the board as needed, using stakes to hold it in place.

4 Extend another reference board from the house at the other end of the ledger, following the same procedure.

5 Measure out along both boards, and mark the centerline of the footings (see *Framing Plan,* page 210).

6 Lay a straight 2 × 4 between the centerline marks, and drive stakes to mark the footing locations *(photo C).*

D

Insert the footing form into the hole, leaving 2" above the ground. Level the top, and pack soil around the form to hold it in place.

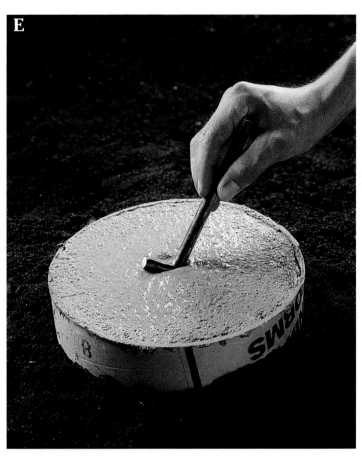

E

Insert a J-bolt into wet concrete at the center of the footing.

7 Remove the boards and dig the post footings, using a clamshell digger or power auger. Pour 2" to 3" of loose gravel into each hole for drainage. NOTE: When measuring the footing size and depth, make sure you comply with local building codes, which may require flaring the base to 18".

8 Cut the footing forms to length, using a reciprocating saw or handsaw, and insert them into the footing holes, leaving 2" above ground level *(photo D).* Pack soil around the forms for support, and fill the forms with concrete, tamping with a long stick or rod to eliminate any air gaps.

9 Screed the tops flush with a straight 2 × 4. Insert a J-bolt into the center of each footing *(photo E)* and set with ¾" to 1" of thread exposed. Clean the bolt threads before the concrete sets.

Set the Posts

1 Lay a long, straight 2 × 4 flat across the footings, parallel to the house. With one edge tight against the J-bolts, draw a reference line across the top of each footing to help orient the post anchors.

2 Place a metal post anchor on each footing, centering it over the J-bolt and squaring it with the reference line. Attach the post anchors by threading a nut over each bolt and tightening with a ratchet wrench.

3 The tops of the posts (B) will eventually be level with the bottom edge of the ledger, but initially cut the posts several inches longer to allow for final trimming. Position the posts in the anchors and tack into place with one nail each.

4 With a level as a guide, use braces and stakes to ensure that the posts are plumb *(photo F).*

5 Determine the height of the beam by using a chalk line and a line level. Extend the chalk line out from the bottom edge of the ledger, make sure that the line is level, and snap a mark across the face of a post. Use the line and level to transfer the mark to the remaining posts.

Plumb each post with a level, then use braces and stakes to hold in place until the beam and joists are installed.

Fasten the beam to the posts with carriage bolts fitted with a washer and nut. Tighten with a ratchet wrench.

Notch the Posts

1 Remove the posts from the post anchors and cut to the finished height.
2 Measure and mark a 3" × 11¼" notch at the top of each post, on the outside face. Use a framing square to trace lines on all sides. Rough-cut the notches with a circular saw, then finish with a reciprocating saw or handsaw.
3 Reattach the posts to the post anchors, with the notch-side facing away from the deck.

Install the Beam

1 Cut the beam boards (C) to length, adding several inches to each end for final trimming after the deck frame is squared up.
2 Join the beam boards together with 2½" galvanized deck screws. Mark the post locations on the top edges and sides, using a combination square as a guide.

3 Lift the beam, one end at a time, into the notches with the crown up. Align and clamp the beam to the posts. NOTE: Installing boards of this size and length, at this height, requires care. You should have at least two helpers.
4 Counterbore two ½"-deep holes using a 1" spade bit, then drill ⁵⁄₁₆" pilot holes through the beam and post.
5 Thread a carriage bolt into each pilot hole. Add a washer and nut to the counterbore-side of each bolt and tighten with a ratchet wrench *(photo G).* Seal both ends of the bolts with silicone caulk.
6 Cut the tops of the posts flush with the top edge of the beam, using a reciprocating saw or handsaw.

Install the Frame

1 Measure and cut the end joists (E) to length, using a circular saw.

2 Attach the end joists to the ends of the ledger with 16d galvanized nails.
3 Measure and cut the rim joist (F) to length with a circular saw. Fasten to the ends of end joists with 16d nails.
4 Square up the frame by measuring corner to corner and adjusting until the measurements are equal. When the frame is square, toenail the end joists in place on top of the beam.
5 Trim the ends of the beam flush with the faces of the end joists, using a reciprocating saw or a handsaw.

Install the Braces

1 Cut the braces (D) to length (see *Elevation*, page 211) with a circular saw or power miter saw. Miter both ends at 45°.
2 Install the braces by positioning them against the beam boards and against

the posts. Make sure the outside faces of the braces are flush with the outside faces of the beam and the posts. Temporarily fasten with deck screws.

3 Secure the braces to the posts with 5" lag screws. Drill two ¼" pilot holes through the upper end of each brace into the beam. Counterbore to a ½"-depth using a 1" spade bit, and drive lag screws with a ratchet wrench. Repeat for the lower end of the braces into the posts.

Install the Joists

1 Measure and mark the joist locations (see *Framing Plan*, page 210) on the ledger, rim joist, and beam. Draw the outline of each joist on the ledger and rim joist, using a combination square.

2 Install a joist hanger at each joist location. Attach one flange of the hanger to one side of the outline, using joist nails. Use a spacer cut from scrap 2 × 8 lumber to achieve the correct spread for each hanger, then fasten the remaining

side flange with joist nails. Remove the spacer and repeat the same procedure for the remaining joist hangers.

3 Measure, mark, and cut lumber for joists (G), using a circular saw. Place joists in hangers with crown side up and attach with joist hanger nails *(photo H).* Align joists with the outlines on the top of the beam, and toenail in place.

Lay the Decking

1 Measure, mark, and cut the decking boards (H) to

Fasten the joists in the joist hangers with 10d joist hanger nails. Drive nails into both sides of each joist.

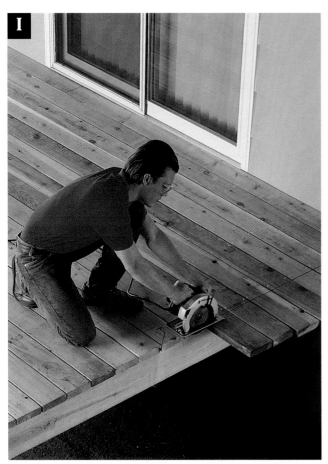

Snap a chalk line flush with the outside edge of the deck, and cut off overhanging deck boards with a circular saw.

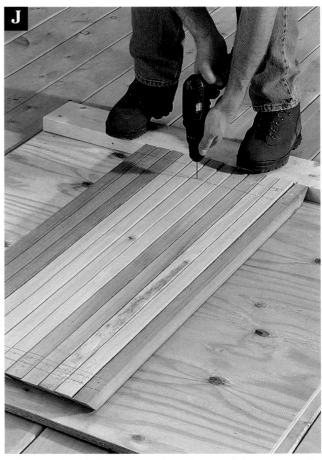

After cutting balusters to length, gang them up and drill ⅛" pilot holes through the top and bottom.

length as needed.

2 Position the first row of decking flush against the house, and attach by driving a pair of galvanized deck screws into each joist.

3 Position the remaining decking boards, leaving a ⅛" gap between boards to provide for drainage, and attach to each joist with deck screws.

4 Every few rows of decking, measure from the edge of the decking to the outside edge of the deck. If the measurement can be divided evenly by 5⅝", the last board will fit flush with the outside edge of the deck as intended. If the measurement shows that the last

board will not fit flush, adjust the spacing as you install the remaining rows of boards.

5 If your decking overhangs the end joists, snap a chalk line to mark the outside edge of the deck and cut flush with a circular saw set to a 1½" depth **(photo I).** If needed, finish the cut with a jig saw or handsaw where a circular saw can't reach.

Build the Railing

1 Measure, mark, and cut the balusters (I) to length, with 45° miters at both ends.
2 Gang the balusters together and drill two ⅛" pilot holes at both ends **(photo J).**

3 Clamp a 1½" guide strip flush with the bottom edge of the deck platform to establish the baluster height (see *Railing Detail*, page 210).
4 To ensure that the balusters are installed at equal intervals, create a spacing jig, less than 4" wide, from two pieces of scrap material.
5 Attach the corner balusters first (see *Face Board Detail*, page 210), using a level to ensure that they are plumb. Then use the spacing jig for positioning, and attach the remaining balusters to the deck platform with 3" deck screws **(photo K).**
6 Measure, mark, and cut the top rail sections (J) to

Rest the balusters on a 1 × 2 guide strip, and use a spacing jig to position them at equal intervals. Attach them with 3" deck screws.

length. Round over three edges (see *Railing Detail*, page 210) using a router with a ½" round-over bit. Cut 45° miters on the ends that meet at the corners.

7 Hold or clamp the top rail in position, and attach with 2½" deck screws driven through the balusters.

8 If you need to make straight joints in the top rail, cut the ends of the adjoining boards at 45°. Drill angled ⅛" pilot holes and join with deck screws **(photo L).**

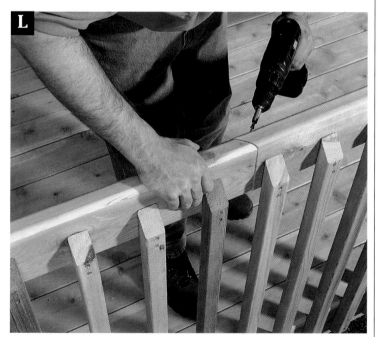

To make a joint in the top rail, cut the ends at 45° and drill a pair of pilot holes. Then fasten the ends together with deck screws.

Inside Corner Deck

A distinctive pattern gives this deck visual appeal.

With the help of a diamond decking pattern, this inside corner deck provides a focal point for recreational activities and social gatherings. At the same time, the corner location can offer intimacy, privacy, shade, and a shield from the wind.

The design calls for double joists and blocking for extra strength and stability where decking boards butt together. Joists are spaced 12" on center to support diagonal decking.

It takes a little more time to cut the decking boards and match the miter cuts, but the results are spectacular and well worth the effort.

Cutaway View

Lumber List			
Qty.	Size	Material	Part
6	2 × 8" × 14'	Trtd. lumber	Short ledger (A), Long ledger (B), Beam boards (D)
14	2 × 8" × 16'	Trtd. lumber	Joists (G), Single blocking (I)
3	2 × 8" × 8'	Trtd. lumber	Double blocking (H)
3	4 × 4" × 8'	Trtd. lumber	Deck posts (C)
1	2 × 8" × 16'	Cedar	End joist (E)
1	2 × 8" × 14'	Cedar	Rim joist (F)

Lumber List			
Qty.	Size	Material	Part
42	2 × 6" × 8'	Cedar	Decking (J), Railing caps (Q)
16	2 × 6" × 14'	Cedar	Decking (J)
1	4 × 4" × 10'	Cedar	Stair posts (K)
6	2 × 6" × 8'	Cedar	Treads (M)
4	4 × 4" × 8'	Cedar	Railing posts (N)
2	2 × 10" × 8'	Cedar	Stringers (L)
33	2 × 2" × 8'	Cedar	Balusters (O)
6	2 × 4" × 8'	Cedar	Top rails (P)

Supplies: 8"-diameter footing forms (8); J-bolts (8); 4 × 4" metal post anchors (8); 2 × 8" single joist hangers (50); 2 × 8" double joist hangers (30); 1½ × 10" angle brackets (12); 3" galvanized deck screws; 2½" galvanized deck screws; 16d galvanized nails; joist hanger nails; ⅜ × 4" lag screws and washers (78); ¼ × 1¼" lag screws (96); ½ × 7" carriage bolts, washers, and nuts (12); exterior silicone caulk (6 tubes); concrete as needed.

Framing Plan

1½"
170"
[14'-2"]
1½"

1½" Blocking
3" Double blocking

15½"
75"
75"
1½"

F
18"
G
B
12" 3¾"

58¼"
ℂ

12"

60"
74"
D
D
A
12"

53¼"
I
60"
H
12"

ℂ

D
D
12"

K
L
39½"
12"

36"
ℂ
1½"

12"

156"
[13'-0"]

60"
60"
12"

58¼"
12"

ℂ

12"

18"
12" 3¾"

E
ℂ

77¼"
1½"

17"
78"
78"

ℂ 156"
[13'-0"]

173"
[14'-5"]

Elevation

Q
P
N
O

36"

1½"

7¼"

P
F
D
D
E
J
49"

P
L
C
C
7¼"

K

17¾"
77¼"
78"

173" [14'-5"]

220

Railing Detail

Stairway Detail

Directions: Inside Corner Deck

Attach the Ledgers

The inside angle of the house should form a right angle. If there is a slight deviation, use shims behind the ledger to create a 90° angle in the corner.

1 To show where the ledgers will be attached to the house, draw outlines on the wall, using a level as a guide. To locate the top of the ledger outline, measure down from the indoor floor surface 1" plus the thickness of the decking boards. This height difference prevents rain and melting snow from seeping into the house.

2 Measure and cut the ledgers to length. They will be shorter than the outline on the wall to allow for the width of the rim joist and end joist.

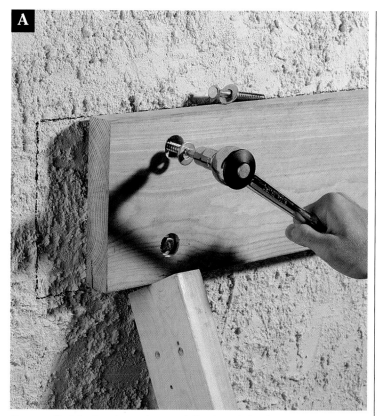

Once pilot holes have been drilled and the ledger has been positioned and braced against the wall, use a ratchet wrench to attach the ledger with lag screws and washers.

B

To locate the centerpoints of the footings on the ground, drop a plumb bob from the intersections of the mason's strings. Then, drive a stake into the ground to mark each centerpoint.

C

Post anchors keep the post above the footing to discourage rot. The post rests on a metal pedestal that fits over a J-bolt mounted in the footing.

3 Drill pairs of ¼" pilot holes through the ledgers at 16" intervals. Counterbore the pilot holes ½" with a 1" spade bit.
4 Brace the short ledger (A) in place, and insert a nail or an awl through the pilot holes to mark the hole locations on the wall.
5 Repeat the process to mark the hole locations for the long ledger (B).
6 Remove the ledgers and drill pilot holes into the stucco with a ⅜" masonry bit. Then, use a ¼" bit to extend each pilot hole through the sheathing and into the header joist.
7 Position and brace the ledgers against the walls. Use a ratchet wrench to attach the ledgers to the walls with ⅜ × 4" lag screws and washers *(photo A).* Seal the screw heads and all cracks between the wall and ledger with silicone caulk.

Pour the Deck Footings

To locate the footings, stretch mason's strings between the ledgers and 2 × 4 supports, known as *batterboards.*

1 Referring to the measurements shown in the *Framing Plan,* page 220, mark the centerlines of the footings on the ledgers, and drive a nail into the ledger at each location.
2 Set up temporary batterboards and stretch a mason's string out from the ledger at each location. Make sure the strings are perpendicular to the ledger.
3 Check the mason's strings for square, using the 3-4-5 triangle method. From the point where each string meets the ledger, measure 3' along the ledger and make a mark. Next, measure 4' out along the string and mark with tape. The distance between the points on the ledger and the string should be 5'. If it's not,

adjust the string position on the batterboard accordingly.
4 Drop a plumb bob to transfer the footing centerpoints to the ground, and drive a stake to mark each point *(photo B).* Remove the strings.
5 Dig the post footings, using a clamshell digger or power auger. Pour 2" to 3" of loose gravel into each hole for drainage. NOTE: Make sure the footing size and depth comply with your local building code, which may require flaring the base to 12".
6 Cut the footing forms to length, using a reciprocating saw or handsaw, and insert them into the footing holes so that they extend 2" above grade. Pack soil around the forms for support, and fill the forms with concrete, tamping with a long stick or rod to eliminate any air pockets.
7 Screed the tops of the footings flush, using a 2 × 4. Insert a J-bolt into the wet concrete of each footing,

and set it, with ¾" to 1" of thread exposed. Retie the mason's strings and position each J-bolt at the exact center of the post location, using the plumb bob as a guide. Clean the bolt threads before the concrete sets.

Set the Posts

1 Lay a long, straight 2 × 4 flat across each row of footings, parallel to the short ledger. With one edge tight against the J-bolts, draw a reference line across the top of each footing.

2 Center a metal post anchor over the J-bolt on each footing, and square it with the reference line. Attach the post anchors by threading a nut over each bolt and tightening with a ratchet wrench.

3 Cut the posts, leaving an

extra 6" for final trimming. Place each post in an anchor **(photo C)** and tack it in place with one nail.

4 With a level as a guide, use braces and stakes to ensure that each post is plumb. Finish nailing the posts to the anchors.

5 Determine the height of the inside beam by extending a straight 2 × 4 from the bottom edge of the long ledger across the row of posts. Level the 2 × 4, and draw a line on the posts. Use the same method to determine the height of the outer beam.

Install the Beams

1 Cut the beam boards (D), leaving an extra few inches for final trimming.

2 Position one beam board, crown up, against the row of

posts. Tack the board in place with deck screws **(photo D).**

3 Attach the remaining beam boards to the posts in the same way.

4 Drill two ½" holes through the boards and posts at each joint, and counterbore the pilot holes ½" with a 1" spade bit. Secure the beam boards to the posts with carriage bolts, using a ratchet wrench.

5 Cut the tops of the posts flush with the tops of the beams, using a reciprocating saw or handsaw.

Install the Joists

A double joist at the center of the deck provides extra support for the ends of the decking boards.

1 Measure, mark, and cut the end joist (E) and the rim joist (F), using a circular saw.

2 Attach the end joist to the short ledger and the rim joist to the long ledger, using 16d galvanized nails.

3 Nail the rim joist to the end joist **(photo E).**

4 Toenail the end joist to the tops of the beams, and cut the ends of the beams flush with the end joist.

5 Measure, mark, and install the double center joist at the precise center of the deck with double joist hangers.

6 Measure both ways from the double joist, and mark the centerpoints of the remaining joists at 12" intervals. Using a combination square, mark the outlines of the joists on the ledger, beams, and rim joist.

7 Nail the joist hangers to the short ledger and rim joist, using a scrap 2 × 8 as a spacer to achieve the correct spread for each hanger.

8 Cut the joists (G) to

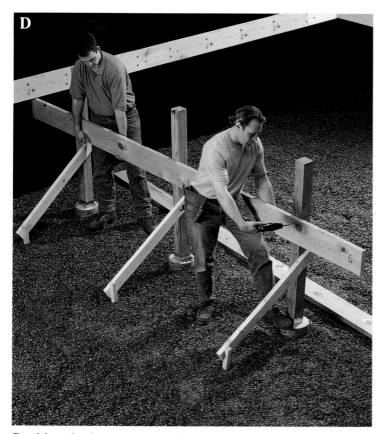

Position the beam against the posts, and attach it temporarily with deck screws.

Drive 16d galvanized nails through the rim joist and into the end joist.

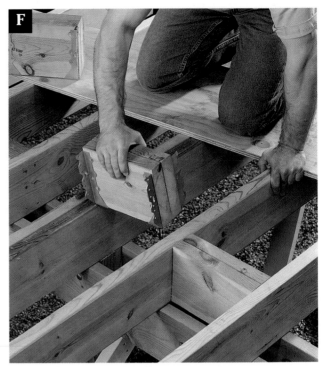

Working from a plywood platform, install double blocking to support the ends of the deck boards. Attach the blocking by alternating end nailing with using joist hangers.

length. Insert the joists into the hangers with the crown up, and attach them with joist hanger nails. Align the joists with the marks on the beams and toenail them in place.

Install the Blocking

The ends of the decking boards in the diamond pattern are supported by a row of double blocking at the center of the pattern and a row of single blocking at the edge of the pattern.

1 To locate the rows of blocking, measure from the inside corner of the house along the long ledger (see *Framing Plan*, page 220). Drive one screw or nail at 78", and another at 156". Make corresponding marks across from the ledger on the end joist.
2 Snap chalk lines across the joists, between the ledger and the end joist.

The line at 78" is the center-line of the double blocking. The line at 156" is the outer edge of the single blocking. Don't be concerned if the blocking is not directly over the beams.
3 Cut double blocking pieces from 2 × 8s nailed together with 16d galvanized nails.
4 Install the blocking by alternating end nailing using galvanized joist hangers *(photo F)*.

Lay the Decking

Except for the three rows of straight decking at the top of the stairway, the decking is laid in a dia-mond pattern.

1 Begin at the center of the diamond pattern, where the double joist and the double blocking intersect. Cut four identical triangles, as large as possible, from 2 × 6" cedar stock.
2 Drill ⅛" pilot holes in the ends, position the pieces as

shown, and attach with 3" deck screws.
3 To install the remaining courses, measure, cut, drill, and attach the first three boards in each course. Then, measure the actual length of the last board *(photo G)* to achieve the best fit. For best results, install the decking course by course. Maintain a ⅛" gap between courses.
4 Once the diamond deck-ing pattern is complete, cut and install the three remain-ing deck boards.

Build the Stairs

1 For the position of the stairway footings, refer to the *Framing Plan* on page 220. Locate the footings by extending a 2 × 4 from the deck, perpendicular to the rim joist, dropping a plumb bob, and marking the centerpoints on the ground with stakes.

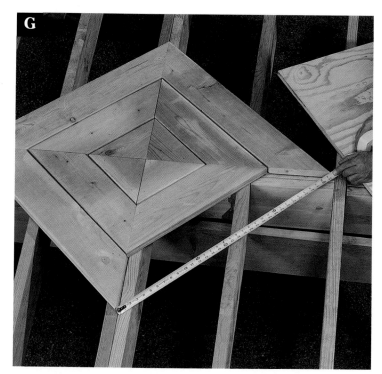

To achieve the best fit, measure the actual length of the last deck board in each course before cutting.

2 Dig postholes with a clamshell digger or an auger, and pour footings using the same method as for the deck footings. Insert J-bolts, leaving ¾" to 1" of thread exposed. Allow the concrete to set. Attach metal post anchors.

3 Cut the stairway posts (K) to length, adding approximately 6" for final trimming. Place the posts in the anchors.

4 Use a level to ensure that the posts are plumb, and attach the posts to the anchors with 16d galvanized nails.

5 Cut the stringers (L) to length and use a framing square to mark the rise and run for each step (see *Stairway Detail*, page 221). Draw the tread outline on each run. Cut the angles at the ends of the stringers with a circular saw. (For a more detailed description of stairway construction, see pages 94 to 99.)

6 Position an angle bracket flush with the bottom of each tread outline. Drill ⅛" pilot holes in the stringers, and attach the angle brackets with 1¼" lag screws.

7 The treads (M) fit between the stringers, and the stringers fit between the stairway posts. Measure and cut the treads (M) to length, 3" shorter than the distance between the stairway posts.

8 Assemble the stairway upside down on sawhorses. Mark and drill ⅛" pilot holes at the ends of the treads. Position each front tread with its front edge flush to the tread outline, and attach to the angle brackets with ¼ × 1¼" lag screws.

9 Attach the rear treads in similar fashion **(photo H),** leaving a ⅛" gap between treads.

10 Position the stairway in place against the edge of the deck, making sure the top of the stringer is flush with the surface of the deck. From underneath the deck, drill ¼" pilot holes through the rim joist into the stringers. Attach the stringers to the rim joist with 4" lag screws, using a ratchet wrench **(photo I).**

11 To fasten the stairway to the stair posts, drill two ¼" pilot holes through each stringer into a post. Counterbore the pilot holes ½" deep with a 1" spade bit, and use a ratchet wrench to drive 4" lag screws with washers. Seal the screw heads with silicone caulk.

Install the Deck Railing

1 Cut the railing posts (N) and balusters (O) to length (see *Railing Detail*, page 221) with a power miter saw or circular saw. Cut the tops square and the bottoms at 45° angles.

2 Drill two ¼" pilot holes at the bottom end of each railing post, positioned so the lag screws will attach to the rim joist. Counterbore the holes ½" deep with a 1" spade bit.

3 Drill two ⅛" pilot holes near the bottom of each baluster, spaced 4" apart. At the top of each baluster, drill a pair of ⅛" pilot holes spaced 1½" apart.

Tip

When laying decking, install boards that have a flat grain with the bark side down. Flat-grain boards tend to cup to the bark side, and if installed bark-side-up, often trap water on the deck.

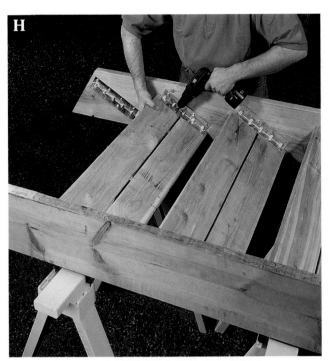

Drill pilot holes and then attach the treads to the stringers, using 1¼" lag screws and angle brackets.

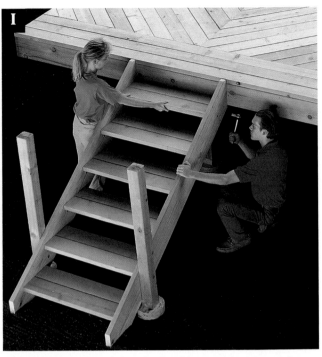

Fasten the stair to the deck with a ratchet wrench, using 4" lag screws.

4 With the help of a combination square, draw the outlines of the railing posts around the perimeter of the deck. The posts at the corner must be spaced so there is less than 4" between them.

5 Hold each railing post in its position, with the end 1½" above the bottom edge of the deck platform (see *Railing Detail*, page 221). Make sure the post is plumb, and insert an awl through the counterbored holes to mark pilot hole locations on the deck.

6 Set the post aside and drill ¼" pilot holes at the marks. Attach the railing posts to the deck with ⅜ × 4" lag screws and washers. Seal the screw heads with silicone caulk.

7 Cut the top rails (P) to length with the ends mitered at 45° where they meet in the corner. Attach them to the railing posts with 3" deck screws, keeping the edges

of the rails flush with the tops of the posts.

8 To position the balusters, measure the total distance between two railing posts, and mark the centerpoint on the top rail. The two railing sections on the long side of this deck will have a baluster at the centerpoint; the two railing sections on the stairway side will have a space at the centerpoint. NOTE: If the dimensions of your deck vary from the plan, calculate whether you will have a baluster or a space at the center of each section.

9 Cut a spacer slightly less than 4" wide. Start at the center of each railing section, and position either a baluster or a space over the line. Measure out from the center both ways, marking the outlines of the balusters on the top rail. The end spaces may be narrow, but they will be symmetrical.

10 To install the balusters, begin next to a railing post and make sure the first baluster is plumb. Install the remaining balusters, holding each one tight against the spacer and flush with the top rail. Attach the balusters with 2½" deck screws.

11 Cut the deck railing cap (Q) to length, with the ends mitered at 45° where they meet in the corner. Position the railing cap sections so the inside edge overhangs the inside edge of the top rail by ¼" *(photo J).* Attach the cap with 3" deck screws.

Install the Stairway Railing

1 Determine the exact size and shape of the stairway top rail. Tack a cedar 2 × 4 across the faces of the stairway post and deck post with 10d galvanized nails. Make sure the angle of the 2 × 4 is parallel with the angle of the stringer below.

After the top rail and balusters have been installed, install the railing cap with its inside edge overhanging the inside face of the top rail by ¼".

With the stairway top rail cut to size and installed, attach the railing cap with deck screws.

2 On the back side of the 2 × 4, mark the outline of the deck railing post and the end of the deck top rail. On the stairway post, mark a diagonal cutoff line at the top edge of the 2 × 4. At the lower end of the 2 × 4, use a level to mark a plumb cutoff line directly above the end of the stringer.

3 Remove the 2 × 4 and make the cuts.

4 Drill ⅛" pilot holes through the stairway top rail. Place in position and attach with 2½" deck screws.

5 To trim the top ends of the stairway balusters, hold a baluster against the stairway post and draw a diagonal cut line along the top edge of the rail. Trim the baluster. Using this baluster as a template, mark and cut the remaining stairway balusters.

6 Install the stairway balusters with 2½" deck screws, using the same procedure as for the deck balusters.

7 Measure the railing caps for the stairway. Cut the caps to size, with the upper ends beveled to fit against the deck posts, and the lower ends beveled to align with the end of the top rail. Install the caps by drilling ⅛" pilot holes and attaching them with 2½" deck screws **(photo K)**.

Island Deck

The perfect place to visit when you need to relax.

An island deck can transform any area of your yard into a virtual oasis. Since it's not attached to your house, you can position your island deck wherever you like—to capitalize on a spectacular view or to catch the cool afternoon breeze in a shady glen.

Accessible and inviting with its three-sided landing, this deck welcomes visitors of all ages. And it can readily serve as a cornerstone for a total landscaping plan; one that will make your entire yard a more comfortable and attractive space for enjoying the great outdoors.

Cutaway View

Lumber List			
Qty.	**Size**	**Material**	**Part**
4	2 × 4" × 16'	Pine	Site chooser sides (A)
2	2 × 4" × 12'	Pine	Site chooser diagonals (B)
2	4 × 4" × 12'	Trtd. lumber	Deck posts (C), Landing posts (H)
10	2 × 8" × 14'	Trtd. lumber	Beam boards (D)
			Long joists (E)
2	2 × 8" × 12'	Trtd. lumber	Mitered joists (F)
6	2 × 8" × 10'	Trtd. lumber	Mitered joists (F), Inner rim joists (I), Outer rim joists (J), Landing joists (K)
9	2 × 8" × 6'	Trtd. lumber	Deck rim joists (G), Landing joists (K)
25	2 × 6" × 14'	Cedar	Deck decking (L), Railing cap (S)

Lumber List			
Qty.	**Size**	**Material**	**Part**
23	2 × 6" × 14'	Cedar	Deck decking (L), Railing cap (S)
7	2 × 6" × 12'	Cedar	Deck decking (L)
13	2 × 6" × 10'	Cedar	Deck decking (L), Landing decking (N), Treads (U)
4	2 × 6" × 8'	Cedar	Deck decking (L)
11	2 × 10" × 6'	Cedar	Deck face boards (M), Landing face boards (O)
8	2 × 4" × 8'	Cedar	Railing posts (P)
42	2 × 2" × 8'	Cedar	Balusters (Q)
7	2 × 4" × 6'	Cedar	Top rail (R)
3	2 × 10" × 6'	Cedar	Stringers (T)

Supplies: 8"-diameter footing forms (12); J-bolts (12); 4 × 4" metal post anchors (12); 90° 2 × 8" joist hangers (10); 45° 2 × 8" joist hangers (8); joist ties (16); post-beam caps (4); joist hanger nails; 1½" × 10" angle brackets (12); 3" galvanized deck screws; ¼ × 1¼" galvanized lag screws and washers (96); 16d galvanized box nails; ½ × 7" carriage bolts, washers, and nuts (16); ⅜ × 5" lag screws and washers (32); concrete as required.

Framing Plan

229½"
[19'-1½"]

169½"
[14'-1½"]

163½"
[13'-7½"]
Upper beams

60"

3"

3"

12"

12"

36"

1½"

M

G

See Detail A

See Detail B

F

D

1¾"

13"

See Detail A

See Detail B

62" 36"

U

J

K

53" Joist

59" Deck boards

55½"

17¾"

69" Rim joist

70¼" face board

169½"
[14'-1½"]

13"

T

C 6¾"

17½"

166½" lower beam

O

C 6¾"

17"

5"

51½"

17"

5¼"

17⅜"

1½"

Elevation

S

Q

36"

O

T

C

9¼"

28"

36"

57¾"

51½"

70¼"

115½"

230

Detail A

M

2⅛"

½"

P

G ⅝"

O

6¾"

J H C̶L̶

I G

M

½"

5¼"

C̶L̶

Detail B

G

G

D

G

1¾"

3½"

⅝"

E

67¾"
Rim
joist,
inner
face

69"
Rim
joist,
outer
face

51¼"

70¼"
Face
board

D

M

3½"

1¾"

⅝"

G

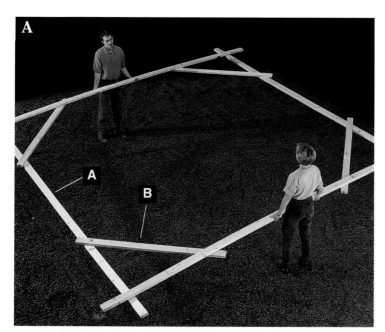

A

A

B

Use the site chooser to experiment with possible deck locations and to find the site you like best.

Directions: Island Deck

Position the Deck

1 Measure, mark, and cut to length the site chooser frame (A) and diagonal braces (B), (see *Site Chooser Detail*, page 232).

2 Fasten the frame together with 3" deck screws, and check for squareness by measuring corner to corner. Adjust the frame so measurements are identical, and attach the diagonal braces with deck screws.

3 With a helper, move the site chooser to select the exact deck location *(photo A).*

4 When you've established

B

C

Locate the deck footings by stretching mason's strings across the site chooser, marking footing locations with tape, and dropping a plumb bob from each mark.

Insert a J-bolt, then drop a plumb bob to check for exact center of the footings.

the deck position, set the site chooser on sawhorses and tack or clamp in place to conveniently find the footing locations.

Locate the Footings

1 Mark the footing centerlines on the frame and stretch mason's string across the site from mark to mark. Measure along the strings, marking the footing locations with tape.

2 Drop a plumb bob from each marked location, and drive stakes into the ground to mark the centers of the deck footings *(photo B)*.

Pour the Footings

1 Remove the mason's strings and dig the footing holes, using a clamshell digger or power auger.

2 Pour 2" to 3" of loose gravel into each hole for drainage. Make sure hole dimensions comply with your local building code, which may require flaring the base to 12".

3 Cut concrete tube forms to length, using a reciprocating saw or handsaw. Insert tubes into holes, leaving 2" of tube above ground level.

4 Pack soil around tubes and fill tubes with concrete. Tamp with a long stick or rod to eliminate air gaps.

5 Screed the concrete flush, using a straight 2 × 4, and insert a J-bolt into each footing, leaving ¾" to 1" of the thread exposed. Retie

Site Chooser Detail

After trimming the lower posts to length, permanently attach the deck beams to the posts with carriage bolts, using a ratchet wrench. The upper deck beams will be perpendicular to, and rest on top of, the lower deck beams.

the mason's strings and position the J-bolt at the center of the footing, using a plumb bob as a guide *(photo C)*.
6 Clean bolt threads before concrete sets.

Set the Deck Posts

1 Lay a straight 2 × 4 flat across each pair of footings, with one edge tight against the J-bolts. Draw a line across the top of each footing to help orient the post anchors.
2 Place a metal post anchor on each footing, centering it over the J-bolt and squaring it with the reference line. Thread a nut over each J-bolt and tighten the post anchors in place.
3 Cut the deck posts (C), several inches long to allow for final trimming. Set the posts in the anchors, brace the taller posts plumb, and nail the posts in place.
4 Establish the height of the

taller posts by measuring up 26½" from ground level and marking one post. Using a mason's string and a line level, transfer this mark to the remaining tall posts.
5 To establish the height of the lower beam posts, measure down 7¼" from the first line and transfer a level mark to the four lower posts.

Install the Deck Beams

This deck uses two sets of beams. The lower beams are three inches longer than the upper beams, because the rim joists rest on them. The lower beams support the upper beams and the deck platform.

1 Measure, mark, and cut the four lower beam boards (D) to length.
2 Mark the post locations on the tops and sides of the lower beams, using a combination square as a guide.

3 Position the lower beams crown-side-up on their posts. Make sure they are level, and fasten them with deck screws.
4 Trim the tops of the posts flush with a reciprocating saw or a handsaw.
5 Drill two ½" holes through the beams at each post. Securely attach the lower beams with joist ties, carriage bolts, and washers, using a ratchet wrench *(photo D)*.
6 Measure, mark, and cut the upper beams (D) to length. Mark post locations and attach, following the same steps as for the lower beams.

Install the Rim Joists

1 Cut four of the eight rim joists (G) to length (see *Detail B*, page 231), using a circular saw. Make 22½° miter cuts on the ends.
2 Attach one rim joist to each end of the upper

Angle bracket

beams (see *Detail B*, page 231) by nailing through the rim joist into the beams with box nails. Toenail the remaining two rim joists to the tops of the lower beams.
3 Verify the measurements of the remaining rim joists, cut to length, miter the ends at 22½°, and install. At the corners, drill pairs of ⅛" pilot holes, and fasten the adjacent rim joists to each other with deck screws.

Pour Landing Footings and Install Posts

1 Locate the landing footings by stretching a mason's string out from the rim joist to a batterboard, according to the measurements on the *Framing Plan*, page 230, and *Detail A*, page 231. Make sure the strings are perpendicular to the rim joist and are parallel with each other.
2 Mark the footing locations with tape. Use a plumb bob and stakes to transfer the

locations to the ground *(photo E)*.
3 Remove the mason's strings and dig holes for the footings, using a clamshell digger or power auger. Pour 2" to 3" of loose gravel into each hole for drainage, making sure hole dimensions comply with your local building code.
4 Use a reciprocating saw or handsaw to cut concrete tube forms to length. Insert tubes into holes. Leave 2" of tube above ground level, pack soil around tubes, and fill tubes with concrete. Tamp the concrete to eliminate air gaps.
5 Screed the tops flush and insert a J-bolt into each footing, leaving ¾" to 1" of the thread exposed. Retie the mason's strings and position the J-bolt at the centerpoint of the footing, using a plumb bob. Clean bolt threads before concrete sets.
6 Install post anchors, cut the landing posts to length (see *Detail*, above), and at-

tach the posts to the post anchors.

Install Landing Beams and Rim Joists

1 Attach post-beam caps to the tops of the landing posts.
2 Verify size, mark, and cut the beam boards (J) and rim joists (I) to length, using a circular saw (see *Framing Plan*, page 230).
3 Hold one pair of beam boards together, then measure and mark the post-beam cap locations on the tops and sides of the boards, using a combination square. Repeat for the second pair of boards.
4 Place beams, crown side up, into the post-beam caps and align. Drill pilot holes and fasten the caps to the beams with deck screws.
5 Position the rim joists flush with the side and top of the beams (see *Detail A*, page 231), drill ⅛" pilot holes

Locate the landing footings with mason's string and a plumb bob.

Measure, mark, and cut the landing beams. Attach them to the landing posts, using post-beam caps.

through the rim joists, and fasten with deck screws *(photo F)*.

Install Deck and Landing Joists

For the deck, the inner joists are installed with joist hangers and toe-nailed to the tops of the lower beams. This deck uses 90° joist hangers for the landing and for the two deck joists between the upper beams. For the angled deck joists, we used 45° joist hangers.

1 Using the plan, measure along the deck rim joists and lower beams, marking where joists attach. Draw the outline of each joist on the beams, using a combination square as a guide.
2 Measure, mark, and cut lumber for long joists (E) and mitered joists (F), using a circular saw. Mark the ends of the mitered joists with a 22½° angle, using a speed square, and cut the ends.

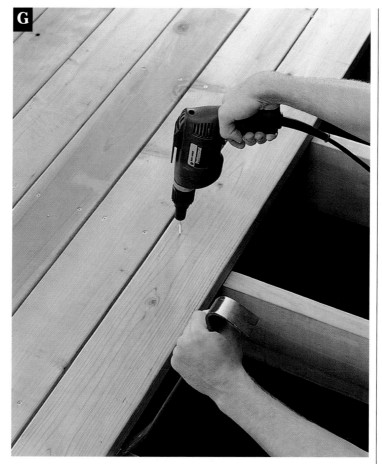

Straighten out any bowed decking boards with a pry bar and attach, using decking screws, leaving a ⅛" gap between boards.

Railing Detail

Face Board Detail

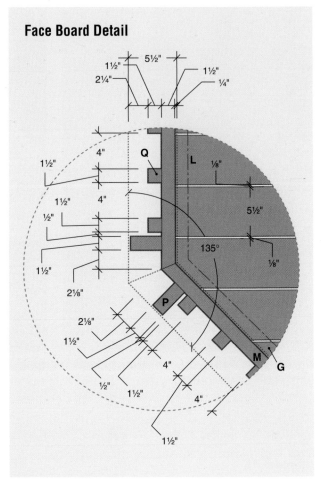

3 Place joists in hangers with crown side up, and attach with nails. Align joists with the outlines on the top edges of the lower beams and toenail in place.

4 Measure and mark locations of landing joists (K) on landing beams. Position joist hangers and attach with nails. Install landing joists and nail in place.

Lay the Deck Decking

1 Measure, cut, and position the first row of decking (L) next to the landing, and attach by driving a pair of deck screws into each joist.

2 Position the remaining decking boards so ends overhang the rim joists, leaving a ⅛" gap between the boards to provide for

drainage **(photo G)**. Attach boards to each joist with a pair of deck screws.

3 After installing every few rows of decking, measure from the edge of the decking to the far edge of the deck. Adjust the spacing between the remaining boards so the final board can be full width.

4 Snap a chalk line on the decking to mark a line flush with the outside edge of the deck, and trim the deck boards with a circular saw.

Install the Face Boards

1 Measure, mark, and cut deck face boards (M). Miter-cut the ends at 22½°. Position face boards flush with decking and attach to rim joists, using deck screws.

2 Verify the measurements, mark, and cut the landing face boards (O) to length. Position top edges flush with decking, and attach to landing beams and front rim joist, using deck screws.

Build the Railing

1 Measure, mark, and cut the railing posts (P) to length (see *Railing Detail*, above).

2 At the bottom of each post, counterbore two holes ½" deep, using a spade bit slightly larger than the diameter of the washers.

3 Drill two ¼" pilot holes through the bottom of each post. Position posts (see *Face Board Detail*, above), mark and drill pilot holes in deck, and attach to the face

Drill ⅛" pilot holes, then screw the top rail sections together where they meet at the corners.

After attaching angle brackets, turn stringers upside down and install treads, using 1¼" lag screws.

board and rim joist, using lag screws.

4 Cut each top rail section (R) the same length as the face board below it. Miter the ends of each section at 22½°.

5 Fasten the top rails to the posts with screws.

6 Measure, mark, and cut railing balusters (Q) to length.

7 Drill ⅛" pilot holes in the balusters, and attach them to the face boards and the top rails with screws.

8 To strengthen the corners, drill ⅛" pilot holes at an angle and screw the top rail sections together *(photo H).*

9 Verify the measurements for the railing cap sections (S), and cut them to length with 22½° miters where the ends meet. Attach to the posts and top rail with deck screws.

Build the Stairways

1 Measure, mark, and cut the stringers (T) to size (see *Landing & Stairway Detail,* page 234).

2 Using a framing square, lay out the top step with a 6" rise (the top of the stringer is installed 1" below the surface of the decking) and 12" run. Extend the rise line to both edges of the stringer, and cut along this line.

3 Lay out the bottom step with a 7" rise and a 12¾" run. At the end of the run, draw a perpendicular line 7" long and make a mark. Draw another perpendicular line to the bottom edge of the stringer and cut to size (see *Landing & Stairway Detail,* page 234).

4 Position the angle brackets

in place and attach to the stringers, using 1¼" lag screws.

5 Measure, mark, and cut the treads (U) to length, and attach to the stringers with lag screws through the angle brackets, leaving a ⅛" gap between treads *(photo I).*

6 Install the stairways by propping them in position against the landing, and drilling ¼" pilot holes through the rim joists and face boards into the top end of the stringers. Attach with a pair of lag screws at each stringer.

Lay the Landing Decking

After installing the stairways, cut the landing decking (N) to length and attach with deck screws.

Wraparound Deck

Combine multiple seating possibilities with an expansive view.

By wrapping around an outside corner of your house, this versatile deck increases your living space and lets you take advantage of views in several directions. The plan also creates two symmetrical areas for sitting or relaxing, providing space for two distinct activities. Our plan also calls for a front stairway for easy access to your yard or garden. The horizontal rails and notched posts provide striking visual elements that enhance the deck's overall design and add to its intimate nature. By adding a box or rail planter (see pages 296 to 299), you can bring your garden right up to the deck.

Cutaway View

Lumber List			
Qty.	Size	Material	Part
9	2 × 8" × 16'	Trtd. Lumber	Joists (D)
6	2 × 8" × 12'	Trtd. Lumber	Ledgers (A), Beam boards (C), End joist (E), Rim joist (F)
13	2 × 8" × 10'	Trtd. Lumber	Beam boards (C), Joists (D), End joist (E), Rim joists (F), Lower gusset (L)
1	2 × 6" × 4'	Trtd. Lumber	Stairway nailer (I)
1	2 × 4" × 4'	Trtd. Lumber	Upper gusset (L)
3	4 × 4" × 8'	Trtd. Lumber	Deck posts (B)
9	4 × 4" × 8'	Cedar	Deck railing posts (G), Stairway railing posts (N)

Lumber List			
Qty.	Size	Material	Part
28	¾ × 6" × 16'	Cedar	Decking (H)
2	2 × 10" × 12'	Cedar	Face boards (J)
2	2 × 10" × 10'	Cedar	Face boards (J)
1	2 × 10" × 6'	Cedar	Face boards (J)
1	2 × 12" × 12'	Cedar	Stringers (K)
5	2 × 6" × 12'	Cedar	Railing cap (Q)
5	2 × 6" × 8'	Cedar	Treads (O)
10	1 × 4" × 12'	Cedar	Rails (P)
11	1 × 4" × 10'	Cedar	Rails (P)
8	1 × 4" × 6'	Cedar	Rails (P)

Supplies: 8"-diameter footing forms (8); J-bolts (8); 4 × 4" metal post anchors (8); post-beam caps (8); 90° 2 × 8" joist hangers (26); 45° 2 × 8" joist hangers (3); 1½ × 1½" galvanized metal angle brackets (26); joist hanger nails; ⅜ × 4" lag screws and washers (20); ⅜ × 3" lag screws and washers (32); 6 × 30" mending plate (1); silicone caulk (3 tubes); 3" masonry screws; 3" galvanized deck screws; 1½" galvanized deck screws; ⅝" galvanized screws; concrete as required.

Framing Plan

Elevation

Railing Detail

Stairway Detail

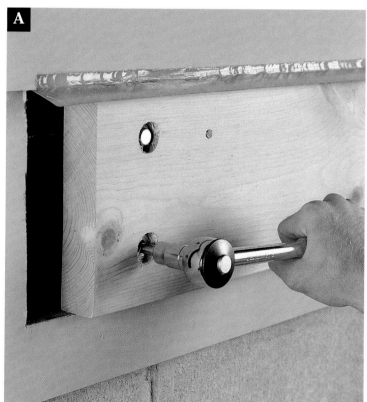

A

Attach the ledgers to the walls with ⅜ × 4" lag screws and washers, using a ratchet wrench.

Directions: Wraparound Deck

Attach the Ledgers

1 Draw a level outline on the siding to show where the ledgers and the adjacent end joist and rim joist will fit against the house.

2 Position the top edge of the ledgers so that the surface of the decking boards will be 1" below the indoor floor level. This height difference prevents rainwater or melted snow from seeping into the house. Draw the outline long enough to accommodate the thickness of rim joist F-1 and end joist E-2.

3 Cut out the siding along the outline with a circular saw. To keep the blade from cutting the sheathing underneath the siding, set the blade depth to the same

Footing Location Diagram

Set the post anchors in place, squaring them with the reference line scribed in the footings.

thickness as the siding. Finish the corners of the cutout with a chisel, holding the beveled side in to ensure a straight cut.

4 Cut galvanized flashing to the length of the cutout, using metal snips, and slide the flashing up under the siding.

5 Measure and cut the ledgers (A) to length from pressure-treated lumber, using a circular saw. Remember, the ledger boards should be shorter than the overall length of the cutouts.

6 Position the ledgers in the cutout, underneath the flashing, and brace them in place. Fasten them temporarily with deck screws.

7 Drill pairs of ¼" pilot holes through the ledger and sheathing and into the house header joist at 2' intervals. Counterbore each

pilot hole ½" deep, using a 1" spade bit. Attach the ledgers to the wall with ⅜ × 4" lag screws and washers, using a ratchet wrench *(photo A).*

8 Apply a thick bead of silicone caulk between the siding and the flashing. Also seal the lag screw heads and any gaps between the wall and the ledger.

Pour the Footings

1 Referring to the *Footing Location Diagram* (above), stretch mason's strings across the site, using 2 × 4 batterboards. Check the mason's strings for square, using the 3-4-5 triangle method. From the point where each string meets the ledger, measure 3' along the ledger and make a mark. Next, mea-

sure 4' out along the mason's string and mark with tape. The distance between the points on the ledger and the string should be 5'. If not, adjust the mason's strings accordingly. Measure along the strings to locate the centerpoints of the footings. Mark the locations with tape.

2 Drop a plumb bob at the tape locations, and drive stakes into the ground to mark the centerpoints of the footings.

3 Remove the mason's strings and dig holes for the footings, using a clamshell digger or power auger.

4 Pour 2" to 3" of loose gravel into each hole for drainage. Make certain the hole dimensions comply with your local building code, which may require flaring the footings to 12" at the base.

5 Cut the footing forms to length, using a reciprocating saw or handsaw. Insert the forms into the holes, leaving 2" of each form above grade. Pack soil around the forms.

Use a speed square to mark a 22½° miter cut where the ends of beams C-3 and C-4 fit together.

Install the Beams

1 Cut the beams from 2 × 10" lumber, adding several inches to each beam for final trimming. Position the beam boards (C) so the crowns face the same direction, and fasten them together with 10d galvanized nails spaced every 16".

2 Position beams C-1 and C-2 in their post-beam caps and attach them with nails.

3 Mark and cut the angled end of beam C-3 by mitering it at 22½° **(photo C).** Position the beam in the post caps.

4 Make a 22½° miter cut at one end of beam C-4 to form a 45° corner with beam C-3. Leave the other end long for final trimming. Place beam C-4 in the post-beam caps **(photo D).**

5 Fit the beams tightly together, fasten them with 3" deck screws, and attach them to the post caps with 8d nails.

6 Fill the forms with concrete and tamp the concrete with a long stick to eliminate any air pockets. Screed the tops flush with a flat 2 × 4. Insert a J-bolt into each footing, leaving ¾" to 1" of thread exposed.

7 Retie the mason's strings and drop a plumb bob to position each J-bolt at the exact center of the footing. Clean the bolt threads before the concrete sets.

Set the Deck Posts

1 Start by laying a long, straight 2 × 4 flat across each pair of footings. With one edge tight against the J-bolts, draw a reference line across each footing.

2 Place a metal post anchor on each footing, center it over the J-bolt, and square it with the reference line **(photo B).** Thread a nut over each J-bolt and tighten each of the post anchors in place.

3 Cut the posts (C) to their approximate length, adding several inches for final trimming. Place the posts in the anchors and tack them into place with one nail each.

4 With a level as a guide, use braces and stakes to plumb the posts. Once the posts are plumb, finish nailing them to the anchors.

5 To determine the height of the posts, make a mark on the house, 7¼" down from the bottom edge of the ledger. Use a straight 2 × 4 and a level to extend this line across a post. Transfer this line to the remaining posts.

6 Cut the posts off with a reciprocating saw or a handsaw and attach post-beam caps to the tops, using 8d nails.

Fit beam C-4 tightly against beam C-3 and attach the two beams to each other with deck screws.

Install the Joists

1 Referring to the *Framing Plan* on page 240, cut rim joist F-1 to final length, and cut end joist E-1 generously long, to allow for final trimming.

2 Fasten one end of rim joist F-1 to the ledger with 16d galvanized nails. Rest end joist E-1 in place on beams C-1 and C-2. Fasten F-1 and E-1 together with deck screws.

3 Use a framing square to finalize the location of E-1 on the beams. Mark the beams and trim them to length. Toenail E-1 in place on the beams.

4 Cut end joist E-2 to length. Install it by nailing it to the end of the ledger, checking for square, and toenailing it to the top of beam C-3. Trim the beam to length.

5 Mark the outlines of the inner joists (D) on the ledger, beams and rim joist F-1 (see *Framing Plan*, page 240), using a tape measure and a combination square.

6 Attach joist hangers to the ledger and rim joist F-1 with 1¼" joist hanger nails, using a scrap 2 × 8 as a spacer to achieve the correct spread for each hanger. NOTE: Spacing between the joists is irregular to accommodate the installation of railing posts.

7 Place the inside joists in the hangers on the ledger and on rim joist F-1, crown up, and attach them with 1¼" joist hanger nails. Be sure to use all the nail holes in the hangers. Toenail the joists to the beams and leave the joists long for final trimming.

8 Mark the final length of the inside joists by making a line across the tops of the joists from the end of end joist E-2. Check for square. Brace the inside joists by tacking a board across

Mark the three remaining inside joists for cutting by snapping a chalk line. Brace and miter-cut the three inside joists.

their edges for stability. Cut them to length with a circular saw.

9 Cut rim joist F-2 long to allow for final trimming, and nail into position with 16d galvanized nails.

10 To mark the remaining joists for trimming at a 45° angle, make a mark 139" from the 90° corner on end joist E-1. Make a second mark 139" from the other 90° corner along rim joist F-2. The distance between these two points should be at least 70". If necessary, move the line back until it measures 70". Regardless of the overall dimensions of your deck, this length will ensure adequate space for mounting the railing posts at the top of the stairway.

11 Mark the last three joists for cutting by snapping a chalk line between the marked points on end joist E-1 and rim joist F-2 *(photo E).* Transfer the cut marks to the faces of the

joists with a combination square, and cut the miters with a circular saw.

12 Measure, cut, and attach rim joist F-3 across the angle with deck screws.

Install the Railing Posts

1 Cut the railing posts (G) to size and notch the lower ends to fit around the rim joists (see *Railing Detail*, page 241).

2 Clamp all but two of the posts together to lay out and cut ¾" × 3½" notches, or dadoes, for the horizontal rails. NOTE: The posts at the stairway are not notched for rails.

3 Cut the dadoes by making a series of parallel ¾"-deep cuts within each 3½" space, about ¼" apart, with a circular saw. Knock out the waste wood between the cuts, using a hammer. Then, chisel smooth the bottom of each dado.

4 To locate the railing posts

Drill pilot holes through the posts and into the rim joists, and attach the posts with lag screws. Note the unnotched stairway post.

on the diagonal corner, find the centerline of rim joist F-3 and measure 18" in both directions. These points are the inner faces of the railing posts and the outer faces of the stringers. Drill ¼" pilot holes through the railing posts into the rim joist, and secure the posts with lag screws.

5 To position the corner railing posts, measure 3" both ways from the outside corners of rim joist F-3. Predrill the posts, and use a ratchet wrench to attach them to the rim joists with lag screws **(photo F).**

6 Use the *Framing Plan*, page 240, and the *Corner Post Detail*, page 246, to locate the remaining railing posts.

Install the Decking

If possible, buy decking boards that are long enough to span the deck.

1 Measure, mark, and cut the decking (H) to size,

making notches to fit around the railing posts. Position the first board above the stairway **(photo G),** and attach it by driving a pair of deck screws into each joist.

2 Position the remaining

decking boards so that the ends overhang the deck, leaving a ⅛" gap between the boards to allow for drainage.

3 Where more than one board is required to span the deck, cut the ends at 45° angles and make the joint at the center of a joist.

4 Snap a chalk line flush with the edge of the deck, and cut off the overhanging ends of the deck boards with a circular saw set for a 1½"-deep cut.

Install the Nailer & Face Boards

1 Measure, mark, and cut the stairway nailer (I) to size and attach it to the rim joist with a mending plate and deck screws (see *Stairway Detail*, page 241).

2 Measure, mark, and cut the face boards (J) to length, making 45° miter cuts at the right angle corners and 22½° miter cuts at the stairway corners. Attach the face boards to the rim and end joists with pairs of deck screws at 2' intervals.

Cut the notches for the first decking board and position it above the stairway.

Drill ⅛" pilot holes through the treads to prevent splitting. Then, attach the treads to the stringers with deck screws, using a power driver.

Clamp the long rails, mark the ends, and transfer the lines across the face of the board with a combination square to ensure a tight-fitting 22½° miter with the short rail.

Corner Post Detail

¾"
3¾"
Post
Railing
Face board
3¼"
4"
5" 5"
Rim joist
End joist

page 240). Level the form at 42" below the finished surface of the deck, to accommodate six 7" stairway rises. Stake the form into place.

4 Fill the form with concrete, screed it flush with a 2 × 4, and let the concrete set overnight.

Build the Stairway

1 Lay out and cut the stringers (K) to size, according to the *Stairway Detail*, page 241. The center stringer is notched at the top and bottom to fit around the gussets. Mark the rises and runs with a framing square. Cut the notches with a circular saw, using a reciprocating saw or handsaw to finish the corners.

2 Measure, mark, and cut the gussets (L) to length. Assemble the stairway framework by nailing the gussets in place between the outer

Pour the Concrete Pad

1 Determine the location for the pad. Add 6" in each direction, and excavate the area approximately 8" deep.

2 Lay and tamp a 4" base of compactable gravel.

3 Build a form from 2 × 6 lumber (see *Framing Plan*,

stringers with 16d nails. Turn the framework upside down and attach the center stringer by nailing through the gussets.

3 Position the framework against the deck, and attach with deck screws driven through the upper gusset into the face board and nailer. Drill pilot holes through the lower gusset into the concrete pad; attach with masonry screws.

4 Cut the stairway railing posts (N) to length. To install the railing posts, clamp them in place against the stringers, drill pilot holes through the stringers into the posts, and attach the posts with ⅜ × 4" lag screws.

5 Measure, mark and cut the treads (O) to length. For the bottom treads, use a piece of railing post scrap to trace a line for the notch. Then, cut the notch with a circular saw. Attach the treads to the stringers with deck screws **(photo H)**.

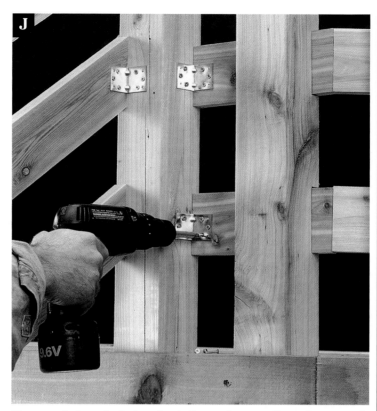

Use angle brackets to attach the stairway railing pieces and angled rails. To attach the brackets to the rails, use ⅝" galvanized screws.

Build the Railing

1 Measure and cut to length the 10' rails, each with one end mitered at 45°. Install the rails, using 1½" deck screws.

2 Miter one end of the long rails at 45°. Leave the other end long for final trimming.

3 Clamp each long rail in place and use a straight-edge to mark cut lines at the angled corner **(photo I)**. Transfer this line to the face of each rail, using a combination square. Remove the rails and miter-cut the ends for the angled corners at 22½°.

4 Reposition the rails and attach them to the railing posts with 1½" deck screws.

5 Measure, mark, and cut the short rails to length with one end mitered at 22½° and the other end cut square.

6 Fasten the ends of the short rails to the railing posts

above the stairway with angle brackets **(photo J)**. Use ⅝" galvanized screws to attach the brackets to the rails and 1½" deck screws to attach them to the posts. Attach them to the notched post as well, using 1½" deck screws.

7 Measure, mark, and cut the deck railing cap (Q), and install it with 3" deck screws.

Build the Stairway Railing

1 To mark the stairway posts for trimming, hold the edge of a straight 2 × 4 across the deck post at the top of the stairs and the stairway post below. With the upper end of the 2 × 4 against the underside of the deck railing cap, and the 2 × 4 parallel to the stairway stringer, mark a cut line on the stairway post along the underside of the 2 × 4. Cut the post to length.

2 Repeat the process to mark and cut the other stairway post to length.

3 Measure, mark, and cut the stairway railing caps (see *Stairway Detail*, page 241). Place a cedar 2 × 6 on top of the stairway posts, mark the angles for the ends, and cut to length, allowing for a 1" overhang at the end of the stairway.

4 Install the stairway railing caps with 3" deck screws.

5 To cut the stairway rails, hold each one tight against the bottom of the cap and mark the ends. Cut the rails to length so that they fit tight between the posts.

6 To install the rails, mark the positions of the rails on the posts and attach them with angle brackets, using ⅝" screws and 1½" deck screws.

Angled Deck

Give yourself a commanding view from this unique angled deck.

Expand your living space with style. This attractive deck makes creative use of simple geometry to achieve both practicality and pizzazz.

The railing adds interest with its combination of vertical balusters, horizontal rails, and shaped railing posts. And the straight staircase — anchored to a concrete pad

for stability — provides direct, convenient access.

Though designed for construction at medium height on level ground, this deck uses heavy-duty posts, beams, joists, and footings. By simply lengthening posts and modifying the stairway, it's readily adaptable for installation at a higher level or on a sloped site.

Cutaway View

Lumber List			
Qty.	**Size**	**Material**	**Part**
4	2 × 10" × 20'	Trtd. lumber	Ledger (A), Primary beam boards (C)
1	2 × 10" × 18'	Trtd. lumber	Joists (G)
4	2 × 10" × 16'	Trtd. lumber	Joists (G)
5	2 × 10" × 14'	Trtd. lumber	Joists (G)
8	2 × 10" × 12'	Trtd. lumber	Joists (G)
5	2 × 10" × 10'	Trtd. lumber	Joists (G), End joists (E), Rim joists (F)
4	2 × 10" × 8'	Trtd. lumber	Secondary beam boards (D)
2	2 × 10" × 6'	Trtd. lumber	Rim joists (F)
2	6 × 6" × 8'	Trtd. lumber	Deck posts (B)

Lumber List			
Qty.	**Size**	**Material**	**Part**
1	2 × 6" × 8'	Trtd. Lumber	Gussets (J)
6	4 × 4" × 8'	Cedar	Railing posts (H)
4	4 × 4" × 10'	Cedar	Stair railing posts (K)
3	2 × 12" × 8'	Cedar	Stringers (I)
7	2 × 6" × 8'	Cedar	Treads (L)
38	2 × 6" × 16'	Cedar	Decking (M)
8	2 × 4" × 10'	Cedar	Top & bottom rails (N)
2	2 × 4" × 8'	Cedar	Top & bottom rails (N)
11	1 × 3" × 10'	Cedar	Top & bottom inner rails (O)
20	2 × 2" × 10'	Cedar	Balusters (P)

Supplies: 12"-diameter footing forms (4); J-bolts (4); 6 × 6" metal post anchors (4); 90° 2 × 10" joist hangers (22); 45° double 2 × 10" joist hangers (2); 3" galvanized deck screws; 1¾" galvanized deck screws; 3" masonry screws (4); joist hanger nails; 16d galvanized casing nails; ⅜ × 4" lag screws and washers (60); ⅜ × 5" carriage bolts, washers and nuts (22); silicone caulk (3 tubes); concrete as required.

Framing Plan

Post Detail

198 ¾" [16'-6¾"]
108"   48¾"   42"
1"   4½"

E
H   H   H
1½"   12"
18"
9¼"
C   12"
C   12"
80 ¼"
C   12"
77¼"
C   12"
H
B
C   12"
24"
G   D
C   12"
100½"
C   12"
C   12"
C   12"
56" Pad
C   12"
C
24"
C   12"
8"
D
41"
C   10½"
7"
C   10½"
C   12"
F
61" Pad
C   10"
54"
C   14"
H
C   12"
1½"   12"
E   H   18"   F
108"   9"
117"   49¾"
[9'-9"]

240"
[20'-0"]
237"
[19'-9"]

78¾"
120"

ELEVATION POINT OF VIEW

Elevation

H   4"   P   O   N

36"

E   F   9¼"   1½"
C   9¼"
I   D
58"   B   56"
B   B
B   L
B
2"
71⅜"
3½"   3⅞"
78¾"
120" [10'-0"]

250

Railing Detail

Stairway Detail

After attaching the ledger, drop a plumb line to a convenient height and stretch mason's strings. Mark footing locations with tape, and use the 3-4-5 triangle method to verify that the strings are square.

Directions: Angled Deck

Attach the Ledger

The ledger anchors the deck and establishes a reference point for building the deck square and level.

1 Draw a level outline on the siding to show where the ledger and the end joists will fit against the house. Install the ledger so that the surface of the decking boards will be 1" below the indoor floor level. This height difference prevents rainwater or melted snow from seeping into the house.

2 Cut out the siding along the outline with a circular saw. To

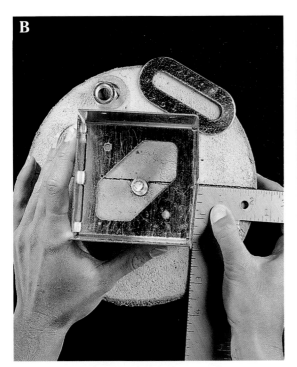

Square the post anchors to the reference lines on the top of each footing to ensure that the posts are aligned with each other.

Determine the finished post height by leveling a straight 2 × 4 from the bottom edge of the ledger.

prevent the blade from cutting the sheathing that lies underneath the siding, set the blade depth to the same thickness as the siding. Finish the cutout with a chisel, holding the beveled side in to ensure a straight cut.

3 Cut galvanized flashing to the length of the cutout, using metal snips. Slide the flashing up under the siding at the top of the cutout.

4 Measure and cut the ledger (A) from pressure-treated lumber. Center the ledger end to end in the cutout, with space at each end for the end joist.

5 Brace the ledger into position under the flashing. Tack the ledger into place with galvanized nails.

6 Drill pairs of ¼" pilot holes at 16" intervals through the ledger and into the house header joist. Counterbore each

pilot hole ½", using a 1" spade bit. Attach the ledger with lag screws and washers, using a ratchet wrench.

7 Apply a thick bead of silicone caulk between siding and flashing. Also

seal lag screw heads and the cracks at the ends of the ledger.

Pour the Footings

1 To locate the footings,

After marking the notches for the primary beam, cut out the tops of the posts with a circular saw and a handsaw.

E

Use a ratchet wrench to tighten the lag screws that secure the primary beam to the notched posts.

drop a plumb bob from the end of the ledger down to a level that's comfortable for making measurements and stretching mason's strings.

2 Measurements for the footing centerpoints are shown on the *Framing Plan*, page 250. Construct, position, and install temporary 2 × 4 batterboards.

3 Stretch three strings perpendicular to the house; one at each end of the ledger, and one at the centerline of the footing for the secondary beam, 80¼" from the right end of the ledger.

4 Make sure that the strings are square to the house **(photo A)** by using the 3-4-5 triangle method. Measuring from the point where the string meets the house, make a mark on the house at 3'. Then measure out along the string and make a mark at 4'. When the string is truly perpen-

dicular, the diagonal line connecting the two marked points will measure 5'. Adjust the string on the batterboard as needed.

5 Stretch the fourth string between batterboards, parallel to the house, at the centerline of the primary beam.

6 Measure along the parallel string and use tape to mark the three centerpoints of the footings for the primary beam.

7 To locate the footing for the secondary beam, use tape to mark a point on the middle perpendicular string that is 48¾" out from its intersection with the parallel string.

8 Transfer the locations to the ground by dropping a plumb bob from each tape mark and driving a stake into the ground at each point.

9 Remove the mason's strings and dig holes for the footings, using a clamshell

digger or power auger. Pour 2" to 3" of loose gravel into each hole for drainage. NOTE: When measuring the footing size and depth, make sure you comply with your local building code, which may require flaring the base to 18".

10 Cut the footing forms to length, using a reciprocating saw or handsaw, and insert them into the footing holes, leaving 2" of tube above ground level. Pack soil around the forms for support, and fill with concrete, tamping with a long stick or rod to eliminate any air gaps.

11 Screed the tops flush, using a straight 2 × 4. Insert a J-bolt into the center of each footing, leaving ¾" to 1" of thread exposed. Retie the mason's strings and use the plumb bob to position the J-bolts at the exact center of each footing. Clean the bolt threads before the concrete sets.

Set the Posts

1 To provide a reference line for orienting the post anchors so the posts will be aligned with each other, lay a long, straight 2 × 4 flat across the primary beam footings, parallel to the ledger. With one edge tight against the J-bolts, draw a line across the top of each footing.

2 To mark the post anchor position on the footing for the secondary beam, mark a line across the footing at a 45° angle to the primary beam.

3 Place a metal post anchor on each footing, centering it over the J-bolt and squaring it with the reference line **(photo B).** Thread a nut over each J-bolt and securely tighten the post anchors in place.

After the secondary beam boards have been cut, assembled, and attached with deck screws, secure the beam to the post with lag screws.

Cut the 45° angles on the ends of the joists with a circular saw.

4 Estimate the height of each post, and cut the posts slightly long to allow for final trimming. Set the posts in the anchors and tack into place with one nail.

5 With a level as a guide, use braces and stakes to ensure that the posts are plumb.

6 Determine the top of the posts by extending a straight 2 × 4 from the bottom edge of the ledger and marking a line on the posts level with the bottom of the ledger *(photo C).*

7 Outline a 4½" × 9¼" notch (see *Post Detail*, page 250) at the top of each of the primary-beam posts.

8 Remove the posts from the anchors, cut to finished height, and cut the notches, using a circular saw and handsaw *(photo D).*

9 Reposition the posts with

the notches facing away from the house, brace them plumb, and nail them securely to the post anchors.

Install the Beams

We used 20' boards for the primary beam. However, for reasons of cost or availability, you may need to use 10'-long boards. Check with your local building inspector regarding acceptable joining hardware and techniques.

1 Construct the primary beam from 2 × 10" boards. Position the primary beam boards (C) so the crowns face the same direction, and fasten together with 16d galvanized nails. Drill pairs of ⅜" holes through the beam at 24" intervals, and secure with carriage bolts,

washers, and nuts.

2 Measure, mark, and cut the beam to length. Position the beam in the post notches, crown-side-up. Make sure the beam is square to the ledger by measuring the diagonals; adjust the beam position so the diagonal measurements are equal.

3 Drill two ¼" pilot holes through each post into the beam. Fasten with lag screws and washers, using a ratchet wrench *(photo E).*

4 Measure, mark, and cut the post for the secondary beam slightly long to allow for final trimming. Install the post in the post anchor.

5 Locate and mark the points where the secondary beam butts against the primary beam. Run a straight 2 × 4 across the face of the post to the primary beam in both directions. Outline the ends of the secondary beam on the face of the primary beam, and install 45° 2 × 10 double joist hangers at each point.

6 Measure, mark, and cut secondary beam boards (D) to length, using a circular saw.

7 Install the boards one at a time, verifying that they are level and attaching them with deck screws.

8 Drill pilot holes through the assembled beam and into the post. Counterbore the holes ½" deep with a 1" spade bit, and secure the secondary beam to the post with lag screws *(photo F)*.

9 Fasten the secondary beam to the joist hangers with 10d galvanized nails.

Install the Joists

1 Measure and cut the end joists (E), leaving them several inches long for final trimming. Install by nailing into the ends of the ledger with 16d galvanized nails and toenailing to the top of the primary beam.

2 The joists are not all evenly spaced. Referring to the *Framing Plan* (page 250) use a combination square and draw the joist outlines on the face of the ledger and the top of the beams.

3 Install a joist hanger on the ledger at each location. Attach one flange of a hanger to one side of each outline, using joist hanger nails. Use a spacer cut from scrap 2 × 10" lumber to achieve the correct spread for each hanger, then fasten the re-

maining side flange with joist hanger nails. Remove the spacer and repeat the procedure to install the remaining joist hangers.

4 Measure, mark, and cut the joists (G), using a circular saw. Be sure to leave the joists long to accommodate final angled trimming. Place joists in hangers with crown side up and attach with nails. Align joists with the outlines on the top of the beam and toenail in place.

5 Snap chalk lines along the top edges of the joists (see *Framing Plan*, page 250) to mark the perimeter of the deck. All the angles are either 45° or 90°. Allow for the 1½" thickness of the rim joists. Extend the cutoff lines to the faces of the joists, and make the cuts, using a circular saw *(photo G)*.

6 Referring to the *Framing*

Pour the concrete into the staircase pad form, and screed flush, using a straight 2 × 4.

255

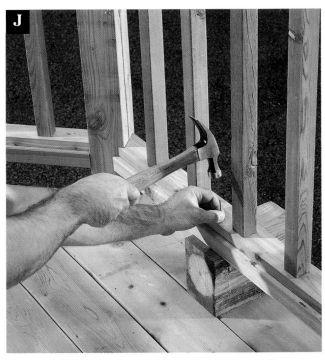

Drill pilot holes through the gusset and into the concrete pad, then attach with masonry screws, using a power drill.

Use a nailing block to support the bottom rail, and attach the baluster assembly with nails. Notice the notch where the rails join the post at a 45° angle.

Plan and confirming the actual dimensions of your deck, measure, mark, and cut the rim joists (F) to size and attach them to the joists with deck screws.

Install the Railing Posts

Locate railing posts in the corners of the deck, then center the intermediate posts between them (see *Framing Plan*, page 250).

1 Cut railing posts (H) to length (see *Railing Detail*, page 251). Cut a 60° pyramid on the top of each post, and rout a ½" × ½" groove on all four sides 1" below the pyramid.
2 To install the railing posts, clamp them one at a time into position, and drill ¼" pilot holes through the rim joist into the post. Counterbore the holes ½" using a 1" spade bit, and secure the posts to the rim joists with lag screws.

Pour the Pad

1 Determine the location of the concrete pad. Add 6" in each direction, and excavate approximately 8" deep.
2 Lay and tamp a 4" base of compactible gravel.
3 Build a form from 2 × 6 lumber, and align the inside of the form with the outside rim joists as shown in the *Framing Plan*, page 250. Level the form at 56" below the finished surface of the deck, to accommodate eight 7" stairway rises. Stake the form into place.
4 Fill the form with concrete, screed with a straight 2 × 4 **(photo H),** and let the concrete set up overnight.

Install the Stairway

1 Lay out the stringers (I), according to the *Stairway Detail*, page 251. Notch the center stringer at the top and bottom to fit around the gussets. Mark the rises and

runs with a framing square. Cut the notches with a circular saw, using a reciprocating saw or handsaw to finish the corners.
2 Measure, mark, and cut the gussets (J) to length. Assemble the stairway framework by nailing the gussets in place between the outer stringers with 16d nails. Turn the framework upside down and attach the center stringer by nailing through the gussets.
3 Position the stairway framework against the deck rim joist, and attach with deck screws driven through the top gusset into the rim joist. Drill pilot holes through the bottom gusset into the concrete pad and attach with masonry screws **(photo I).**
4 Cut the stair railing posts (K) to length. Shape the top ends. Install the posts by clamping them into place against the stringers, drilling pilot holes through the stringers into the posts, and

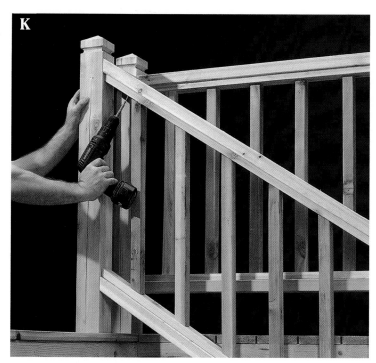

Drive deck screws up through the top inner rail to attach the top rail to the baluster assembly.

attaching with lag screws and washers.

5 Measure and cut the treads (L) to length, using a circular saw. The bottom treads are notched to fit around the posts.

Install the Decking

If possible, buy decking (M) long enough to span the deck. When joints between deck boards are necessary, center them above joists so the ends of both boards are supported.

1 Position the first deck board along the outer 45° rim joist, and mark the railing post locations. Cut notches for the railing posts, using a circular saw, handsaw, and chisel. Attach the board by driving two deck screws into each joist.

2 Cut and attach the remaining deck boards, leaving a ⅛" gap between the boards for drainage.

Install the Railing

The railing for this deck is assembled in sections and then installed. The balusters are first fastened between the inner rails, then the baluster assembly is cut to exact length and attached to the outer rails.

1 Verify the measurements between your railing posts. Measure, mark, and cut the top and bottom rails (N) to length.

2 Install the bottom rails by drilling angled ⅛" pilot holes into the posts at the ends, and attaching with deck screws. NOTE: Where the railings meet the posts at a 45° angle, you'll need to notch the ends to fit.

3 Measure, mark, and cut the top and bottom inner rails (O), leaving them several inches long for final trimming.

4 Measure, mark, and cut the deck balusters (P) to length.

5 Assemble each railing section by positioning the balusters between the top and bottom inner rails, drilling ⅛" pilot holes, and attaching them with deck screws. Trim the section to final length with an equal space at each end.

6 Position the baluster assembly on the bottom rail and nail in place **(photo J)**.

7 Position the top rail above the baluster assembly, drill pilot holes through the top inner rail into the top rail, and attach with deck screws from below.

8 To determine the angle for the ends of the stairway rails and balusters, as well as the length of the inner and outer stairway rails, hold a straight 2 × 4 across one pair of stairway posts. With the top edge of the 2 × 4 crossing each post at the routed groove, mark the angle on the back of the board. NOTE: The angle will be approximately 32°, but you'll get the best fit by marking it from your actual railing posts.

9 Measure, mark, and cut the top and bottom rails to length, with the ends angled to fit against the posts. Install the bottom rails.

10 Cut inner rails and balusters to size with mitered ends.

11 Build the stairway railing assemblies using the same procedures as used for the deck railing assemblies, taking care that the space between balusters is 4" or less.

12 Install the stairway railing assemblies by positioning them on the bottom rails and nailing with 6d casing nails.

13 Install the stairway top rails by positioning them above the railing assemblies, drilling pilot holes through the top inner rails, and driving deck screws from below **(photo K)**.

Low-Profile Deck

*An attractive alternative
to a plain patio.*

This low-profile deck creates a distinctive focal point for homes with ground-level entries. The composite decking complements the rich tones of the cedar, and the V-pattern directs your view to the centerpoint of the deck. This deck is ideal for flat, level lots or for covering up an old cement patio, and requires no posts, so construction is easier than building a higher deck. Since this deck is less than 24"-high, there's also no requirement for a railing. This deck can hold a BBQ, table, and chairs. Our plan also calls for a suspended step that's perfect for areas with snow and frost.

Cutaway View

Lumber List			
Qty.	Size	Material	Part
5	2 × 8" × 20'	Trtd. lumber	Ledger (A) & Beam bds (B)
2	2 × 8" × 16'	Trtd. lumber	End joists (C)
40	2 × 8" × 8'	Trtd. lumber	Joists (D)
3	2 × 4" × 8'	Trtd. lumber	Step support spacers (E)
2	2 × 6" × 8'	Trtd. lumber	Interior step supports (F)
1	2 × 6" × 6'	Cedar	End step supports (G)

Lumber List			
Qty.	Size	Material	Part
2	2 × 6" × 6'	Cedar	Step riser (H)
74	2 × 6" × 10'	Composite	Decking (I)
2	2 × 6" × 6'	Composite	Tread (L)
1	2 × 10" × 20'	Cedar	Front face bd (J)
2	2 × 10" × 16'	Cedar	Side face bds (K)

Supplies: 8"-diameter footing forms (6); 3" direct bearing hardware (6); 2 × 8" double joist hangers (4); 2 × 8" joist hangers (72); 2½" composite decking screws; joist hanger nails; 16d galvanized box nails; 12d galvanized casing nails; ⅜ × 4" carriage bolts, washers, and nuts (12); ⅜ × 4" lag screws (22); lead masonry anchors (22); ledger flashing (20 ft.); exterior silicone caulk (3 tubes); concrete as required.

Framing Plan

192" [16'-0"] Deck

189" [15'-9"] End joists

3"

1½"

91½" Joists

91½" Joists

K

C

B

A

9¾"

D

26¼"

12"

₵

12"

₵

12"

₵

12"

1½"

₵

48"

12"

₵

11¼"

12"

85½"

₵

12"

G

₵

12"

₵

12"

69"

₵

12"

₵

F

12"

E

1½"

12"

₵

12"

H

₵

12"

G

₵

96"

12"

₵

12"

J

₵

12"

₵

12"

B

₵

12"

₵

26¼"

₵

9¾"

K   C

234" [19'-6"]

240" [20'-0"]

94½"

94½"

₵

₵

Footing

Footing

Elevation and Details

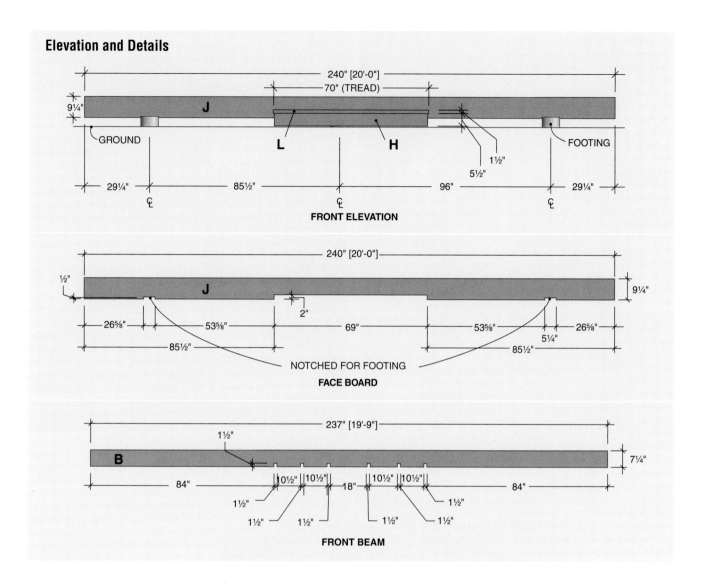

240" [20'-0"]
70" (TREAD)
9¼"
J
GROUND
L
H
FOOTING
1½"
5½"
29¼"
85½"
96"
29¼"

FRONT ELEVATION

240" [20'-0"]
½"
J
9¼"
2"
26⅝"
53⅝"
69"
53⅝"
26⅝"
85½"
5¼"
85½"
NOTCHED FOR FOOTING

FACE BOARD

237" [19'-9"]
1½"
B
7¼"
84"
10½" 10½"
18"
10½" 10½"
84"
1½"
1½"
1½"
1½"
1½"
1½"

FRONT BEAM

Directions: Low-Profile Deck

Attach the Ledger

1 Measure and cut the ledger (A) to length. Drill pairs of ¼" pilot holes at 2 ft. intervals. Counterbore each hole ½", using a 1" spade bit.

2 Determine ledger location and draw its outline on the wall. Make sure you include a 3" space at each end of the ledger for the end joists and side face boards. Temporarily brace the ledger in position, using 2 × 4s. Make sure the ledger is level and mark the hole locations on the wall with an awl or nail.

A

Attach the ledger to the masonry wall with lag screws and washers, using a ratchet wrench.

261

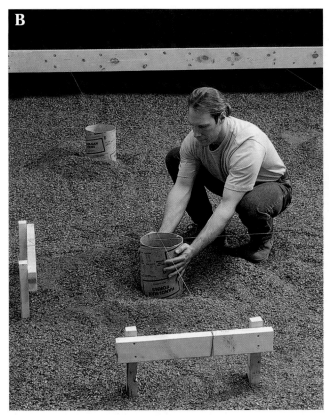

Stretch level mason's strings between the bottom of the ledger and temporary batterboards. Level the footing forms against the strings.

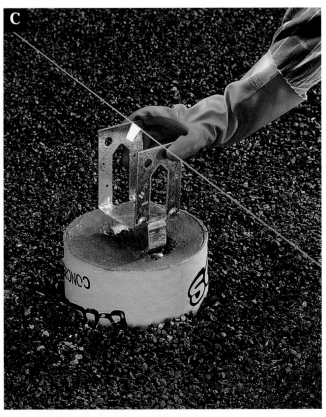

Set the direct-bearing hardware into the wet concrete, using layout strings to ensure accurate alignment.

3 Remove the ledger and drill anchor holes 3" deep, using a ⅜" masonry bit. Drive lead anchors into the drilled holes, using a rubber mallet, and attach the ledger to the wall with lag screws and washers, using a ratchet wrench **(photo A).**
4 Seal the screw heads and the joint between the wall and ledger with silicone caulk.

Pour the Footings

1 To locate the footings, refer to the measurements in the *Framing Plan* (page 260) and mark the centerline for each pair of footings on the ledger.
2 Construct three temporary 2 × 4 batterboards. Position the batterboards out from the footing marks, approximately 19 ft. from the

ledger. Stretch mason's string from the bottom of the ledger at each mark to the corresponding batterboard, making sure that the strings are level and perpendicular to the ledger.
3 Check for square, using the 3-4-5 triangle method. From the point where each string meets the ledger, measure 3 ft. along the ledger and make a mark. Next, measure 4 ft. out along the string and mark with tape. The distance between the points on the ledger and the string should be 5 ft. If it's not, adjust the string position on the batterboard accordingly.
4 To locate the centers of the six footings, build four more batterboards and stretch two additional mason's strings parallel to the house (refer to the

Framing Plan on page 260 for measurements). Use a plumb bob to transfer the footing centerpoints to the ground, and drive a stake to mark each point.
5 Remove the mason's strings and dig the footings, using a clamshell digger or power auger. Pour 2" to 3" of loose gravel into each footing hole for drainage. NOTE: When measuring the footing size and depth, make sure you comply with your local building code, which may require flaring the base to 12".
6 Cut the footing forms to length, using a reciprocating saw or handsaw, and insert them into the footing holes.
7 Retie the mason's strings, making sure they are level.
8 Level the tops of the forms by setting them flush with the mason's strings

Set the beams in the direct-bearing hardware on the footings. Note the "notch" for the end joist at the end of the outer beam.

Measure, cut, and install the joists with joist hangers, verifying the length of each one as you go.

(photo B) and packing soil around them to hold them securely in place.

9 Remove the mason's strings and fill the footing forms with concrete, tamping with a long stick or rod to eliminate any air gaps.

10 Screed the concrete flush, using a straight 2 × 4, then insert direct-bearing hardware into each footing while the concrete is still wet. Reattach the layout strings to ensure that the hardware is aligned correctly *(photo C)*.

Install the Beams

1 Measure, mark, and cut the beam boards (B) to length, using a circular saw. NOTE: Three of the beam boards are the same length as the ledger. The fourth board is 3" longer to accommodate the 1½" end joist on each end.

2 Make each beam by fastening two beam boards together with pairs of box nails driven at 16" intervals. At both ends of the outer beam, the long beam board overhangs 1½", creating a notch for attaching the end joist.

3 Position the beams crown-side-up on the direct-bearing hardware *(photo D).* Double-check that both beams are correctly aligned with the ledger, and attach to the hardware with carriage bolts.

Install the Joists

1 Measure, mark, and cut the end joists (C) to length. The end joists extend from the house to the notch in the end of the outer beam. In our plan the end joists are 189" long, but verify this measurement before cutting. Attach the end joists to the ledger and beams with box nails.

2 Measure, mark, and cut double center joists (D). Mark the centerline of the deck on the ledger and beams, install double joist hangers at each mark, and nail the joists in place. Seal the seam between the beam boards in the double joists with silicone caulk to protect against moisture.

3 Locate the remaining joists by measuring along the ledger and beams from the center joists, and marking centerlines at 12" intervals (see *Framing Plan*, page 260). Install a joist hanger at each centerline.

4 Measure, mark, and cut the inner joists (D), verifying the actual lengths, and install in joist hangers with joist nails *(photo E).*

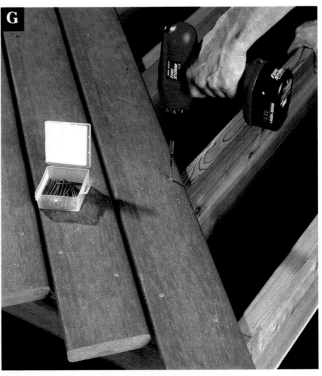

Cut 1½" × 1½" notches for the step supports in the outer beam with a reciprocating saw or handsaw. Finish the notches with a hammer and chisel.

Lay composite decking boards with a ⅛" to ¼" gap to allow for drainage, and expansion and contraction.

Build the Step

Our plan includes a cantilevered step suspended from the underside of the deck. This step is constructed with 2 × 6 step supports (F, G) attached to the lower portions of the deck joists. Notches in the bottom edge of the outer beam (see *Detail*, page 261) allow the supports to run through. A long notch in the front face board (see *Detail*, page 261) accommodates all the step supports. Spacers (E) offset the step supports from the joists to avoid the joist hangers.

1 Measure, mark, and cut the step support spacers (E). Set the spacers back approximately 1" from the front beam, and attach to the deck joists with deck screws (see *Step Detail*, page 265).

2 Cut 1½" × 1½" notches in the bottom edge of the front beam, adjacent to the step support spacers. Use a reciprocating saw or handsaw to make the vertical cuts, and finish each notch with a chisel and hammer *(photo F)*.

3 Measure, mark, and cut the step supports (F) and end step supports (G) to length. Make a 45° miter cut at the front of the end step supports where they meet the step riser. Attach the step supports to the spacers with deck screws. The interior step supports extend 11¼" beyond the beam, while the end step supports extend 12¾" to allow for the miter joints at the riser.

4 Measure, mark, and cut the step riser (H) to length, with 45° mitered ends. Attach the riser to the step supports with casing nails.

Lay the Decking

1 To create reference lines, mark a point in the center of the front of the deck. Measure equal distances along the double center joist, and along the outer beam, then snap a chalk line between these points. As you progress with rows of decking, periodically measure between the ends of the decking boards and the reference line to help you maintain a consistent angle.

2 Begin laying the composite decking at the front center of the deck. Cut one end of the first decking board at a 45° angle and leave the other end slightly long. Position it above the step, aligning the 45° cut with the centerline of the double joist, and fasten with 2½" composite screws.

3 Cut and attach the next deck board in similar fashion, leaving a ⅛" space between the boards.

4 Cut and attach the remaining deck boards **(photo G),** periodically checking the angle of the decking against the reference lines and making any necessary adjustments.

5 After installing the decking, trim the excess that overhangs the deck ends. For boards 16 ft. or smaller, leave a gap at the deck ends and at any butt joints—¹⁄₁₆" for every 20°F difference between the temperature at the time of installation and the expected high for the year—as composite decking will expand and contract. Set the blade depth on your circular saw at slightly more than 1½", and trim the decking to size.

Step Detail

Install the Face Boards

1 Measure, mark, and cut the front face board (J) to size (see *Detail*, page 261), and notch it to fit around the step supports. Cut 45° miters on both ends.

2 Temporarily clamp the face board in place and mark for notching around the footings. Also mark the points where the carriage bolts in the direct-bearing hardware contact the back of the board.

3 Remove the board, cut the footing notches, and chisel out the back of the board to accommodate the carriage bolts. Attach the face board with casing nails.

4 Measure, mark, and cut the side face boards (K) to length, making 45° miter cuts at the front ends. Attach the face boards to the end joists with deck screws.

Install the Step Treads

Complete the suspended step by cutting the composite treads (L) to length and attaching them to the step supports, using 2½"composite screws. Leave a ½" gap at the front face board, and a ¼" gap between the treads **(photo H).**

Cut the composite step treads to length and attach with composite screws, leaving a ½" gap between the first tread and the face board.

2 × 6 decking
spaced ⅛" apart

2 × 6
hand rail

2 × 2s
spaced 4" apart

2 × 6
side joist

2 × 6
joist

Precast concrete
footings

2 × 6
rim joist

12" sleepers

Adjust until the diagonal measurements are equal, which means the footings are square.

3 Place a 2 × 6 across the corner footings for the back row, setting it in the center slots. Check this joist with a level, then add or remove soil beneath footings as necessary to level it.

4 Center a footing between these corner footings. Use a level to recheck the joist, then add or remove soil beneath the center footing, if necessary **(photo A)**. Remove the joist.

5 Repeat the process described in #3, #4 and #5 to set and level the footings for the front row.

6 Position the remaining 12 footings at equal intervals, aligned in three rows. Position a 2 × 6 from the front row of footings to the back, and adjust soil as necessary to bring the interior footings into alignment with the front and back rows.

Platform Deck

A freestanding platform deck is a low-maintenance option for creating an outdoor floor. Because it can be constructed virtually anywhere, in almost any size, a platform deck works in nearly any landscape. The wood can be left natural, stained or painted to blend with your house and other landscape elements.

You'll be able to build this deck over a single weekend. It uses lumber in standard lengths, so you won't need to do a lot of cutting. In addition, this deck uses precast concrete footings, rather than poured footings. These precast footings are available at home improvement centers and lumberyards.

This 12 × 12-ft. deck rests on a 10 × 10-ft. base formed by 18 concrete footings arranged in three rows of six footings each. Joists are secured in slots in the tops of the footings, simplifying the building process.

Directions: Platform Deck

Install & Level the Footings

1 Measure a 10 × 10-ft. area for the deck foundation, and mark the corners with stakes.

2 Position a footing at each corner, then measure from corner to corner, from the center of each footing.

Install the Joists

1 Seal the ends of each 2 × 6 with wood sealer/protectant and let them dry completely.

2 Center a 12-ft. joist across each row of footings. Using a level, check the joists once again and carefully adjust the footings if necessary **(photo B)**.

Add the Side Joists & Rim Joists

1 Line up a 2 × 6 flush against the ends of the joists along the left side of the deck, with the ends extending equally past the front and back joists.

2 Attach the side joist by driving a pair of deck screws into each joist.

3 Repeat this process to install the right side joist.

4 At the front of the deck, position a 2 × 6 rim joist flush between the ends of the side joists, forming a butt joint on each end.

5 Attach the rim joist to the side joists by driving a pair of deck screws through the faces of the side joists, into the ends of the rim joist *(photo C)*.

6 Repeat #4 and #5 to install the other rim joist.

Position the Sleepers

1 Measure and cut six 2 × 6 sleepers to fit between the front and back joists and the rim joists. Seal the cut ends with wood sealer/protectant and let them dry completely.

2 Position one sleeper in each row of footings, between the first joist and the rim joist *(photo D)*. Attach each sleeper by driving a pair of galvanized deck screws through each of the joists and into the sleeper.

Square Up the Frame

1 Once the framing is complete, measure the diagonals from corner to corner. Compare the measurements to see if they are equal *(photo E)*.

2 Adjust the framing as necessary by pushing it into alignment. Have someone help you hold one side of the framework while you push against the other.

Framing Plan

12 ft. × 12 ft. decking

12 ft. 2"

10 ft.

CONSTRUCTION MATERIALS

• *Precast concrete footings (18)*

• *12-ft. 2 × 6s (38)*

• *2 lbs. galvanized 3" deck screws*

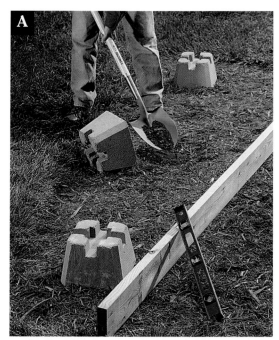

A

Position the corner footings and the center footing for the back joist. Remove or add soil beneath the footings to level them.

B

Position the remaining footings and insert the joists. Check to make sure the framework is level, and adjust as needed.

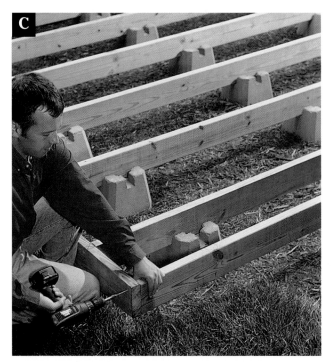

Install the front and back rim joists between the ends of the side joists, securing them with pairs of deck screws.

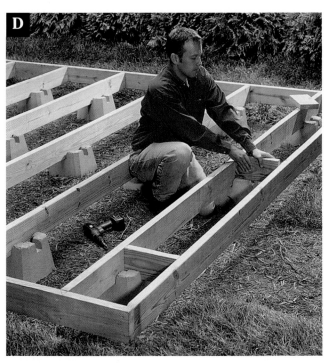

Position the sleepers in the slots of the footings, then attach them to both joists with pairs of deck screws.

Lay the Decking

1 Seal the 2 × 6 decking boards with wood sealer/protectant and let them dry. Seal all exposed framing members as well.

2 Lay a 2 × 6 over the surface of the deck, perpendicular to the joists and flush with the rim joist. Secure this board with deck screws.

3 Repeat # 2 to install the rest of the decking *(photo F).* Use a framing square to set a ⅛" space between boards. Rip cut the last decking board if needed.

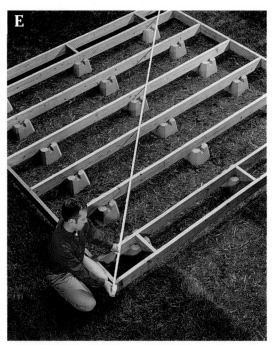

After the framing is completed, measure the diagonals and adjust the frame until it's square.

Install the decking by driving a pair of screws into each joist. Use a framing square to leave a ⅛" space between boards.

Variation: Adding a Railing

Although this platform deck rests low to the ground, you may want to add a hand rail around two or three sides of the deck, especially if the deck will be used by young children or an elderly person. For each side of the deck to which you're adding railings, you'll need 25 2 × 2s, 42" long.

Prepare the Balusters

1 Place the 2 × 2s flush together, adjust them so the ends are even, and draw a pair of straight lines, 3" apart, across each board, 1½" above the beveled end. Repeat the process and draw a single line 2¾" from the top of the other end. Using the lines as guides, drill pilot holes into the 2 × 2s *(photo A)*.
2 Apply wood sealer/protectant to the ends of the 2 × 2s.

Attach the Balusters

1 Position a 2 × 2 flush with the bottom of the joist, then clamp it in place to use as a placement guide.
2 Position the corner 2 × 2s against the side joists, beveled end down, 4" in from the corner. Check for plumb, then drive deck screws through the pilot holes.
3 Attach the remaining 2 × 2s for each side, spacing them 4" apart *(photo B)*.

Attach the Hand Railing

1 Hold a 12-ft. 2 × 6 that forms the top of the railing in place, behind the installed 2 × 2s.
2 Attach the 2 × 2s to the 2 × 6 top rails by driving deck screws through the pilot holes *(photo C)*.
3 Connect the top rails at the corners, using pairs of deck screws.
4 Finish the railing by applying a coat of wood sealer, according to the manufacturer's directions.

> CONSTRUCTION MATERIALS
> • *12-ft. 2 × 6s (3)*
> • *42" 2 × 2s (75, one end beveled)*
> • *2½" galvanized deck screws*

Gang together the 2 × 2s, then drill a pair of pilot holes into the beveled ends, and a single pilot hole in the opposite end.

Attach the 2 × 2s to the side joists, leaving a 4" gap between them.

Level the 2 × 6 railing behind the 2 × 2s, then attach it by driving screws through the pilot holes.

Multilevel Deck

Create a multitude of possibilities with this multilevel design.

This multilevel deck is ideal where you need access from different areas and levels of your home. The size and shape also provide many functional spaces for entertaining, privacy, or relaxation, as well as unobtrusive storage areas for recreational accessories.

The lower deck in this plan has been built around a patio. If you want this as a deck area instead, simply extend the lower ledger board across the house and run joists between the ledger and the center beam. You can remove the spa area from the plans and adjust the shape of the lower deck if you wish, too.

With some modification, this design also can help you make use of an otherwise unusable steep slope. However, you may need to eliminate or reduce the storage and small deck area underneath the landing. Some excavation of the existing slope area might also be required.

OVERALL SIZE:
27'-2" LONG
20'-6½" WIDE
8'-9" HIGH

Deck plans courtesy of handymanplans.com

Lumber List			
Qty.	Size	Material	Part
18	4 × 4" × 8'	Trtd. lumber	Post (A, B, C, D, F, G)
5	4 × 4" × 10'	Trtd. lumber	Post (E)
40	2 × 6" × 4'	Trtd. lumber	Rim joist (J), joist (K)
52	2 × 6" × 6'	Trtd. lumber	Beam (I), rim joist (J), joist (K) tread (O), kick plate (T)
27	2 × 6" × 8'	Trtd. lumber	Ledger (H), beam (I), rim joist (J), joist (K), cross bracing (N)
12	2 × 6" × 10'	Trtd. lumber	Ledger (H), rim joist (J), joist (K)
2	2 × 6" × 12'	Trtd. lumber	Beam (I)
76	2 × 6" × 16'	Trtd. lumber	Decking (M)
1	2 × 6" × 18'	Trtd. lumber	Rim joist (J)
6	2 × 8" × 4'	Trtd. lumber	Face board (L)
5	2 × 8" × 8'	Trtd. lumber	Face board (L)

Lumber List			
Qty.	Size	Material	Part
3	2 × 8" × 10'	Trtd. lumber	Face board (L)
1	2 × 10" × 6'	Trtd. lumber	Stair hanger (U)
2	2 × 12" × 8'	Trtd. lumber	Stair face board (S)
1	2 × 12" × 10'	Trtd. lumber	Stair face board (S)
3		Trtd. lumber	7-tread precut Stair stringer (Q)
4		Trtd. lumber	5-tread precut Stair stringer (R)
16	2 × 4" × 4'	Trtd. lumber	Top & bottom rails (V)
8	2 × 4" × 6'	Trtd. lumber	Top & bottom rails (V)
2	2 × 4" × 8'	Trtd. lumber	Top & bottom stair rails (W)
2	2 × 4" × 10'	Trtd. lumber	Top & bottom stair rails (W)
12	1 × 8" × 6'	Trtd. lumber	Riser (P)
68	2 × 12" × 10'	Trtd. lumber	Balusters (X)

Supplies: 2 × 6" metal joist hangers (138); 2 × 6" double metal joist hangers (2); 4 × 4" metal post anchors (28); 16d galvanized nails (3½", 25 lbs); 10d galvanized nails (3", 30 lbs); 3" galvanized screws (15 lbs.); 60 lb. dry concrete in bags (62); ⅜ × 6" galvanized carriage bolts, washers, and nuts (26); ⅜ × 4" galvanized lag screws (26); ⅜ × 6" galvanized lag screws (12); ⅜ × 4" galvanized expansion bolts (8); weather-resistant hinges* (4); weather-resistant door latch* (2); metal ledger flashing (34 ft.); decorative post cap* (19).

*optional

Cutaway View - Upper Deck and Landing

Deck plans courtesy of handymanplans.com

Upper Deck Framing Plan

Front Elevation

Cut and attach a ledger, using carriage bolts or lag screws, in the cutout area you have made in the siding. Make sure you allow space for the rim joists that will be attached at each end of the ledger.

Dig code-approved footings, insert footing tube forms, and fill them with concrete. Screed each footing top level with the form, using a piece of 2 × 4.

Directions: Multilevel Deck

Attach the Ledgers

1 Draw a level outline on the siding in both locations to show where the ledgers and the end joists will fit against the house (See the *Lower Deck Framing Plan* and *Upper Deck Framing Plan,* pages 273 and 274). Position the top edge of each ledger so that the surface of the decking boards will be 1" below the indoor floor level. This height difference prevents rainwater or melted snow from seeping into the house.

2 Cut out the siding along the outline with a circular saw. To keep the blade from cutting too deeply into the sheathing underneath the siding, set the blade depth the same thickness as the siding. Finish the corners of the cutouts with a hammer and chisel, holding the beveled side in to ensure a straight cut.

3 Install new building felt over the existing felt exposed by siding removal. Cut galvanized flashing to the length of each cutout using metal snips, and slide it up under the siding.
4 Measure and cut the ledgers to length from pressure-treated 2 × 6 lumber. Center the ledgers in the cutouts, underneath the flashing, with space at the ends for the end joists. Brace ledgers in place, fastening them temporarily to the house with 3" deck screws.
5 Drill pairs of ¼" pilot holes through the ledger and sheathing and into the house header joist at 16" intervals. Counterbore each pilot hole ½" deep, using a 1" spade bit. Attach the ledgers to the wall with ⅜ × 4" lag screws and washers, using an impact driver or a ratchet wrench *(photo A).*
6 Apply a thick bead of silicone caulk between the siding and the flashing. Also seal the lag screw heads and any gaps between the wall and the ledgers.

Pour the Footings

1 Referring to the *Post Location Plan* on page 275, stretch mason's strings across the site, using 2 × 4 batterboards. Check the mason's strings for square, using the 3-4-5 triangle method (see page 57). Adjust as necessary until they are square. Measure along the strings to locate the centerpoints of the footings. Mark the locations with tape.
2 Drop a plumb bob at the tape locations and drive stakes into the ground to mark the centerpoints of the footings.
3 Remove the mason's strings and dig holes for the footings, using a clamshell digger or power auger. Make certain the hole sizes and depths comply with your local building code, which may require flaring the footings at their base.
4 Pour 2" to 3" of loose gravel into each hole for drainage.
5 Cut the footing tube forms to length, long enough so

Plumb each post in its post anchor, temporarily securing it in place with braces and stakes.

Cut @ 22½°

45°

Cut 45°-miters at the ends of rim joists that meet posts at a 45° corner. Cut 22½°-miters at the ends of face boards that meet at a 45° corner.

they will extend 2" above grade, using a reciprocating saw or handsaw. Insert the forms into the holes and backfill with soil.

6 Layout and mark the location for a concrete pad within the hexagonal spa area (see *Lower Deck Framing Plan*, page 273). Excavate and build forms for the pad (see pages 65 to 67).

7 Fill the tube forms with concrete in stages, tamping the concrete at each stage with a long stick to eliminate any air pockets. Screed the tops flush with a flat 2 × 4 *(photo B)*.

8 Retie the mason's strings and drop a plumb bob to establish centerpoint of the footing. Insert a J-bolt into each footing, leaving ¾" to 1" of thread exposed. Clean the bolt threads before the concrete sets. NOTE: With the large number of footings needed, you will need one or more helpers to install the J-bolts before the concrete begins to set. Another option is to install threaded rods with epoxy after the concrete has cured (see

pages 64 to 65).

9 Pour concrete into the spa pad form and tamp to remove air pockets. Screed the top flush with the form (no other finishing techniques are necessary for this pad) and allow the pad to cure (see pages 66 to 67).

Set the Posts

1 Lay a long, straight 2 × 4 flat across pairs of footings. With one edge tight against the J-bolts, draw a reference line across each footing. Do this in both directions for pairs of footings where necessary.

2 Place a metal post anchor on each footing, center it over the J-bolt, and square it with the reference line. Thread a nut over each J-bolt and tighten each of the post anchors in place.

3 Cut deck support posts A through E to their approximate length, adding several inches for final trimming (see *Elevation*, page 274 and *Upper Stair Detail*, page 280). (NOTE: The finished height of post C is 40" above the lower decking surface and the fin-

ished heights of posts D and E are 36" above the decking. The top post B is flush with the rim joists of the stair landing. Also note that, because the lower level deck is close to the ground, you may need to use low-profile deck building methods, see pages 130 to 133.) Place the posts in the anchors and tack them into place with one nail each.

4 With a level as a guide, plumb the posts, using braces and stakes to hold posts B through E plumb *(photo C)*. Once the posts are plumb, finish nailing them to the anchors.

Install the Beam, Rim Joists & Face Boards for the Lower & Upper Decks

1 Using a string, water, or laser level, mark the top edge of the lower deck rim joists and center beam locations on posts A and at the footing ends of appropriate posts B through E (see *Lower Deck Framing Plan*, page 273). Make mark level with the top edge of the lower ledger.

Cut a 45°-miter at the ends of rim joists and face boards that meet the center beam of the lower deck at a 45° corner.

Use 45°-angled joist hangers where joists meet the angled rim joists. Space joists 22⅝" on center.

2 Mark posts E for the upper deck rim joists, using the top edge of the upper ledger as the reference. (NOTE: Marking posts B and D for the stair landing rim joists will occur during stair construction.)

3 Measure, cut, and install rim joists for the upper deck from pressure-treated 2 × 6 lumber. Do this one piece at a time to ensure accurate measuring. Cut 45° miters at the ends of the pieces that meet posts at the 45° corners. Attach rim joists by toenailing them to the post faces, using 3½" deck screws.

4 Measure, cut, and install face boards from pressure-treated 2 × 8 lumber. Do this one piece at a time as with the rim joists. Cut 22½° miters at the ends of the pieces that meet at the 45° corners **(photo D)**. Attach face board pieces that fit flush with the post faces using ⅜ × 6" carriage bolts, washers and nuts. Attach pieces that don't fit flush with the post faces at the 45° corners with ⅜ × 4" lag screws and washers. Make sure to stagger the bolt and/or screw locations on posts where two pieces attach. At-

tach the face boards to the rim joists with pairs of 3" deck screws driven at 24" intervals.

5 Build the center beam from doubled 2 × 8 pressure-treated lumber. Measure, cut, and attach it to the posts with ⅜ × 8" carriage bolts, washers, and nuts. Cut 45° miters in the ends of the pieces that will meet the rim joist face at a non-perpendicular junction.

6 Measure, cut, and install the rim joists and face boards for the lower deck in the same manner you followed for the upper deck. However, cut 45° miters in the ends of the pieces that will meet the center beam face at a non-perpendicular junction **(photo E)**.

7 Cut the tops of posts A flush with the top edges of the rim joists and center beam using a reciprocating saw.

Install the Rim Joists & Face Boards for the Landing

1 Measure 42" up from the top of the lower deck rim joists attached to posts B and D and mark the posts (see *Upper Stair Detail*, page 280).

2 Measure, cut, and attach the landing rim joists, aligning their top edges with the 42" marks, and the face boards in the same manner you followed for the lower and upper decks.

3 Cut the tops of posts B flush with the top edges of the rim joists, using a reciprocating saw.

Install the Joists

1 Measure and mark the outlines for joist locations spaced 16" on center on the ledger and rim joists of the upper deck (see *Upper Deck Framing Plan,* page 274), using a tape measure and speed square. The spacing of the joists measured along the 45° angled rim joist will be 22⅝" on-center. Measure and mark the outlines for joist locations for the stair landing in the same manner.

2 Measure and mark the outlines for joist locations spaced 16" on center on the ledger, rim joists, and center beam of the lower deck (see *Lower Deck Framing Plan,* page 273). As with the upper deck, the joist spacing will

Lower Stair Details

D V

W

3"

V 3"

3"

X

C

L

O

Stair
landing

7"

U

11"

P

W R

T

Lower deck

Grade

5'-2"

be 22⅝" on-center measured on the 45° angled rim joist.

3 Attach the joist hangers to the ledgers, rim joists, and center beam with 10d joist hanger nails, using a scrap 2 × 6 as a spacer to maintain the correct spread for each hanger. Use 45° joist hangers of the proper direction where joists meet the angled rim joists *(photo F).*

4 Measure, mark, and cut 2 × 6 pressure-treated lumber for the joists. Make certain to cut a 45° miter in the joist ends that will fit the 45° joist hangers. Determine which edge has the crown before measuring and making a miter cut.

5 Insert the joists into the hangers with crown side up, and attach at both ends with 10d joist hanger nails. Be sure to drive a nail in every hole in the hangers.

6 Add cross bracing for the joists in the upper deck as necessary.

Install the Railing Posts

1 Cut railing posts F and G to their approximate length, adding several inches for final

trimming. (The final height between the top of the decking and the top of the posts should be a minimum of 36".

2 Mark the position of these posts on the inner faces of the rim joists for the upper deck and stair landing (see *Upper Deck Framing Plan,* page 274).

3 Clamp each post in place to the inner face of the rim joist. Drill pilot holes for two ⅜ × 6" carriage bolts through the rim joist and the post. Counterbore the holes in the rim joist ½"-deep, using a 1" spade bit. Attach the posts to the rim joists with the carriage bolts, washers, and nuts *(photo G).*

Install the Decking

If possible, buy decking long enough to span the deck and landing areas. When joints between deck boards are necessary, center them above joists so the ends of both boards are supported. The decking for this plan is installed diagonally, so make sure to cut these ends at a 45° angle.

G

Attach the railing posts to the upper deck rim joists with carriage bolts, washers, and nuts.

279

Upper Stair Detail

- 3"
- W
- V   X
- 3"
- 3"
- 7"
- 11"
- O
- U
- Upper deck
- W   P
- Q
- T
- 3"
- **Stair landing**
- V
- D
- B
- E
- D
- 19½"
- 6'-0"
- 8'-11"
- 4'-3"
- 9"
- **Lower deck**
- **Grade**

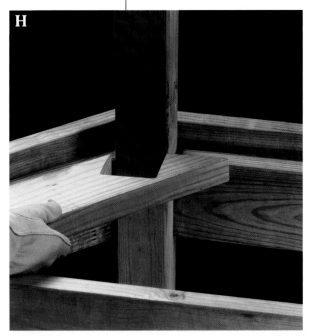

Cut notches in the decking boards that meet the railing posts. Test fit the board: the leading edge should be flush with the face boards.

1 Position a deck board along the outer 45° rim joist on the upper deck. It should be long enough to completely overhang the rim joists at both ends. Mark the railing post locations.

2 Cut notches for the railing posts, using a jigsaw. Test fit the board: its leading edge should be flush with the front face of the 45° rim joist *(photo H)*. Adjust as necessary. Attach the board by driving two deck screws into each joist.

3 Cut and attach the remaining deck boards, again letting ends overhang the rim joists wherever possible. Leave a ⅛" gap between the boards for drainage. Cut notches for railing posts as necessary.

4 Mark and snap lines across the overhanging board ends that are aligned with the outer faces of the rim joists. Set the depth of the circular saw blade ⅛" deeper than the thickness of the decking and cut along the line, and complete cuts at

corners or walls with a jigsaw, and a hammer and sharp chisel.

5 Remove all braces and stakes supporting posts.

6 Install the decking on the stair landing and lower deck following the same methods.

Building the Stairs

1 Cut the stair stringers for the upper stairs to length and use a framing square to mark the rise and run for each step. (See *Upper Stair Detail,* above. If you need to alter the plans to accommodate the height of your deck, see pages 142 to 151.) Cut the notches and the angles at the ends of the stringers with a circular saw, then complete the cuts at corners with a jigsaw.

2 Measure and cut a stair hanger and attach it to the posts E at the stair location with deck screws. Its top edge should butt against the bottom edge of the rim joist.

3 Position the middle stringer so the bottom end is flat

Attach the center stair stringer to the kick plate, using deck screws driven at an angle.

Cut and install railings into notches cut into the inner faces of the railing posts.

against the middle of the stair landing and the upper end is against the stair hanger. Mark the spot where the front edge of the stringer meets the landing. Measure and cut a 2 × 6 kick plate to fit between the outer stringers. Align the front edge of the kick plate with the mark you made, making sure the board is parallel to the near edge of the landing. Fasten it to the stair landing with deck screws.

4 Cut a notch for the 2 × 6 kick plate in the middle stringer.

5 Position each outer stringer against one end of the kick plate and against the stair hanger. Drive a screw through each stringer into the kick plate. Square each stringer to the hanger, using a framing square, and mark its position. Attach the upper ends of the stringers to the hanger with angle brackets. Position the middle stringer evenly between the outer stringers. Attach it to the stair hanger with a skewable joist hanger and to the kick plate, using deck screws driven at an angle **(photo I)**.

6 Measure and cut riser boards from pressure-treated

1 × 8 lumber. Attach the riser boards to the stringers with two deck screws per each stringer. Drill pilot holes for the screws at the ends of the boards.

7 Measure and cut two 2 × 6 stair treads for each step. Their ends should be flush with the outer faces of the stringers. Attach the treads with two deck screws per tread at each stringer, leaving a ¼" gap between treads. The back tread should touch the riser on each step.

8 Measure, layout, cut, and install the lower stairs following the same methods.

Install the Railing

For railing installation, refer to the *Upper Stair Detail* on page 280. For additional railing installation techniques, refer to pages 100 to 107.

1 Level and trim the post tops to final height. Make any decorative cuts for the post tops at this time. Cut notches for the top and bottom rails in the inner faces of the railing posts using a jigsaw, a hammer, and a chisel. Make certain the space between the

decking and the bottom rail complies with your local building code.

2 Measure, cut, and install pairs of rails to fit between the centerpoints of the notches **(photo J)**.

3 Cut and install balusters, making certain the space between them complies with local building code. NOTE: Building codes may require a grippable handrail for the stairs on this deck.

Enclose the Spa & Storage Areas

Install the spa on the pad and connect it to the utilities following the manufacturer's instructions. Have a professional do the installation if you are not comfortable working on plumbing, wiring, or gas systems.

After the spa is installed, follow the methods on pages 176 to 179 for enclosing the framing. You can use the same basic techniques to create storage enclosures beneath the stairway landings.

Casual Curved Deck

Simple in design but stylish in appearance.

Gentle, sweeping curves define this delightful design. Easily adapted to other dimensions, this plan offers a great deal of functional appeal without a large outlay of time or money.

If your local building code requires a concrete pad at the base of the large stair area, consider hiring a professional to install it, unless you have a high degree of skill at installing large concrete areas. Stair railings shouldn't be necessary with the height and step design of this plan, but check with your local building inspector. A simple metal railing could be installed without affecting the visual appeal of this design.

Cutaway View

Deck plans courtesy of handymanplans.com

Lumber List			
Qty.	Size	Material	Part
3	4 × 4" × 8'	Trtd. lumber	Posts (A)
6	2 × 8" × 8'	Trtd. lumber	Beam (B), rim joists (D)
3	2 × 8" × 8'	Trtd. lumber	Beam (B), blocking (F)
1	2 × 8" × 12'	Trtd. lumber	Joists (C)
6	2 × 8" × 16'	Trtd. lumber	Joists (C), rim joist (D)
7	1 × 8" × 10'	Trtd. lumber	Curved rim joist (E), stair risers (K)
2	1 × 8" × 12'	Trtd. lumber	Stair risers (K)

Lumber List			
Qty.	Size	Material	Part
32	¼ × 6" × 8'	Trtd. lumber	Decking (G)
4	5/4 × 6" × 10'	Trtd. lumber	Decking (G)
8	5/4 × 6" × 12'	Trtd. lumber	Decking (G)
3	2 × 6" × 10'	Trtd. lumber	Stair treads (H)
9	2 × 12" × 8'	Trtd. lumber	Stair stringers (J)
8	2 × 12" × 10'	Trtd. lumber	Curved stair tread (I)

Supplies: 8"-diameter footing forms (6); 3" direct bearing hardware (6); 2 × 8" double joist hangers (4); 2 × 8" joist hangers (72); 2½" composite decking screws; joist hanger nails; 16d galvanized box nails; 12d galvanized casing nails; ⅜ × 4" carriage bolts, washers, and nuts (12); ⅜ × 4" lag screws (22); lead masonry anchors (22); ledger flashing (20 ft.); exterior silicone caulk (3 tubes); concrete as required.

Framing Plan

Side Stair Detail

Curved Stair Detail

Note: glue and screw stringer to side of blocking

A

Pour 2" to 3" of loose gravel into each footing hole for drainage, then cut and insert a footing tube form so it extends 2" above grade.

Directions: Casual Curved Deck

Pour the Footings

A ledger isn't used for this deck plan. If you alter these plans to include a ledger board, see pages 46 to 53 for ledger installation methods.

1 Mark the deck location on the wall of the house (see *Framing Plan,* page 284), then stretch mason's strings across the site, using 2 × 4 batterboards. Temporarily attach batterboards to the wall with deck screws. Check the mason's strings for square, using the 3-4-5 triangle method (see page 57). Adjust as necessary until they are square. Measure along the strings to locate the centerpoints of the foot-

ings and mark each with tape. (NOTE: Allow yourself room to dig the footings at the house wall; the centerpoint of the posts can be up to 16" from the end of the beam.)

2 Drop a plumb bob at the tape locations and drive stakes into the ground to mark the centerpoints of the footings.

3 Remove the mason's strings and dig holes for the footings, using a clamshell digger or power auger. Make certain the hole sizes and depths comply with your local building code, which may require flaring the footings at their base.

4 Pour 2" to 3" of loose gravel into each hole for drainage.

5 Cut the footing tube forms to length, so they extend 2" above grade, using a recip-

rocating saw or handsaw. Insert the forms into the holes and backfill with soil *(photo A).*

6 Fill the tube forms with concrete in stages, tamping the concrete at each stage with a long stick to eliminate any air pockets. Screed the tops flush with a flat 2 × 4.

7 Retie the mason's strings and drop a plumb bob to establish centerpoint of the footing. Insert a J-bolt into each footing, leaving ¾" to 1" of thread exposed. Clean the bolt threads before the concrete sets. NOTE: Another option is to install threaded rods with epoxy after the concrete has cured (see pages 64 to 65).

Set the Posts

1 Start by laying a long straight 2 × 4 flat across pairs of footings. With one edge tight against the J-bolts, draw a reference line across each footing. Do this in both directions for pairs of footings where necessary.

2 Place a metal post anchor on each footing, center it over the J-bolt, and square it with the reference line. Thread a nut over each J-bolt and tighten each of the post anchors in place.

3 Cut 30"-long posts from pressure-treated 4 × 4 lumber. Place each post in a post anchor and tack it in place with one nail. With a level as a guide, plumb the posts, using braces and stakes to hold them in place. Finish nailing the posts to the anchor.

4 At the centermost post along the wall, measure down from the door, allowing 7¼" for the joists, 1¼" for the decking, and 1" between the decking surface and the interior floor, then mark the post at this measurement *(photo B).*

5 Use a string, water, or laser level to transfer this

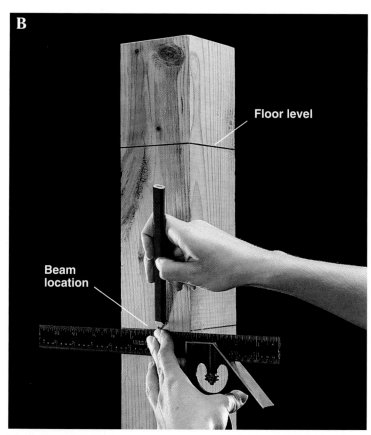

B

Floor level

Beam location

Mark the posts for the height of the beam, allowing 7¼" for the joists, 1¼" for the decking, and 1" between the decking surface and the interior floor of the house.

mark to the other posts. Each mark will be level with the top edge of the beams.

Install the Beams

1 Measure and cut two pressure-treated 2 × 8s to length for each of the three beams (see *Framing Plan,* page 284). Place their faces together so that their crown sides are aligned and attach them together with pairs of galvanized nails or deck screws driven every 12".

2 Position the crown (top) edge of each beam against the level marks on the appropriate posts and clamp it in place. Drill pairs of holes for ⅜ × 8" carriage bolts through the beam and post at each location. Attach each beam to the posts with the carriage bolts, washers, and nuts, inserting the bolts through the beam.

Install the Rim Joists

1 Measure and cut the two outer rim joists. Provide a 1 × 2" space between one end of each joist and the wall and a 2" extension beyond the outer corner post at the other end. Position their bottom edges so they are level with the top edges of the beams and attach them to the posts with 3" deck screws.

2 Measure, cut, and attach the wall-side rim joist between the ends of the outer rim joists. Align the wall-side rim joist face that is nearest the wall so it is flush with the ends of the outer joists. Drill pilot holes through the outer rim joist and drive deck screws through into the wall-side rim joist ends.

3 Cut and install the inner joist between the outer rim

joists on the front faces of the outer corner posts. Attach it to the posts with deck screws and to the beams with rafter ties.

Install the Curved Rim Joist

1 Measure and cut a pressure-treated 1 × 8 a few inches longer than needed to span from the outer rim joist to the centerpoint of the middle post at the front of the deck. This will be the first piece of the curved rim joist. Cut numerous ¼"-deep kerfs along the back width of this board. See pages 166 to 171 for more information on cutting kerfs.

2 Place one end of the board in the intersection of an outer rim joist and inner joist at an outer corner post, with the kerfed face against the inner joist and its top edge flush with the top edges of the joists. Drill pilot holes and drive 3" deck screws through the end of the board into the joist and post.

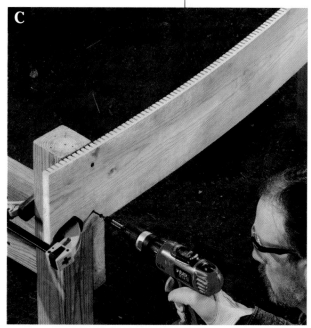

C

Cut ¼"-deep kerfs along the back width of the first 1 × 8 for the curved rim joist. Bend and attach it to the posts, using clamps to hold it in position.

D

Install the next layer of kerfed 1 × 8s, driving pairs of screws every 12" and at each post location.

E

Mark the profile of the inner face of the curved rim joist on each end of the 2 × 8 for the inner joist at the curve. Cut the joist at the marks, then fasten to the posts with carriage bolts and to the curved rim joist with deck screws.

3 Bend the other end of the board until it meets the face of the center post and attach it to the post with deck screws driven 1" from the centerpoint *(photo C)*. Make sure the bottom edge of the curved joist is level with the top edge of the beam. Mark a straight cut line at the centerpoint of the post on the curved joist, using a speed square. Cut the board with a circular saw with its blade set ⅛" deeper than the thickness of the board.

4 Measure, cut, and kerf another 1 × 8 a few inches longer than needed to complete the span. Attach one end in the intersection of the other outer rim joist and corner post. Bend and clamp the board into position. Mark a cutting line for the board to meet the other curved joist at the center post. Cut it with the circular saw, drill pilot holes, and drive deck screws to attach it to the post before removing the clamps.

5 Measure, cut, and kerf another pair of 1 × 8s. Clamp them to the first layer, staggering the joints so they do not fall on the center post and aligning the ends so they protrude rim joists. Drill pilot holes and fasten with deck screws every 12" and at post locations *(photo D),* then trim the ends of the rim joists flush with the outer face of the curved rim joist, using a reciprocating saw.

Install the Joists

1 Measure, cut, and install the remaining inner joists with 16" on-center spacing beginning at the wall side of the deck.

2 Select a 2 × 8 for the inner joist closest to the curved rim joist that is about 12" longer than necessary. Position it so its ends overlap the curved rim joist with its inner face aligned with the adjacent posts. Mark the profile of the inner face of the curved rim joist each end of the inner joist *(photo E).* Cut the inner joist at these marks with a reciprocating saw, then install it with deck screws driven through it and into the curved rim joist.

3 Cut and install 2 × 8

blocking at the midpoints of the joist spans to provide support for the diagonal decking. Also install blocking between the curved rim joist and adjacent joists as necessary to help support the curved profile.

4 Cut the tops of the posts flush with the top edges of the joists.

5 Remove all braces and stakes supporting posts.

Build the Stairs

If the height and grade level for your deck won't accommodate these stairs, see pages 94 to 99 to determine layout dimensions for stairs that will fit your deck.

1 Cut the stair stringers to length from pressure-treated 2 × 12 lumber and use a framing square to mark the rise and run for each step. (See *Side Stair Detail* and *Curved Stair Detail,* page 285). Cut the notches and the angles at the end of the stringers with a circular saw, then use a jigsaw to complete the corners.

Cut a 2"-wide piece of 2 × 6 lumber and use it as a spacer to mark the outside curve for the inner tread.

Use a jigsaw to trim the decking boards overhanging the curved rim joist.

2 Attach the side stair stringers to the joist ends. Attatch the stringers for the curved stair to the blocking between the inner joists and the curved rim joist. Install additional blocking as necessary.

3 Rip ¼"-thick plywood sheets into 2 × 8-ft.-long pieces and trace the profile of the curved rim joist onto them. Cut out this profile, using a jig saw, and use the plywood templates to mark the inside curve for the inner tread of the top step onto 10-ft.-long pieces of 2 × 12 lumber. Cut a 2"-wide piece of 2 × 6 lumber and use it as a spacer to mark the outside curve for the inner tread. Guide one end of the spacer along the inside curve line while holding a pencil point at the other end *(photo F)*.

4 Cut the curved inner tread pieces, using a jigsaw. Use the outside curved edge of the inner tread to mark the inside curve of the outer tread for the top step. Use the spacer to mark the outside edge, then cut the treads, using a jigsaw.

5 Use the outside curved edge of the outer tread for the top step to mark the inside curved edge on the inner tread of the bottom step. Repeat the process used to mark and cut the top step treads to complete the bottom step treads.

6 Install the curved treads, drilling pilot holes and using deck screws. Make sure joints between tread pieces are supported by stringers.

7 Measure and cut treads from 2 × 6 lumber, and attach them to the side stair stringers.

Install the Decking

If possible, buy decking long enough to span the distance between the midpoint of the deck and its edges. When joints between deck boards are necessary, center them above joists so the ends of both boards are supported.

1 Cut a 45° angle at the end of a deck board and position it with the long point ¼" from the wall and centered on the midpoint blocking.

The other end should overhang the rim joists at the opposite corner. Attach the board by driving two deck screws into each joist.

2 Cut and attach the rest of the deck boards on this side of the deck, first installing those ending at the midpoint blocking, then those ending at the joist adjacent to the wall. Leave a ⅛" gap between the boards for drainage.

3 Cut and attach the deck boards for the other side of the deck, again letting ends overhang the rim joists wherever possible.

4 Mark and snap chalk lines across the overhanging board. Set the depth of the circular saw blade ⅛" deeper than the thickness of the decking and cut along the lines. Complete the cuts at the wall with a jigsaw, and a hammer and sharp chisel.

5 Use the plywood templates you cut for the stair installation to mark the curve on the ends of the decking boards overhanging the curved rim joist and trim, using a jigsaw *(photo G)*.

Deck Accessories

Elements that add personal style and charm to your deck

Lumber for arbor provided by P & M Cedar Products, Inc.

OVERALL SIZE:
16" HIGH
18" WIDE
48" LONG

A

C

A

⅜"
TYP.

B

D

E

D

E

E

F

F

F

1½"

5½"

1½"
TYP.

E

E

F

F

F

Deck Bench

A handsome and comfortable bench that's easy to make.

Due to its modular design, this bench can be mixed or matched with planters or other benches. Cedar wood enables this bench to withstand sun, rain, and even snow. This bench will enhance your enjoyment of your deck and its beauty.

CONSTRUCTION MATERIALS

Quantity	Lumber
1	2 x 4" x 8' cedar
1	2 x 4" x 6' cedar
4	2 x 2" x 8' cedar
1	2 x 6" x 6' cedar
1	4 x 4" x 6' cedar

Cutting List				
Key	Part	Dimension	Pcs.	Material
A	Sides	1½ x 3½ x 48"	2	Cedar
B	Ends	1½ x 3½ x 15"	2	Cedar
C	Slats	1½ x 1½ x 45"	8	Cedar
D	Stretchers	1½ x 3½ x 15"	2	Cedar
E	Braces	1½ x 5½ x 15"	4	Cedar
F	Legs	3½ x 3½ x 13"	4	Cedar

Supplies: 3" gold-colored deck screws (60), 2½" gold-colored deck screws (16).

Note: Measurements reflect the actual thickness of dimensional lumber.

Use spacers to help you position the slats. Then, holding each slat firmly against the spacers, secure the slats with 3" screws driven through pilot holes.

With the stretchers positioned between the reference lines, attach the stretcher to each slat using 2½" screws.

Directions: Deck Bench

Make the Frame

The butt joints make this bench sturdy and easy to construct. For strength and good looks, we used gold-colored deck screws.

1 Measure, mark, and cut the sides (A) and ends (B) to length, using a circular saw.
2 Position the ends between the sides so the edges are flush. Measure from corner to corner. When the diagonals are equal the frame is square.
3 Drill ⅛" pilot holes through the sides and into the ends. Fasten the sides to the ends by driving 3" gold-colored screws through the pilot holes.

Build the Seat

The slats that make up the seat are spaced ⅜" apart to allow rain water to run off.

1 Cut the slats (C) to length using a circular saw.
2 Set the frame on a flat surface and place ⅜" spacers against one side. Place the first slat in the frame against the spacers. Drill ⅛" pilot holes through both ends into the slat. Secure the slat to the ends with 3" deck screws. Repeat this process of positioning and attaching slats until all the slats are in place **(photo A)**.
3 Measure, mark, and cut the stretchers (D) to length.
4 To mark the stretcher outlines, measure in 5" and 3½" from the inside of each end piece on the back of the slats and make a mark.
5 Position the stretchers between the marks. Drill ⅛" pilot holes through the stretchers into the slats. Attach the stretchers with 2½" screws **(photo B)**.

Assemble the Bench

The braces hold the legs in place against the stretchers.

1 Measure, mark, and cut the braces (E) to length.

2 To shape the ends of each brace, mark the angle by measuring down 1½" from the top edge and 1½" along the bottom edge. Draw a line between the two end points and cut along that line **(photo C)**. Repeat this step at the other end of the brace.

3 On each brace, measure down ¾" from the top edge and draw a reference line across the stretcher for the screw positions. Drill ⅛" pilot holes along the reference line. Position a brace on each side of the stretchers and fasten it with 3" screws driven through the braces and into the stretchers.

4 Measure, mark, and cut the legs (F) to length, using a circular saw. If needed, finish any cuts with a handsaw.

5 Position each leg between the braces and against the sides of the bench frame. Drill pilot holes through each brace and attach the leg to the braces by driving 3" screws through the braces and into the leg. Repeat the process for each leg until all legs are installed **(photo D)**.

Apply the Finishing Touches

1 Sand all surfaces with 150-grit sandpaper. Be sure to sand edges thoroughly to remove all splinters and rough edges.

2 Because cedar is naturally resistant to decay, it will age to a natural gray. To preserve its reddish color, you can apply a clear sealer as we did. Cedar is also suitable for painting.

Measure and mark the angles on the braces, then cut the angles using a circular saw or a power miter saw.

Position each leg between the braces and against the sides. Fasten the legs to the braces with 3" screws.

OVERALL SIZE:
18" HIGH
20½" WIDE
59" LONG

Integral Deck Bench

This simple bench design provides permanent seating.

Build this bench from the same type of lumber that will be used for the decking. It can be installed either perpendicular or parallel to the joists. It should be added to a deck design after the support members are installed, but before the surface decking is laid.

CONSTRUCTION MATERIALS

Quantity	Lumber
1	2 × 10" × 6' cedar
6	2 × 6" × 6' cedar

CONSTRUCTION MATERIALS

Quantity	Lumber
2	2 × 10" × 6' cedar
7	2 × 6" × 6' cedar

Cutting List - Perpendicular Bench			
Key	**Part**	**Dimension**	**Pcs.**
A	Support	1½ × 9¼ × 25"	2
B	Cleat	1½ × 3½ × 9¼"	2
C	Brace	1½ × 5½ × 17½"	2
D	Seat Board	1½ × 5½ × 56"	3
E	Seat Endcap	1½ × 5½ × 17½"	2
F	Seat Length cap	1½ × 5½ × 59"	2

Supplies: ⅜ × 5" carriage bolts (4) with washings & nuts, 3" deck screws (42).

Note: Measurements reflect the actual thickness of dimensional lumber.

Cutting List - Parallel Bench			
Key	**Part**	**Dimension**	**Pcs.**
A	Support	1½ × 9¼ × 25"	4
B	Cleat	1½ × 3½ × 9¼"	4
C	Brace	1½ × 5½ × 17½"	4
D	Seat Board	1½ × 5½ × 56"	3
E	Seat Endcap	1½ × 5½ × 17½"	2
F	Seat Length cap	1½ × 5½ × 59"	2

Supplies: ⅜ × 8" carriage bolts (4) with washings & nuts, 3" deck screws (50).

Note: Measurements reflect the actual thickness of dimensional lumber.

Drill holes and attach the seat supports and cleats to the joists with carriage bolts, washers, and nuts. Seat supports are installed for benches that are perpendicular to the joists (left) or that are parallel to the joists (right).

Directions: : Integral Deck Bench

Install the Seat Supports

1 Determine whether the bench is to be built perpendicular or parallel to the joists (opposite page), and what seat height you want. A comfortable height is 18" above the decking.

2 Measure and cut supports (A) from 2 × 10 lumber. Supports will span from the bottom edge of the joists to 1½" short of seat height. Space the supports no more than 48" apart (maximum distance when using 2× lumber installed flat for the seat).

3 Clamp the supports to the joists, aligning the bottom ends with the bottom edges of the joists. Seat supports should be plumb. Drill holes and attach the supports to the joists with carriage bolts, washers, and nuts before removing clamps **(photos A and B).**

Install Seat Braces and Decking Cleats

1 Cut and install 2 × 4 cleats (B) on the faces of the seat supports as necessary to provide support for decking boards. Attach them with 3" decking screws. Make sure the top edges of the cleats are level with the top edges of the adjacent joists.

2 Measure and cut seat braces (C) from 2 × 6 lumber. Calculate the length of each brace by counting the number of seat boards you want, multiplying by 5⅝", then subtracting ⅛".

3 Level and attach the seat braces at the top ends of the seat supports, using deck screws. Align the top edges of the braces with the ends of the supports.

Attach the Seat

1 Measure and cut seat boards (D) from 2 × 6 lumber. The ends of the boards should overlap the seat braces by no more than 8". Make sure the boards are of equal length and their ends are aligned. Attach them to the braces with two 3" deck screws driven at each brace. Leave a ⅛" gap between the boards for drainage, making sure to align the outside edges of the outer seat boards with the ends of the braces.

2 Cut two pieces of 2 × 6 lumber 3" longer than the length of the seat boards (F), and two pieces equal in length to the seat braces (E).

3 Attach the shorter pieces to the ends of the seat boards, aligning the top edge of each piece with the surface of the seat. Drill pilot holes and drive 3" deck screws through the short pieces and into the seat boards.

4 Align the top edge of each longer piece with the surface of the seat, and the ends with the outer faces of the short pieces. Drill pilot holes and attach the pieces with deck screws **(photo C).**

5 Sand the surface, corners and sides of the seat, using a random orbit sander with 120-grit sandpaper.

Align the top edge of the seat perimeter with the surface of the seat boards, then attach with deck screws.

OVERALL SIZE:
24½" HIGH
18¾" WIDE
18¾" LONG

Box Planter

The versatile design of this planter offers a variety of uses.

This planter is large enough to hold a potted shrub, mixed flowers, or even a miniature herb garden.

The "tiered" construction process makes it both easy to build and sturdy enough for years of use.

CONSTRUCTION MATERIALS

Quantity	Lumber
8	2 × 4" × 6' cedar
3	2 × 2" × 6' cedar

Cutting List

Key	Part	Dimension	Pcs.	Material
A	Side	1½ × 3½ × 16½"	24	Cedar
B	Stringer	1½ × 1½ × 21½"	4	Cedar
C	Bottom cleat	1½ × 1½ × 12"	4	Cedar
D	Bottom	1½ × 3½ × 14¾"	3	Cedar
E	Frame	1½ × 3½ × 18¾"	4	Cedar
F	Top cleat	1½ × 1½ × 13¼"	4	Cedar

Supplies: 2½" gold-colored deck screws (120), 10d casing nails (10).

Note: Measurements reflect the actual thickness of dimensional lumber.

Place spacers into the corners of the first tier, stand the stringers on end, and attach, using deck screws.

Drill pilot holes through the bottom cleats, and attach with deck screws.

Directions: Box Planter

This planter is assembled upside down. The rows of side pieces, or tiers, are constructed independently, then stacked on top of each other and fastened together from the inside through the stringers.

1 Measure, mark, and cut the side pieces (A) to length from 2 × 4" cedar stock.
2 Drill a pair of ⅛" pilot holes through each side piece, about ¾" from one end.
3 Form each of the six tiers by screwing four side pieces together with deck screws driven through the pilot holes.
4 Measure, mark, and cut the stringers (B) to length.
5 Lay the first tier on a flat worksurface, then position a stringer upright in one corner using a scrap of 2 × 2" lumber as a spacer to raise the stringer off the worksurface.
6 Drill ⅛" pilot holes and attach the stringer to the tier with 2½" deck screws.

Attach the other three stringers in the same fashion *(photo A)*.
7 Add the remaining tiers one at a time, positioning each tier so the butt joints are offset with those of the previous tier. Drill ⅛" pilot holes and attach each tier to the stringers with deck screws as you go.
8 Measure, mark, and cut the bottom cleats (C) to length from 2 × 2" cedar stock.
9 With the planter box still upside down, position a bottom cleat between two stringers, so the edge of the cleat is flush with the edge of the side.
10 Drill angled ⅛" pilot holes, and attach the bottom cleat to the side using deck screws. Attach the remaining bottom cleats in the same fashion *(photo B)*.
11 Measure, mark, and cut bottom pieces (D) to length from 2 × 4" cedar stock.
12 Turn the box assembly right-side-up, and set the bottom pieces into the planter so they rest on the cleats and are evenly spaced.
13 Attach the bottom pieces by drilling pilot holes and

driving deck screws through the bottom pieces into the cleats.
14 Measure, mark, and cut the frame pieces (E) from 2 × 4" cedar stock, mitering the ends at 45°.
15 Dry-fit the frame pieces together, with the miter joints tight. Join the frame pieces with casing nails.
16 Cut top cleats (F) to size from 2 × 2" cedar stock. Position the cleats on the assembled frame so the edges are flush with the inside edge of the framing pieces. Drill pilot holes through the cleats and attach by driving deck screws through the cleats and into the frame.
17 Position the frame on the planter so the cleats fit tightly inside box. Attach the frame by drilling pilot holes and driving deck screws through the inside face of the top cleats.
18 Soften the corners and edges of the box planter with a rasp, then apply a finish of your choice; our planter is protected with a coat of clear sealant-preservative.

OVERALL SIZE:
6¼" HIGH
8½" WIDE
27" LONG

Railing Planter

Grow flowers or herbs in this sturdy cedar planter.

Though this planter is built with inexpensive ¾" cedar, adding a planter to your deck will add a touch of class. Build a few planters and create an attractive, colorful privacy hedge.

CONSTRUCTION MATERIALS

Quantity	Lumber
1	1 x 6" x 8' cedar
1	1 x 2" x 8' cedar

Cutting List

Key	Part	Dimension	Pcs.	Material
A	Sides	¾ × 5½ × 25½"	2	Cedar
B	Ends	¾ × 4⅜ × 5½"	2	Cedar
C	Bottom	¾ × 5½ × 24"	1	Cedar
D	Frame sides	¾ × 1½ × 27"	2	Cedar
E	Frame ends	¾ × 1½ × 8½"	2	Cedar
F	Feet	¾ × 1½ × 1½"	4	Cedar

Supplies: 6d finishing nails (26), 4d finishing nails (28).

Note: Measurements reflect the actual thickness of dimensional lumber.

Assemble the box by predrilling the sides and attaching them to the ends with 6d finishing nails.

After attaching the feet to the bottom, insert the bottom into the planter box so it is flush with the reference line. Fasten with 6d finishing nails.

Directions: Railing Planter

The railing planter is designed with longer sides to fit over a standard size railing. Feet are installed to keep the planter off the railing and allow water to drain and air to circulate.

1 Measure, mark, and cut the sides (A) and ends (B) to size from 1 × 6" cedar stock. NOTE: The grain runs horizontally on the sides and vertically on the ends.
2 Position the ends between the sides with the top edges flush. Drill pilot holes, and fasten with 6d finishing nails **(photo A).** Make sure the end pieces are oriented so the wood grain runs vertically.
3 Measure, mark, and cut the bottom (C) to size, using a circular saw.
4 Draw a reference line down the middle of the

bottom. Use a ½" spade bit to drill three drainage holes evenly spaced along the line.
5 Measure, mark, and cut the feet (F) to size from ¾" cedar. Position the feet flush at the corners of the bottom piece and attach with 4d nails.
6 Draw reference lines on the inside faces of the side pieces, 1½" from the bottom edges.
7 With the box frame on its side, insert the bottom piece into the box, and tap into place until the bottom surface is flush with the reference lines. Drill pilot holes and drive 6d finish nails through the sides and ends to secure the bottom piece in place **(photo B).**
8 Measure, mark, and cut the frame sides (D) and frame ends (E) to size from ¾" cedar, mitering the ends at 45°.
9 Position the frame pieces over the top of the planter

box so the inside edges are flush with the inside surfaces of the box. Drill pilot holes and attach the frame pieces to the side and end pieces with 4d finishing nails. Locknail the miter joints with 4d finishing nails.
10 Recess all nail heads with a nail set, then finish as desired. Cedar will age naturally, but you can also seal it, as we did, with a clear wood preservative to maintain its original color.

Tip

You can prevent rot and extend the life of your planter by adding a plastic insert to hold the soil and plants.

OVERALL SIZE:
8'-7" HIGH
10-0" DEEP
8'-0" WIDE

Arbor

Create a pleasant outdoor shelter.

Arbors provide a cozy feeling of enclosure without boxing you in. Sit back and enjoy the cool summer breeze in this simple structure, personalized with your wind chimes, bird feeders, banners or vines.

CONSTRUCTION MATERIALS

Quantity	Lumber
6	4 × 4" × 10' cedar
1	4 × 4" × 6' cedar
4	2 × 8" × 10' cedar
7	2 × 6" × 8' cedar
17	2 × 2" × 10' cedar
1	1 × 4" × 8' cedar
1	¾ × ¾" × 8' cedar cove

Cutting List				
Key	Part	Dimension	Pcs.	Material
A	Corner posts	3½ × 3½ × 101½"	4	Cedar
B	Beam boards	1½ × 7¼ × 120"	4	Cedar
C	Rafters	1½ × 5½ × 96"	7	Cedar
D	End braces	3½ × 3½ × 34¼"	4	Cedar
E	Side braces	3½ × 3½ × 42"	4	Cedar
F	Slats	1½ × 1½ × 120"	17	Cedar
G	Post trim	¾ × 3½ × 5"	16	Cedar
H	Post molding	¾ × ¾ × 5"	16	Cedar

Supplies: ⅜ × 6" lag screws and washers (16); ½ × 7" carriage bolts, washers, and nuts (8); 2½" galvanized deck screws (200); 4 × 4" metal post anchors (4); galvanized metal rafter ties (6); 6d galvanized casing nails (12); 3d finishing nails (8).

A

Fasten the corner posts in the post anchor hardware with 10d joist hanger nails.

B

Use string and a line level and transfer the height of the beams to each corner post. Note temporary bracing on posts.

Directions: Arbor

Even though this arbor is structurally independent and not attached to your house, it's designed to be built next to a wall. If you want to build it away from your house, on a far corner of your deck, simply lengthen the rafters and angle-cut both ends.

Locate the Arbor

When positioning the arbor, make sure the back posts are at least 6" from the house (see *Side Eleva-*tion, page 302) to allow room for attaching the back beam boards. The corner posts should rest on joists. If necessary, add blocking between the joists at post locations for added support.

Set the Posts

1 Mark the corner post locations on your deck (see *Elevations*, page 302). Position the post anchor hardware and attach to the decking with 10d joist hanger nails.
2 Measure, mark, and cut the corner posts (A) to length. You may wish to cut the posts slightly longer than the final height to allow for leveling the beams and rafters.

3 Cut eight temporary braces, approximately 6' long, with a 45° angle on one end.
4 Set the posts in the post anchors and attach with 10d joist hanger nails *(photo A)*. Use a level to ensure that the posts are plumb, and fasten in position by tacking two temporary braces to the deck and each post. Leave the temporary braces in place until the permanent braces are installed.
5 Mark the height of the beam boards on one corner post, using a combination square. Stretch a string between posts and use a line level to transfer this mark to the other corner posts *(photo B)*.

Front Elevation

Side Elevation

Detail A

Drill two ½" holes through the beam boards and post for the carriage bolts.

Install the Beams

The beams are installed between the posts, parallel to the house.

1 Measure, mark, and cut the beam boards to length (see *Front Elevation*, page 302).

2 Stand the beam boards together on edge, ends flush. Measure and mark the outlines of the rafters on the top edges of the boards, using a combination square as a guide.

3 With a helper, hold each beam in position on the corner posts, and tack in place with deck screws. NOTE: If you're working alone, cut four 12"-long 2 × 4s, to use as temporary supports. Attach these pieces to the sides of the posts at the bottom edge of the beam position. Rest the beam boards on the supports.

4 Mark the carriage bolt locations, and drill ½" holes through the beam boards and corner posts *(photo C).*

Attach the inner rafters with galvanized rafter ties and 10d joist hanger nails.

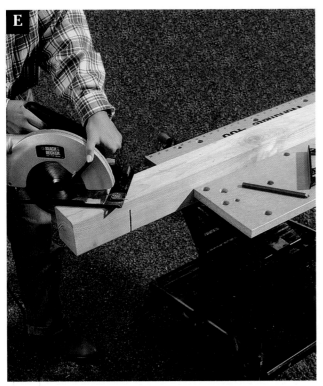

Use a circular saw to cut the 45° angles on the end and side braces.

To secure the top of each brace, drill and countersink a ¼" hole, insert a 6" lag screw, and tighten with a ratchet wrench.

5 Secure the beams to the corner posts with carriage bolts, washers, and nuts.

Install the Rafters

The rafters are installed perpendicular to the house, and overhang the front beam by 6". The front ends of the rafters are cut at a 30° angle (see *Detail A*, page 303).

1 Measure, mark and cut the rafters (C) to size, using a circular saw (see *Side Elevation*, page 302).
2 Set the rafters in position. Attach the outer rafters to the posts with deck screws. Attach the inner rafters to the beams, using metal rafter ties and 10d joist hanger nails *(photo D)*.
OPTION: If you prefer a less visible method of attaching the inner rafters, toenail them with 16d galvanized nails.

3 Trim the posts to final height if necessary, using a reciprocating saw or a handsaw.

Install the Braces

The braces provide lateral support for the canopy. The end braces fit between the beams and the corner posts; the side braces fit between the rafters and the corner posts.

1 Cut the end braces (D) and the side braces (E) to size (see *Elevations*, page 302). Cut 45° angles on both ends with a circular saw *(photo E)*.
2 Position an end brace between the beam boards, with the lower end tight against the post and the upper end flush with the top of the beam. Tack the brace into place with deck screws.

3 Drill a ¼" pilot hole through the lower end of the brace into the post. Countersink the pilot hole ¼" deep with a 1" spade bit, and attach the brace with a lag screw.
4 To fasten the upper end of the brace to the beam, drill a ¼" pilot hole 5" deep. Countersink the hole ¼" deep with a 1" spade bit. Insert a lag screw and tighten with a ratchet wrench *(photo F)*.
5 Use the same procedure to position and install the remaining braces.

Install the Slats

1 Measure, mark, and cut the slats (F) to length.
2 Attach the back slat directly above the back beam board. Attach the remaining slats at 4" intervals, fastening them with deck screws *(photo G)*.

G

Position slats at 4" intervals with a 6" overhang and attach by driving 2½" deck screws through the slats and into the rafters.

Add the Finishing Touches

1 Measure, mark, and cut the post trim (G) and post molding (H) to length, with the ends mitered at 45°.
2 Fit and attach the trim to the posts with 6d galvanized casing nails *(photo H).* You may need to chisel out the back side of the trim to accommodate the post anchor screws.
3 Fit the molding and attach it tight to the posts with 3d finishing nails.
4 Though cedar is naturally resistant to decay and doesn't require an applied finish, you may want to use a coat of clear sealant-preservative for added protection and to preserve the original color of the wood.

H

Attach the post trim and molding with 16d galvanized nails.

Deck Wiring

Lighting and power improve any deck.

The wiring installation shown on the following pages provides step-by step instructions for installing light fixtures and power receptacles on a deck. These instructions are based on the National Electrical Code (NEC), which stipulates minimum standards for outdoor wiring materials. But because climate and soil conditions vary from region to region, always check with your local building and electrical codes for additional restrictions in your area. For example, some codes require that all underground cables be protected with conduit, even though the NEC allows UF cable to be buried without protection at the proper depths.

Note: This project requires general knowledge of electrical materials and techniques beyond the specific instructions shown here. Make certain you know how to do this work before attempting this project.

Check for underground utilities when planning trenches for underground cable runs. Avoid law sprinkler pipes, and consult your electric utility c phone company, gas and water department, an ble television vendor for the exact locations of u ground utility lines. Many utility companies send representatives to accurately locate dangerous derground hazards.

12" minimum

Cutaway view

Bury UF cables 12" deep if the wires are protected by a GFCI and the circuit is no larger than 20 amps. Bury cable at least 18" deep if the circuit is not protected by a GFCI, or if it is larger than 20 amps.

1 ft. minimum
6½ ft. maximum

Install GFCI receptacles in weatherproof electrical boxs at least 1 ft.—and no more than 6½ ft.—above ground level.

Directions: Deck Wiring

Plan the Circuit

1 Visit your electrical inspector to check local code requirements for outdoor wiring and to obtain a permit for your project. Because outdoor wiring is exposed to the elements, it requires the use of special weatherproof materials, including UF cable, rigid metal or schedule 40 PVC plastic conduit, weatherproof electrical boxes and fittings. Some local codes allow either rigid metal or PVC plastic, while others allow only metal.

2 For most homes, an outdoor circuit for a deck is a modest power user. Adding a new 15-amp, 120-volt circuit provides enough power for most needs. However, if your circuit will include more than three large light fixtures (each rated for 300 watts or more) or more than four receptacles, plan to install a 20-amp, 120-volt circuit.

3 Consider the circuit length when choosing cable sizes for the deck circuit. In very long circuits, normal wire resistance leads to a substantial drop in voltage. If your circuit extends more than 50 feet, use cable wire that is one gauge larger to reduce the voltage drop. For example, a 15-amp circuit that extends more than 50 feet should be wired with 12-gauge wire instead of the usual 14-gauge.

4 Plan to bury UF cables 12" deep if the wires are protected by a GFCI and the circuit is no larger than 20 amps. Bury cable at least 18" deep if the circuit is not protected by a GFCI or if it is larger than 20 amps *(Photo A).*

5 Prevent shock by making sure all outdoor receptacles are GFCI protected. A single GFCI receptacle can be wired to protect other fixtures on the circuit. Outdoor receptacles should be at least 12" above ground level and enclosed in weatherproof electrical boxes with watertight covers *(Photo B).*

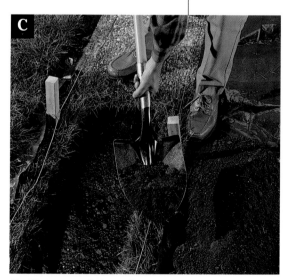

Outline trench locations with stakes and string, then dig the trenches to the depths required by your local code.

Drive conduit beneath sidewalks and other obstacles, using a block of wood and a hammer.

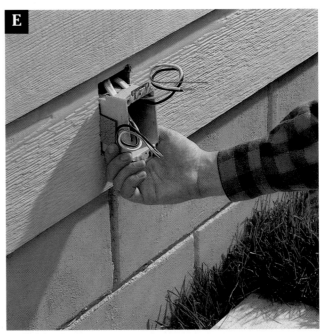

Route cables into the GFCI box, push the box into the cutout, then tighten the mounting screws until the box is secure.

Dig Trenches

When laying underground cables, save time and minimize lawn damage by digging trenches as narrow as possible. Plan the circuit to reduce the length of cable runs. If your soil is sandy, or very hard and dry, water the ground thoroughly before you begin digging.

1 Mark the outline of the trenches with wooden stakes and string.

2 Cut two 18"-wide strips of plastic, and place one strip on each side of the trench outline.

3 Remove blocks of sod from the trench outline, using a shovel. Cut sod 2" to 3" deep to keep roots intact. Place the sod on one of the plastic strips and keep it moist but not wet. It should be replaced within two or three days, otherwise the grass underneath the plastic may die.

4 Dig the trenches to the depth required by your local code. Heap the dirt onto the second strip of plastic **(photo C)**.

5 To run cable under a sidewalk, cut a length of metal conduit about 12" longer than the width of sidewalk, then flatten one end of the conduit to form a sharp tip. Drive the conduit through the soil under the sidewalk, using a ball-peen or masonry hammer and a wood block to prevent damage to the pipe **(photo D).** Cut off the ends of the conduit with a hacksaw, leaving about 2" of exposed conduit on each side. Attach a compression fitting and plastic bushing to each end of the conduit. The plastic fittings will prevent the sharp edges of the conduit from damaging the cable sheathing.

6 If the trenches must be left unattended, temporarily cover them with scrap plywood to prevent accidents.

Install Boxes & Conduit

1 Outline the GFCI receptacle box on the exterior wall of the house. First drill pilot holes at the corners of the box out-line, then use a piece of stiff wire to probe the wall for electrical wires or plumbing pipes. Complete the cutout with a jig saw or reciprocating saw.

Masonry variation: To make cutouts in masonry, drill a line of holes inside the box outline, using a masonry bit, then remove the waste material with a masonry chisel and ball-peen hammer.

2 Install NM cable from the circuit breaker panel to the GFCI cutout. Allow an extra 24" of cable at the panel end and an extra 12" at the GFCI end. Attach the cable to framing members with cable staples. Strip 10" of outer sheathing from the GFCI end of the cable and ¾" of insulation from each wire.

3 Open one knockout for each cable that will enter the GFCI box. Insert the cables so at least ¼" of sheathing reaches into the box. Push the box into the cutout and tighten the mounting screw until the bracket draws the plaster ears tight against the wall **(photo E).**

At the house, install conduit so it extends from the bottom of the extension ring to 4" from the bottom of the trench.

At the deck, attach conduit to the receptacle box so it extends from the bottom of the box to 4" from the bottom of the trench.

4 Position a foam gasket over the GFCI box, then attach an extension ring to the box, using the mounting screws included with the extension ring. Seal any gaps around the extension ring with silicone caulk.

5 Measure and cut a length of IMC conduit to reach from the bottom of the extension ring to a point about 4" from the bottom of the trench. Attach the conduit to the extension ring using a compression fitting **(photo F).** Anchor the conduit to the wall with a pipe strap and masonry screws. Or use masonry anchors and pan-head screws. Drill pilot holes for the anchors, using a masonry drill bit.

6 Attach compression fittings to the ends of the metal sweep fitting, then attach the sweep fitting to the end of the conduit. Screw a plastic bushing onto the exposed fitting end of the sweep to keep the metal edges from damaging the cable.

7 Attach mounting ears to

the back of a weatherproof receptacle box, then attach the box to the deck frame by driving galvanized screws through the ears and into the post.

8 Measure and cut a length of IMC conduit to reach from the bottom of the receptacle box to a point about 4" from the bottom of the trench. Attach the conduit to the box with a compression fitting. Attach a sweep fitting and plastic bushing to the bottom of the conduit, using compression fittings **(photo G).**

9 Cut a length of IMC conduit to reach from the top of the receptacle box to the switch box location. Attach the conduit to the receptacle box with a compression fitting. Anchor the conduit to the deck frame with pipe straps.

10 Attach mounting ears to the back of the switch box, then loosely attach the box to the conduit with a compression fitting. Anchor the box to the deck frame by driving galvanized screws through

the ears and into the wood. Tighten the compression fitting with a wrench. Measure and cut a short length of IMC conduit to reach from the top of the switch box to the deck light location. Attach the conduit with a compression fitting **(photo H).**

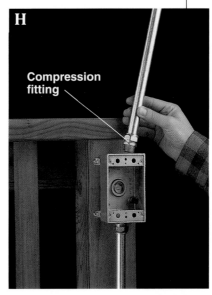

Attach conduit to the switch box so it extends from the box to the deck light location, using a compression fitting.

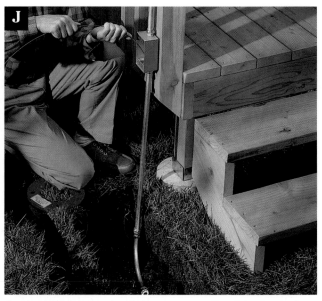

At the house, use fish tape to pull cable through the conduit and into the GFCI box.

At the deck, use the fish tape to pull cable through the conduit and into the receptacle box and switch box.

Install the Cable

1 Measure and cut all UF cables, allowing an extra 12" at each box. At each end of the cable, use a utility knife to pare away about 3" of outer sheathing, leaving the inner wires exposed.

2 Feed a fish tape down through the conduit from the GFCI box. Hook the wires at one end of the cable

Connect a grounding pigtail to each metal box and extension ring and join all grounding wires with the pigtail. Install the coverplates for the rough-in inspection.

through the loop in the fish tape, then wrap electrical tape around the wires up to the sheathing. Carefully pull the cable through the conduit *(photo I).*

3 Lay the cable along the bottom of the trench, making sure it is not twisted. Where cable runs under a sidewalk, use the fish tape to pull it through the conduit.

4 Use the fish tape to pull the end of the cable up through the conduit to the deck receptacle box at the opposite end of the trench *(photo J).* Remove the cable from the fish tape.

5 Cut away the electrical tape at each end of the cable, then clip away the bent wires. Bend back one of the wires in the cable, and grip it with needlenose pliers. Grip the cable with another pliers, then pull back on the wire, splitting the sheathing and exposing about 10" of wire. Repeat with the remaining wires, then cut off excess sheathing with a utility knife. Strip ¾" of insulation from the end of each wire, using a combination tool.

6 Measure, cut, and install a cable from the deck receptacle box to the outdoor switch box, using the fish tape. Strip 10" of sheathing from each end of the cable, then strip ¾" of insulation from the end of each wire, using a combination tool.

7 Attach a grounding pigtail to the back of each metal box and extension ring. Join all grounding wires with a wire connector. Tuck the wires inside the boxes, and temporarily attach the weatherproof coverplates until the inspector arrives for the rough-in inspection *(photo K).*

Connect the Receptacles

1 At the GFCI receptacle, connect the black feed wire from the power source to the brass terminal marked LINE. Connect the white feed wire from the power source to the silver screw terminal marked LINE.

2 Attach the short white pigtail wire to the silver screw terminal marked LOAD, and attach a short black pigtail wire to the brass screw terminal marked LOAD.

Foam gasket

Single-pole switch

Toggle lever

To install a GFCI receptacle, connect the black feed wire from the power source to the brass screw terminal (LINE), and the white feed wire to the silver screw terminal (LINE). Use pigtails and wire connectors to connect the remaining black circuit wires to the brass screw terminal (LOAD), the white circuit wires to the silver screw terminal (LOAD), and the green or copper wires to the grounding screw.

To install a weatherproof switch, connect the black circuit wire to one of the screw terminals on the switch, and the black wire lead from the fixture to the other screw terminal. Use wire connectors to join the white circuit wires and the grounding wires.

3 Connect the black pigtail wire to all the remaining black circuit wires, using a wire connector. Connect the white pigtail wire to the remaining white circuit wires.
4 Attach a grounding pigtail to the grounding screw on the GFCI. Join the grounding pigtail to the bare copper grounding wires, using a wire connector *(photo L).*
5 Carefully tuck the wires into the box. Mount the GFCI, then fit a foam gasket over the box and attach the weatherproof coverplate.
6 At each remaining receptacle in your deck circuit, connect the black circuit wires to the brass screw terminals on the receptacle. Connect the white circuit wires to the silver screw terminals on the receptacle. Attach a grounding pigtail to the grounding screw on the receptacle, then join all grounding wires with a wire connector.
7 Carefully tuck all wires into the box, and attach the receptacle to the box, using the mounting screws. Fit a foam

gasket over the box, and attach the weatherproof coverplate.

Connect the Decorative Light Fixtures

1 Thread the wire leads of the light fixture through a threaded compression fitting. Screw the union onto the base of the light fixture *(photo M).*
2 Feed the wire leads through the conduit and into the switch box. Slide the light fixture onto the conduit, and tighten the compression fitting.

Connect the Switch

Switches for outdoor use have weatherproof coverplates with built-in toggle levers. The lever operates a single-pole switch mounted to the inside of the coverplate.

1 Connect the black circuit wire to one of the screw terminals on the switch, and connect the black wire lead from the light fixture to the other screw terminal.

2 Connect the black wire lead to one screw terminal on the switch, and connect the white wire lead to the white circuit wire *(photo N).* Use a wire connector to join the grounding wires.

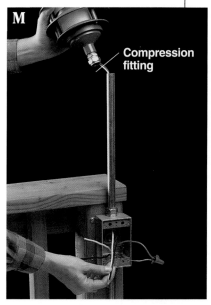

Compression fitting

Feed the wire leads through the conduit into the switch box, then attach the light fixture using a compression fitting.

311

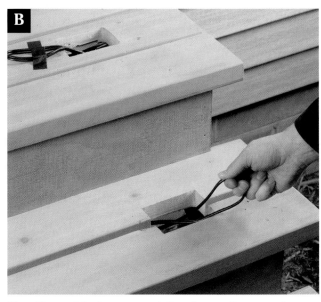

Mark the fixture location, then cut the holes using a jigsaw.

Run the cable from an existing low-voltage system or from a new transformer to the stair location.

Directions: Installing Recessed Low-voltage Step Lights

Low-voltage recessed lights are great for decks. Installed inconspicuously in the deck boards, they provide accent lighting for plant boxes or pathway lighting for stairs.

Cut the Holes for the Fixtures

1 Use the template or trace the bottom of the fixture onto the treads to mark holes for each light. Center the fixture on the tread, 1 to 2" from the edge (the hole will center on the gap between the 2 × 6s on most deck stairs).
2 Drill holes at the corners, then cut the holes with a jig saw *(photo A).*
3 Test the fixtures to be sure they will fit (they should fit snugly), and adjust the holes as necessary.

Run Cable for the Fixtures

1 Run cable from an existing low-voltage system or from a new transformer to the stairs.

Drill a hole in the bottom riser if necessary, and snake the cable under the stairs along the inside edge *(photo B).*
2 Pull a loop of cable through each of the holes for the fixtures and temporarily secure it to the tread with tape.

Wire the Fixture

1 At the middle of the first loop of cable in the series, separate 3 to 4" of the two conductors in the cable by slicing down the center.

2 Strip about 2" of insulation off of each wire. Cut the wire in the center of the stripped section, and twist the two ends and the end of one of the fixture wires into an outdoor wire connector. Secure the connection with electrical tape.
3 Repeat with the other fixture wire and the other circuit wire.
4 Tuck the wires back into the hole, and place the fixture into the hole.
5 Test each fixture before installing the next one.

Join the lead wires of the fixture with the wires of the low-voltage cable, using outdoor wire connectors.

Run low-voltage cable from a transformer or low-voltage circuit to the end of the railing and secure with cable staples.

Fasten U channel to the bottom of the railing, then press the rope light in the channel securely.

Directions: Attaching Low-voltage Railing Lights

Rope light is thin, flexible clear tubing with tiny light bulbs embedded every few inches along its length. Most rope lights are meant to plug into a receptacle and use household current. While this is all right for indoor decorating, it limits their use outdoors. Low-voltage versions, however, are powered by transformers and can be connected inconspicuously to a low-voltage landscape lighting circuit. They are available from specialty lighting stores and catalogs.

Route the Cable

1 Run a cable from a transformer or from a nearby low-voltage circuit using a T connector.
2 Route the cable up a post at the end of the rail, and secure it with cable staples. Leave enough length at the end of the cable to connect it to the rope light *(photo A).*

Secure the Rope Light

1 Secure the rope light to the underside of the railing with U channel. Cut the channel to length, and nail it to the bottom of the railing *(photo B).*
2 Press the rope into the channel.

Wire the Rope Light

1 Connect the fixture cord to the end of the rope with the twist-on fitting.
2 Connect the rope wires to the branch cable with a cable connector designed for low-voltage outdoor cable *(photo C).*
3 Cap the end of the rope with a plastic cap.

Connect the rope wires to the branch cable with a cable connector designed for outdoor cable.

Index

Creative Publishing international, Inc.
offers a variety of how-to books.
For information write or visit our website:
  Creative Publishing international, Inc.
  Subscriber Books
  18705 Lake Drive East
  Chanhassen, MN 55317

www.creativepub.com

Resources

American Wood Council
(general lumber information)
202-463-2700
www.awc.org

Deck Industry Association
(general deck building information)
972-849-1835
www.deckindustry.org

DEKBRANDS, Inc.
(Dek-Block Piers)
(612) 331-4755
800-664-2705

eON ® CPI Plastics Group Ltd.
(composite decking)
866-342-5366
www.eonoutdoor.com

Pultronex Corporation /E.Z.Deck
(fiberglass decking)
800-990-3099
www.ezdeck.com

Simpson Strong-Tie Co.
(metal brackets & hardware)
800-999-5099
www.strongtie.com

Southern Lumber Manufacturers Association (SLMA)
(general lumber information)
404-361-1445, 404-631-5963
www.slma.org

Trex Co. LLC
(composite decking)
800-289-8739
www.trex.com

U.S. Environmental Protection Agency (EPA)
(phase-out of CCA-treated lumber)
202-272-0167
www.epa.gov

Photography Contributors

Photos of redwood decks courtesy of **California Redwood Association:**
Front cover, pp. 143 (top right), 173 (top left, top right, bottom right), 182 (top right).
California Redwood Association
415-382-0662
www.calredwood.org

Photo courtesy of **Lindal Cedar Homes, Inc.:** p. 109 (bottom right).
Lindal Cedar Homes, Inc.
800-426-0536
www.lindal.com

Photo courtesy of **Milt Charno & Associates, Inc.:** p. 143 (bottom left).
Milt Charno & Associates, Inc.
414-475-1965
www.decksbymiltcharno.com

Photo courtesy of **REED Concrete Pumps & Gunite Machines:**
p. 23 (bottom right).
REED Concrete Pumps & Gunite Machines
Toll-Free: 888-779-7333
(outside US: 909-287-2100)
www.reedpumps.com

Photo courtesy of **Western Red Cedar Lumber Association:** p. 4.
Western Red Cedar Lumber Association
To order a brochure or a designers' handbook packet call
866-778-9096 or visit:
www.realcedar.org

Photo courtesy of **Western Wood Products:** p. 109 (bottom left)
Western Wood Products
503-224-3930
www.wwpa.org

Also from

CREATIVE PUBLISHING INTERNATIONAL

Complete Guide to Bathrooms
Complete Guide to Building Decks
Complete Guide to Ceramic & Stone Tile
Complete Guide to Creative Landscapes
Complete Guide to Easy Woodworking Projects
Complete Guide to Finishing Touches
   for Yards & Gardens
Complete Guide to Flooring
Complete Guide to Home Carpentry
Complete Guide to Home Masonry
Complete Guide to Home Plumbing
Complete Guide to Home Storage
Complete Guide to Home Wiring
Complete Guide to Kitchens
Complete Guide to Outdoor Wood Projects
Complete Guide to Painting & Decorating
Complete Guide to Roofing & Siding
Complete Guide to Windows & Doors
Complete Photo Guide to Home Repair
Complete Photo Guide to Home Improvement
Complete Photo Guide to Outdoor Home Repair

ISBN 0-86573-592-1

ISBN 1-58923-202-X

CREATIVE PUBLISHING INTERNATIONAL

18705 LAKE DRIVE EAST
CHANHASSEN, MN 55317

WWW.CREATIVEPUB.COM